Youth and the National Narrative

Also available from Bloomsbury

Citizenship Education in Conflict-Affected Areas, Bassel Akar
Conflict, Education and Peace in Nepal, Tejendra Pherali

Youth and the National Narrative

Education, Terrorism and the Security State in Pakistan

Marie Lall and Tania Saeed

BLOOMSBURY
NEW DELHI • LONDON • OXFORD • NEW YORK • SYDNEY

BLOOMSBURY INDIA
Bloomsbury Publishing India Pvt. Ltd
Second Floor, Building No. 4
DDA Complex LSC, Pocket C – 6 & 7
Vasant Kunj, New Delhi 110070
www.bloomsbury.com

BLOOMSBURY, Bloomsbury Academic India and the Diana logo are trademarks of Bloomsbury Publishing Plc

First published in India 2020
First published in Great Britain 2020

Cover design: Adriana Brioso
Cover Image: Imran Khan, chairman of the Pakistan Tehreek e Insaf (PTI) party, addresses supporters during an election campaign rally in Narowal, Pakistan, 2013.
(© Daniel Berehulak/Getty Images)

This edition published with permission from Bloomsbury Publishing Plc,
50 Bedford Square, London, WC1B3DP, UK

British Library Cataloguing-in-Publication Data
A catalogue record for this book is available from the British Library.

Library of Congress Cataloging-in-Publication Data
A catalog record for this book is available from the Library of Congress

ISBN: 978-93-88912-27-3

For sale in the Indian subcontinent only

Typeset by Deanta Global Publishing Services, Chennai, India
Digitally Printed and bound in India by Replika Press Pvt. Ltd. In 2019.

'for Ali, Mariyam, Alena and Mian – my Pakistani family'

&

'for Ama and Abu'

Contents

Map

Map of Pakistan. This image is derived from a United Nations map.

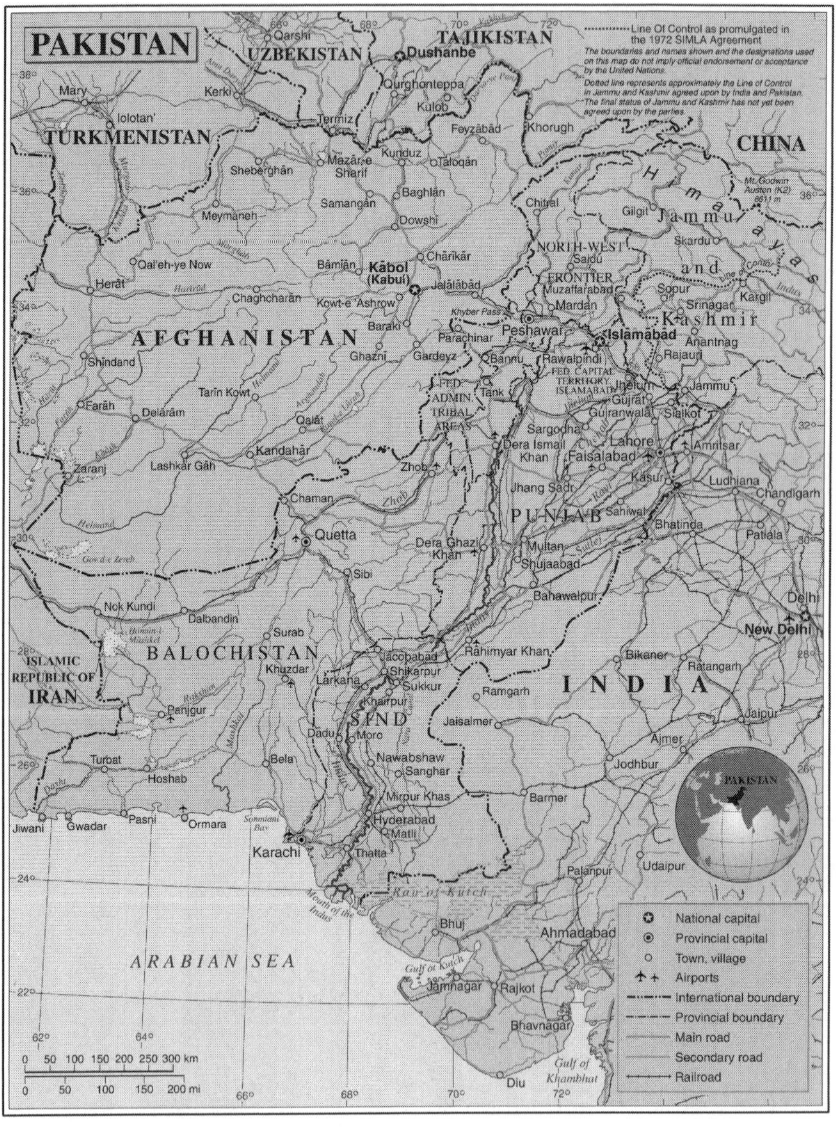

Acknowledgements

The book was conceived at LUMS a decade ago in 2009 during my time there as a visiting professor. It grew over the years that followed; however, the initial idea came over a cup of coffee just after Ramadan 2009 on the LUMS campus whilst I was speaking to a few of my students. I am therefore first and foremost indebted to Dr Ali Khan for inviting me to LUMS, giving me an office, an apartment on campus and the space to conduct my first in-depth study on citizenship and the Pakistani youth. Over the many coffees and my regular stays with them, Ali, Mariyam, Alena and Ali's father Sheriyar Khan became my Pakistani family, and the book is dedicated to them.

LUMS is a truly wonderful place to undertake any kind of research on Pakistan – it is an academic haven, a quiet, studious bubble that allows for intellectual exchanges and has great students who love to engage and exchange ideas. I am deeply indebted to my colleagues at LUMS as well as my various LUMS-based researchers, in particular Farhan Ul Haq and Mariyam Mohiuddin Ahmed, who all contributed time and effort, either with me in the field collecting data or by helping with the data-entering and analysis back on campus.

Tania Saeed joined me a few years later to make this a really remarkable in-depth study. The book would not have had this breadth and depth without her.

I am also indebted to the Citizens Foundation (TCF), in particular Riaz Kamlani and Raheela Fatima, who helped me access many TCF schools and then accompanied me across all four provinces on a number of trips. The TCF directors, in particular Mushtaq Chhapra, have always been supportive of my research work. The British Council in Pakistan has to be mentioned – as it was whilst doing a study on their Connecting Classrooms project that the citizenship book I was starting to give up on got a new lease of life.

Over the years I have worked with many Pakistani researchers and teams drawn from a number of organizations. I am not able to mention them all here, but much of the data would not have been collected without their efforts. Particular thanks go to Adnan Dastgeer, Arifa Bhagat and Rehana Batool.

Many Pakistani families treated me like one of their own, letting me stay, keeping me fed, watered and caffeinated as well as listening to my endless stories from the field. I want to thank Uncle Suhail Sethi for a decade and a half of friendship, Abbas Rachid and Dr Tariq Rehman for many fruitful discussions as well as Arusha Kamlani and Tayyaba Siddiqi for always providing me with a home in Karachi.

I am of course indebted to 1,900+ students, teachers and parents who filled out the forms, sat in focus group discussions or interviews with me across the four corners of Pakistan. It is their voices I have endeavoured to replicate in this book, so that others might read what they had to say about their government over the last decade.

My final thanks go to my husband Viren Lall who has put up with my weeks and months in the field in Pakistan, India and Myanmar for the 22 years that we have been married. I am truly grateful for his patience and unwavering support.

Marie Lall

Tokyo, July 2019

I joined Marie on this book project in 2013 when I returned to Pakistan after finishing my doctorate, and it has been an incredible five years of research and writing. I am grateful to Marie for being so incredibly supportive.

I would also like to thank all those people who supported me during the fieldwork in Karachi and Lahore, some of whom became good friends in the process. Uncle Ishrat, for helping me gain access to universities when I was struggling to find participants, and for his constant encouragement. Amra and Shireen aunty for their consistent support in Lahore. Amina and Mujeeb uncle for being such incredible hosts in Karachi – I truly found another home with them.

For all those individuals who helped find contacts, the teachers who allowed me to speak to their students, and the wonderful students who genuinely engaged in long conversations with me, trusting me with their opinions and points of view – I am truly indebted to you all. I hope I have done justice to your narratives.

I would also like to thank Haroon, Shahid, Zainab, Ayesha, Abdullah and Daneen for reminding me of the importance of having a life beyond work. Bipana, Pegah, Sakina and Asma, thank you for checking up on me, and listening to my rants during this writing process. I am also grateful to my incredible colleagues at LUMS for their constant support and encouragement.

However, none of this would have been possible without the support of my parents, Zareena Saeed and Saeed-uz-Zaman, to whom I dedicate this book. They have patiently supported me during this research. The fieldwork in particular became more personal, as I struggled to find hope through the narratives that students shared with me. While that struggle continues, I am truly indebted to my parents who were always there for me. In particular, Zareena Saeed for engaging in long discussions and for showing me the possibility of hope in my own work. I am also grateful for her meticulous feedback on my writing. She continues to be my most constructive critic and strongest supporter, for which I am eternally grateful.

Tania Saeed
Cambridge, July 2019

Abbreviations

AAT	Allah-o-Akbar Tehreek
AIMSF	All India Muslim Students' Federation
ANP	Awami National Party
APMSO	All Pakistan Mohajir Students' Organisation
APSO	All-Pakistan Students' Organization
BBC	British Broadcasting Corporation
BJP	Bharatiya Janata Party
BLA	Balochistan Liberation Army
BZU	Bahauddin Zakariya University
CCE	Centre of Civic Education
CIA	Central Intelligence Agency
CNIC	Computerized National Identity Card
COAS	Chief of Army Staff
CPEC	China–Pakistan Economic Corridor
DSF	Democratic Students Federation
EUEOM	European Union Election Observation Mission
FATA	Federally Administered Tribal Areas
FIA	Federal Investigation Agency
FIF	Falah-e-Insaniyat Foundation
GCI	Global Competitiveness Index
GRR	Government Request Report

HRCP	Human Rights Commission of Pakistan
HT	Hizb ut-Tahrir
ICG	International Crisis Group
IDEAS	Institute of Development and Economic Alternatives
IDPs	Internally Displaced Persons
IJT	Islami Jamiat-e-Talaba
IMF	International Monetary Fund
INGO	International Non-Governmental Organisations
IS	Islamic State
ISF	Insaf Student Federation
ISI	Inter-Services Intelligence
ISPR	Inter-Services Public Relations
JI	Jamaat-e Islami
JUI-F	Jamiat Ulema-e Islam-Fazlur Rahman
KP	Khyber Pakhtunkhwa
KSF	Karachi Students' Federation
LDBA	Lahore District Bar Association
LeJ	Lashkar-e-Jhangvi
LeT	Lashkar-e-Tayyaba
LHCBA	Lahore High Court Bar Association
LUMS	Lahore University of Management Sciences
MMA	Muttahida Majlis-e-Amal
MML	Milli Muslim League
MQM	Muttahida Qaumi Movement
MSF	Muslim Student Federation

NA	National Assembly
NACTA	National Counter Terrorism Authority
NADRA	National Database Registration Authority
NAP	National Action Plan
NATO	North Atlantic Treaty Organization
NCEPG	National Counter Extremism Policy Guidelines
NCJP	National Commission for Justice and Peace
NEP	National Education Policy
NISP	National Internal Security Policy
NSF	National Students Federation
NSO	National Students' Organization
PAT	Pakistan Awami Tehreek
PATA	Provincially Administered Tribal Areas
PECA	Prevention of Electronic Crimes Act
PML	Pakistan Muslim League
PML(N)	Pakistan Muslim League-Nawaz
PMSF	Pakistan Muslim Students Federation
PRHP	Pakistan Rah-e-Haq Party
PSF	People's Student Federation
PTA	Pakistan Telecommunications Authority
PTI	Pakistan Tehreek-e-Insaf
PTM	Pashtun Tahafuz Movement
RAW	Research and Analysis Wing
SAPs	Structural Adjustment Programmes
SCBA	Supreme Court Bar Association

SSP	Sipah-e-Sahaba Pakistan
TLP/TLYR	Tehreek-e Labbaik Pakistan/Tehreek-e-Labbaik Ya Rasool Allah
TNSM	Tehrike-Nifaz-e-Shariat-e-Mohammadi
TTP	Tehreek-e-Taliban Pakistan
UET	University of Engineering and Technology
UNDP	United Nations Development Programme
UNESCO	United Nations Educational, Scientific and Cultural Organization
YDI	Youth Development Index

Prologue

The 2018 Elections and the illusion of a 'Naya Pakistan'

On 25 July 2018, amidst terrorist attacks and extraordinary levels of national security, Pakistan went to the polls. The 2018 election campaign had been marred by widespread allegations of military interference and marked by terror attacks, the worst of which, in Mastung in Balochistan, killed 151 people. On the Sunday before the election, the Pakistan Tehreek-e-Insaf (PTI)'s Ikramullah Gandapur became the fourth candidate to die when he was killed in a suicide attack. Given the violence in the run-up to the elections, around 400,000 soldiers were stationed inside and outside the country's 89,500 polling stations, a fivefold increase from 2013.

Elections were being held for both the national and the provincial assemblies, with 272 seats up for grabs in Islamabad; sixty of these were reserved for women and ten for minorities. There were nearly 106 million registered voters, 23 per cent more than in the 2013 elections (EUEOM 2018). In total, 95 of the 121 registered parties took part in these elections (EUEOM 2018), but the main battle was between the PML(N) and the PTI to bring about what was only the second civilian transfer of power in Pakistan's 70-year history. Added to this mix was the problematic presence of 'extremist parties' such as the Tehreek-e-Labbaik Pakistan (TLP), the Allah-o-Akbar Tehreek (AAT) and the Pakistan Rah-e-Haq Party (PRHP) which were affiliated 'either to terrorist groups, or individuals linked to organisations that have used, incited or advocated violence' (EUEOM 2018, p. 11).

An all-out win required 137 seats and Imran Khan's PTI won 112, leaving the Pakistan Muslim League (N) (PML(N)) with only 64 and the Pakistan Peoples Party (PPP) with 43 seats. Even in the Punjab Assembly, the PML(N)'s heartland, PTI won 123 out of 297 seats, just 2 short of the PML(N)'s 129 seats.

While PTI's victory can be perceived to have displaced the power of the two prominent political parties, the PML(N) and the PPP, heralding a 'naya Pakistan'[1], the events leading up to the elections, and the electoral process itself, reflect how this 'naya Pakistan' is in line with the existing security state. Khan has been accused by his opponents of being the 'chosen one' of the security establishment, with his victory attributed to a rigged election. The events leading up to the 2018 elections testify to a biased position against the PML(N) and the PPP evident in the actions of the security state that attempted to derail the electoral campaigns of the two main political parties.

The EU Election Observation Mission (EOM) highlights the restrictive environment before the 2018 elections including the manner by which the previously elected prime minister Nawaz Sharif was disqualified on charges of corruption 'that reshaped the political environment ahead of the elections' (2018, p. 10). Sharif was implicated in what came to be known as the 'Panamagate scandal' after the release of the Panama papers[2] that revealed links between the Sharif family and undeclared offshore accounts. The dismissal of Nawaz Sharif by the judiciary led to allegations of the security state's influence over the judicial proceedings especially in the manner in which Sharif was disqualified for life in April 2018, and sentenced to ten years in prison in July, just a few weeks before the elections (Shah 2019; Barker 2018; also see Afzal 2018a). Selective censorship of the media was also problematic. According to EU EOM (2018) media outlets had been contacted by 'state actors' (read: 'khalai makhlooq'[3]) instructing them not to show Nawaz Sharif's return to Pakistan from England for his arrest; nor were they allowed to show interviews with the Sharif family prior to their departure from England. PTI's political rhetoric was in line with the security state, in challenging the position of Nawaz Sharif and the PML(N), given Imran Khan's mandate was anti-corruption. Ironically, despite these accusations of corruption against politicians from other political parties, PTI welcomed many defectors who had previously been on the receiving end of PTI's anti-corruption drive, as they were considered 'electables' (Shah 2019). Yet, prior to the 2018 elections, PML(N) and its workers faced the worst kind of state censorship. Other political parties such as the PPP often faced delays and at times outright denial of licences to hold rallies, a problem that PTI hardly ever encountered (Afzal 2018b).

The problem of election rigging became apparent on election day. The Election Commission of Pakistan had given 'judicial powers to military personnel' who were deployed inside polling stations to ensure 'free and fair elections'. However, there were cases of polling agents being expelled from the polling stations, evident also in 'an audit' by NGOs that found that 'the official document for tabulating results at each polling station… was in 95 percent of cases lacking the polling agent's signature required by law' (Shah 2019, p. 137). Despite the interference by the security state, there were also examples of individuals being elected who were perceived to challenge the security status quo, that is, the case of Mohsin Dawar and Ali Wazir, two leading members of the Pashtun Tahafuz Movement (PTM). The PTM is a peaceful movement led by Manzoor Pashteen, a 25-year-old from South Waziristan, that is voicing its opposition to racial profiling of Pashtuns in the ongoing war against terrorism, demanding the return of the 'disappeared' and their rights under the Pakistani constitution; however, they have faced intimidation from the security state, where their supporters have been 'picked up', arrested and bullied in efforts to stop the movement. While the PTM is not a political party, its members, contesting from the districts of North and South Waziristan, won seats in the general elections for the National Assembly. Their role will be important in highlighting the plight of citizens in Federally Administered Tribal Areas (FATA), yet the space they will have to influence policy on FATA and Provincially Administered Tribal Areas (PATA) remains to be seen.

The decline of right-wing religious parties in this election was also a positive development, but one that needs to be assessed in relation to the success of the TLP, a political party that largely promotes an ideology of 'death to the blasphemer'. The TLP was the 'top fifth party' in 'the National Assembly, outranking major parties like Muttahida Qaumi Movement-Pakistan and Awami National Party among others' (Jahangir 2018). In Punjab, the TLP vote bank was about 69 per cent of the votes that were given to religious parties, while for the NA246 seat[4] in Karachi, the TLP candidate 'secured over 3,000 more votes than the PPP chairman'.

Ironically, these results are reflective of the nature of politics in Pakistan today as discussed in this book. The status quo remains with the security state in charge as parties such as the PML(N) have been removed from the playing field through the PTI; despite the decline of religious right-wing politics, the influence of the religious right has not completely dissipated, evident in the rise of the TLP, a political party that directly spews hatred and advocates violence; while the victory of members of PTM reflect the potential for change, of possibility, yet one that is defined in response to the atrocities of the security state – its narrative thereby shaped by the security narrative that has dominated the lives of Pakistanis for nearly seven decades.

A new political era – youth reflective politics?

PTI's election campaign, particularly in the urban centres, brought in a different middle-class demographic of young people, and families who were seldom seen in political rallies. These rallies were different from the usual political speeches; they included performances by Pakistani pop stars, DJs and celebrities that were there to support and entertain. The target audience were young Pakistanis, as the future of 'naya Pakistan'. Despite the close connection between the security services and the PTI, the party's rhetoric, in particular Prime Minister Imran Khan's inaugural speech, does reflect the sentiments and priorities of young people that are discussed in this book, in particular with regard to the four themes explored across the various chapters: social contract, education, terrorism and the 'right kind' of Islam.

The social contract

Prime Minister Imran Khan's speech drew on Islamic principles of justice and equality and directly addressed concerns regarding corruption, unemployment, education and basic human rights that are discussed in this book. The speech reflected the realization of the need to strengthen the state's ability to deliver basic services and maintain law and order: 'We will establish the supremacy of the law; whoever violates the law, we will act against them.' Khan promised to fix the government so that taxes would benefit the poor and state expenses would be cut. In order to repair Pakistan's fiscal deficit and resolve the economic crisis he promised to halt corruption, which he believes is at the heart of Pakistan's dysfunctional institutions: 'Our state institutions will be so strong that they will stop corruption.' This was directly addressed to the youth who have doubts about the democratic system and lack confidence in state institutions, putting their faith in the army to provide justice and security. It is the first time a Pakistani political party showed any kind of understanding that the Pakistani state in its current form is largely irrelevant in the lives of ordinary Pakistanis, having been unable to provide any economic or social security, and repeatedly accused of corruption and negligence; he also went further and promised to fix it.

Education and unemployment

Beyond governance and state responsibility, Khan addressed issues directly relevant to the youth as he did frequently during his election campaign, thereby getting the support of young voters, especially in the urban centres: 'There are countries with less than 25 million people, and we have that many children out of school.' Not offering a solution, he did link problems in education to another huge issue that Pakistan is facing – unemployment. 'Our second problem is unemployment. We have the second youngest population in the world; they need jobs.' As Chapter 3 shows, education has largely failed the young people of Pakistan. Despite maintaining a strong sense of national identity, they have little understanding of citizenship, nor does what they receive in school provide a sound basis for getting jobs. Today education is linked with the objectives of the security state through the National Counter Extremism Policy Guidelines (NCEPG) of 2018. Higher education institutions are increasingly becoming spaces of surveillance, rather than of critical thinking. It remains to be seen how the PTI-led government will make education relevant to the job market as well as giving young people an understanding of their wider role as citizens.

Security

In his speech Imran Khan also mentioned terrorism, especially the suicide attacks in Balochistan, and thanked the security forces for their service. Despite security and terrorism not featuring much during his first address, PTI's rhetoric is reflective of the National Internal Security Policy 2018–23 that focuses on countering extremism by strengthening the state–citizen relationship. In effect, the 'naya Pakistan' may be nothing more than the old establishment draped in the language of progress and human rights, with the security state remaining at the helm of power in Pakistan.

The problem not addressed here is the security state's record of continuing to mainstream extremist groups into Pakistani politics. Khan's own history points to positions that are more in line with those of the military, including his assertion that militancy in Pakistan was the result of the United States' ill-conceived war on terror rather than a history of support for militant proxies. Until the Pakistani state together with its military disentangles itself from an ideology where geopolitical interests trump the security of its own citizens, the problem of terrorism in Pakistan will continue. It is expected that some of this will be forced on the table as part of a review of Pakistan's relationship with the United States and the aid packages that are needed from the International Monetary Fund. Western institutions and governments are unwilling to continue to support Pakistan unless terrorism is addressed, leaving the PTI the choice between going it alone with China or engaging with the security issues in a meaningful way.

The 'right kind' of Islam

At the basis of the speech is a clear call to Pakistan's conservative religious communities: Imran Khan's vision of Pakistan is steeped in Islamic tradition –

'My inspiration is the Prophet Muhammad, the city of Medina that he founded, how it was based on humanity.' While Khan has been accused of peddling an ideology and beliefs very similar to those of the religious hard right (Dorsey 2018), this theme also pervaded the responses the youth gave when explaining that Pakistan's problems will only subside if and when the 'right kind' of Islam is followed. Like Khan, the 'right kind' of Islam is linked to an Islamic past, yet how this past manifests itself in the present is unclear to many young people today. Khan also spoke of uniting all behind this idea: 'I want all of Pakistan to unite. I want to make it clear that anyone who was against us, who voted against us, I think the kind of personal attacks that I have seen, no one has seen those, but I have forgotten all of those, they are behind me. My cause is far bigger than me.' It is not unusual to hear calls for unity after elections, but again reflecting young people's concerns, these calls showcase that the 'naya Pakistan' can transcend the traditional political divide between PPP and PML(N) supporters.

Khan's inaugural speech reflected the concerns of young people, which partly explains his huge popularity with Pakistan's youth despite the fact that he was the security state's candidate of choice. As this book will show, this paradox can be reconciled when seen through the prism of citizenship and how the country's youth view the Pakistani state.

Notes

1 'Naya Pakistan' literally means 'new Pakistan', a term coined by the PTI election campaign to denote a change from the old corruption ridden government to what the PTI promises will be a new form of government and governance.

2 The Panama Papers include over 11.5 million documents that were leaked showing financial information of individuals across the world including undeclared offshore accounts that could implicate clients for corruption or tax evasion.

3 'Khalai Makhlooq' or 'invisible aliens' – a phrase used by the former prime minister Nawaz Sharif for the military-intelligence nexus that he believed were his main competitors in the elections, given their increasing interference (see Jorgic 2018; BBC News 2018a).

4 National Assemble Seat 246 – it refers to a constituency.

Introduction

Background

Seventy years after its independence Pakistan's struggle with democracy continues. The country achieved its first democratic transition during the elections of 2013, as the elected government of the Pakistan Peoples Party (PPP) handed over power to the PML(N). PML(N)'s rule was not without controversy. Politically, the biggest blow to the PML(N) was the dismissal of the elected prime minister Nawaz Sharif by the Supreme Court of Pakistan on charges of corruption in connection with the Panamagate scandal[1] in 2017.[2] However, the country faced its biggest tragedy in recent history when the Army Public School (APS) Peshawar was attacked by the Tehrik-i-Taliban Pakistan (TTP) in December 2014; 140 people were killed, 132 of whom were children (Boone 2015). This resulted in a public outcry demanding that the government take action against all extremist groups. The Sharif-led government developed a twenty-point National Action Plan (NAP) that included lifting the 2008 moratorium on the death penalty. The twenty-first constitutional amendment passed on 6 January 2015; it empowered special anti-terrorism courts to try all terrorism suspects including civilians, bypassing the normal justice system. Yet the majority of the executions since the lifting of the moratorium have had nothing to do with terrorism and seem only to have reduced the number of convicts on death row (Justice Project Pakistan 2017). Other parallel structures created (such as the provincial apex committees) have allowed the military to play a more direct role in governance and further marginalize civilian institutions in the name of counterterrorism.

In the midst of the wave of violence that has refused to abate, the state felt the need for a national narrative on countering terrorism. This narrative is promoted through the National Counter Extremism Policy Guidelines (NCEPG) with implementable principles for every citizen and institution in the country to reduce the support, felt by some, for acts of terror. To further demonstrate its earnestness towards fighting terrorism the federal state launched a 'Paigham-i-Pakistan' in January 2018; this declaration was signed by more than 1,800 religious scholars from mainstream sects across the country, condemning among other acts 'suicide attacks against the state, spreading sectarianism and anarchy in the name of religion and issuing a call to jihad without the consent of the state' as un-Islamic (Dawn 2018). The state through the NCEPG and declarations like the Paigham-i-Pakistan is using a 'soft' approach to combating terrorism in Pakistan. While Paigham-i-Pakistan has brought religious scholars together, where the message will be promoted through academic and religious institutions, mosques and state institutions, there is also a recognition that other social institutions, such as news and media outlets including social media, need to play their part in assisting the state in its fight against terrorism. However, as the arguments in this book will illustrate, this 'soft' approach is increasingly targeting peaceful citizens who may be challenging the writ of the security state.

While suicide bombers and terrorists were already being targeted by security forces, the nature of the terrorist threat has also evolved, with university-educated individuals being found guilty of engaging in terrorist activities. In September 2017 Minister of Interior Ahsan Iqbal outlined concerns about the evolving nature of the threat, emphasizing the need 'to formulate a national narrative to counter the extremists' agenda', where 'the youth must be imparted with the importance of peace enjoined by Islamic injunctions and the vision of Pakistan'. The danger of the Pakistani-educated youth following the path towards extremism and terrorism was also highlighted in May 2017 by the Inter-Services Public Relations (ISPR) that organized a seminar in the army auditorium entitled 'Role of Youth in Rejecting Extremism'. The keynote address was delivered by the chief of army staff (COAS) Pakistan highlighting the problem of extremism and the importance of the country's youth in challenging this problem. As the COAS observed, 'We are standing at a crossroads; ten years down the line, we will either be enjoying the fruits of a youth dividend or suffering at the hands of a youth bulge, especially with the youth which remains vulnerable to extremism' (Express Tribune 2017b). The various speakers at the seminar, including the chairman of the Higher Education Commission, highlighted the importance of educational institutions in creating an atmosphere of critical learning that would challenge the potential of extremism among the youth (Pakistan Army 2017). The emergence of university-educated individuals such as Omar Sheikh, Saad Aziz, Hafiz Nasir, Azfar Ishrat, Hammad Adil, Tanveer Gondal, Hassan bin Nazeer, Abdul Karim Sarosh Siddiqui and Noreen Jabbar Laghari among others who have turned to terrorism has added another dimension to the discourse on terrorism in Pakistan. The traditional threat from groups in Federally

Administered Tribal Areas (FATA) or South Punjab still exists, where their foot soldiers are recruited either through tribal alliances or through madrassas. But there is an increasing recognition of individuals educated in elite schools or universities taking up the terrorist cause.

Military generals and politicians in the past have pushed narratives through policy agendas – whether it was Ayub Khan's modernization project, Z. A. Bhutto's Islamic socialism, Zia-ul-Haq's Islamization or Pervez Musharraf's Enlightened Moderation – but this 'national narrative' is different. It is being implemented through a counterterrorism authority, the National Counter Terrorism Authority (NACTA), revealing the extent to which the entire national discourse in Pakistan has been securitized. There is a recognition that individuals and communities who are supporting these terrorist causes are being fed a different narrative they have chosen to believe, whether premised on a (mis)interpretation of Islam, or one which questions the legitimacy of a state that has failed to deliver basic services to its citizens – a narrative that needs to be countered not just through traditional counterterrorism means, but also ideologically. In this process, NACTA tried to co-opt universities from across the country to support and promote the national narrative. However, these counterterrorism efforts have increasingly reinforced the emergence of a modern Pakistani 'security state' that recognizes the importance of public opinion in order to defeat these various threats, where any individual or institutional challenge to the security state's 'national narrative' is considered an obstacle in its fight against extremism, sectarianism, terrorism and militancy. If this means clamping down on an individual's freedom to critique or voice opposition to the security state – as evident in the case of bloggers, journalists, students or academics who have been picked up by security agencies and disciplined to follow the state narrative, or even educational institutions that have been urged (if not bullied) into self-censorship – in Pakistan post 9/11, the nexus between security agencies and state institutions has been further strengthened, increasingly weakening an already fallible social contract.

The security state approach has led counterintuitively to the state going after those who are seen as possibly critiquing Islam. An example of this is the Pakistan Telecommunication Authority (PTA) sending a message on all Pakistani mobile phones in 2017 asking users to report anyone who might be committing blasphemy. Also problematic and in the same line of thinking as the monitoring of anti-Islamic discourse on social media is the oxymoronic stance of the security state to mainstream right-wing religious parties into Pakistani politics in an attempt to control their power. The Milli Muslim League, a political party that was formed in 2017 and fought in the NA-120 by-elections, includes representatives and members that are on international lists of most wanted terrorists. The country has on several occasions also been held hostage by right-wing religious groups such as the Tehreek-e-Labbaik Ya Rasool Allah (TLYR or TLP) which together with the Tehreek-e-Khatm-e-Nabuwwat and the Sunni Tehreek Pakistan launched a countrywide three-week protest that ended in November 2017 with the state giving in to the demands of the protestors. The protest was against an amendment made to a clause in the Elections Bill 2017 that relates to the finality of the Prophet of Islam, called the 'Khatm-e-Nabuwwat oath', in which the phrase 'I solemnly swear' was replaced by 'the words "I believe"' (Pakistan Today 2017a). While the law minister defended his reasons for changing these words, clearly stating that it by no means challenged or repealed the 'Khatm-e-Nabuwwat laws' and the Parliament eventually decided that there had been a 'clerical error' and it should be reverted back to the original phrase, the protestors nonetheless demanded that the law minister be sacked. The protestors continued their protests, illegally taking over major cities of Pakistan, ignoring orders from the judiciary to end the protests and further protesting when their leaders and members were arrested, damaging property as well as beating up policemen. With the army refusing to step in at the request of the government, an operation was launched by the government (reminiscent of the disastrous Lal Masjid operation in 2007), which resulted in the killing of six individuals, with the army becoming a mediator between the government and the TLYR protestors and the government caving in to the demands of the protestors (see Chapter 4). Not only was the resignation of the law minister a sign of a weak state giving into these protestors, but the amount of time given to the Faizabad protestors further begs the question whether the Pakistani state is simply paying lip service to the idea of a national narrative against extremism. This is especially questionable in instances where rights activists are immediately stopped from protesting, as was evident in the protest organized by the social activist group FixIT in Karachi at the same time as the Faizabad protest, to raise awareness about the 'poor quality of education'; the protest ended within hours as the police 'used a water-cannon and tear gas to disperse the crowd' (Pakistan Today 2017b). While FixIT protestors were arrested, TLYR announced that it would run for the 2018 elections.

Another example is the security state's treatment of the Pashtun Tahafuz Movement (PTM). The PTM provides the ideal counternarrative to extremism; it is led by young citizens from Waziristan and FATA demanding their rights as Pakistanis. Instead of supporting and promoting this organic narrative, the counternarrative of the security state has been unable to move beyond its good and bad terrorist strategy, supporting groups such as TLYR whose ideology is divisive. In the end the strategy of the counternarrative to terrorism supports many of those it is intended to defeat ideologically.

This book explores these recent dynamics in Pakistan and how Pakistan arrived where it is now through the voices of the youth – exploring young Pakistanis' views and their relationship to this security state. The ideal Western notion of a social contract in relation to such a security state falls through, as the physical and ideological threat of terrorism trumps freedoms of expression and dissent that ought to be guaranteed to all citizens of Pakistan. The focus is on the voices of young Pakistanis, their views on state accountability (or lack thereof), political literacy/participation and the continued problem of terrorism that is transforming their views of both their country and the world today. With 67 per cent of the population under the age of thirty, Pakistan is uniquely poised to evolve in the next couple of decades, and this book provides a window into how that process is likely to unfold.

Explaining Pakistan

Pakistan has been changing over the last decade. One of the least understood concepts in Pakistan is that of citizenship – the relationship between the state and its people. As politics and daily life in Pakistan is increasingly marked by terrorism and violence, ordinary citizens are questioning the role of the state. When examining Pakistani society three main fault lines are usually used as a prism of analysis and as reasons for the country's current socio-economic problems: ethnic/linguistic or provincial identities, sectarian identities and the army versus the rest of the population. While all these fault lines do exist and indeed divide Pakistani society, this book argues that it is state–society relations that need to be examined and better understood in order to explain how Pakistan is evolving today. However, in order to understand state–society relations, it is important to briefly examine the three main fault lines that have shaped Pakistan Studies for the last few decades and see what role the state plays in each one of them (Lall 2012).

Ethnic/linguistic lines – Pakistan through the prism of regionalism

Pakistan was born with a temporary sense of national identity, many suspending their regional, ethnic and linguistic identities during the period immediately preceding independence. Once an independent state had been achieved, Muhammad Ali Jinnah, founder of Pakistan and Pakistan's first governor general, regarded all identities as subservient to Islam, and regionalism was seen as negative and detracting from Islamic unity. 'So what is the use of saying we are Bengalis, or Sindhis, or Pathans, or Punjabis? No, we are Muslims' (quoted in Adeney 2004, p. 166). Although denying the legitimacy of provincial claims for recognition would have been consistent with Jinnah's positive exclusivism, the disparity in the treatment of the regions that developed was not (Adeney 2009). Pakistan struggled with the balance of power between the region and the state, and regional conflicts delayed the first constitution by nine years. Ultimately, the nation was not able to effectively balance the call for regional autonomy with the power of the state. The institutions that rose to power in Pakistan engendered much resentment as they were ethnically dominated. The military in particular was controlled by a disproportionate number of Punjabis. This situation alienated other ethnic groups, especially the Bengali majority group, notably under-represented in the government, and increased the intensity of the divisive forces for regionalism. In addition, a relative paucity of economic wealth was apportioned to Pakistan after partition. This wealth, in turn, was unevenly concentrated and invested in the western wing of the country, only furthering provincial tensions (Talbot 1998). Even the ideology of 'Islamic Socialism' under Zulfikar Ali Bhutto failed to cut across ethnic structures. In the elections of 1970, Bhutto's support was mainly from Punjab and Sindh, not Balochistan, North-West Frontier Province (NWFP – now Khyber Pakhtunkhwa (KP) since 2010) or East Pakistan.

Ethnic Punjabi bias became synonymous with a class bias in the new state. For many Punjabis, there is no conflict between a Punjabi and a Pakistani identity, with the exception of the Siraiki belt, and there is a movement for Siraiki to be declared an independent province from Punjab (Birmani 2018). To this day there are ethnic divisions and grievances based on provincial origin. They are very real, as evident in the renaming of NWFP to KP as well as the flaring up of Balochistan's insurgency, and more recently the PTM. However, there are many cases of compatible and superimposed ethnic identities.

Religious conflict – Pakistan through the prism of sectarian conflict

Pakistan was conceived as a homeland for Muslims in South Asia. The first sectarian conflict emerged in 1953, about the Ahmadiyas in the Punjab. In 1974, under the democratically elected left-leaning Z. A. Bhutto, the government capitulated to a long-standing demand to declare the Ahmadiyas a non-Muslim minority.[3] The issue was intensified under Zia with the blasphemy law (especially Article 295-C) that brought in the death penalty or life imprisonment for blasphemy against the Prophet and effectively put every Ahmadiya at risk by simply practising his or her religion.

More prominent however has been the conflict between Sunnis and Shi'as that increased particularly after General Zia-ul-Haq took over as the chief martial law administrator in 1977, declaring that the Islamic society for which Pakistan had been created would be established and enforcing a Sunni Islam across the country. Zia's Islamization programme was in contrast to popular practice in the culture, in which most people were 'personally' but not 'publicly' religious. An unexpected outcome was that by relying on a policy grounded in Sunni Islam, the state fomented factionalism: by legislating what was Islamic and what was not, Islam itself could no longer provide unity because it was then being defined to exclude previously included groups. This had a particular repercussion in Shi'a–Sunni sectarian disputes as people started to ask 'Who is *really* a Muslim?' – a question that has increasingly haunted all Pakistanis since Zia started narrowing what defined a Muslim.

The fact that Islam could mean different things to different communities is at the bottom of Pakistan's sectarian problems. That Pakistan professed to be an Islamic state meant that Islamic laws would not merely be observed but that the state would enforce them. Which school of Islamic law would hold sway, and how that would affect those who did not recognize its authority, was not taken into account.

The army versus the rest – Pakistan through the prism of democracy

Mohammed Ali Jinnah wanted Pakistan to be a constitutional, parliamentary democracy informed by Muslim values. Yet after independence power was concentrated in the hands of the elite, with Jinnah as the governor general, president of the Muslim League and head of the Constituent Assembly; this created an unfortunate situation when he died thirteen months later because there was no one to fill his shoes.

The army became involved in domestic politics early on, inexorably changing the nature of the Pakistani state. After independence Pakistan suffered from three long periods of army rule starting with General Ayub Khan in 1958, when the parliamentary system came to an end for the first time. He handed over power to General Muhammad Yahya Khan in 1969 who oversaw the 1970 elections and the secession of East Pakistan. After six years of democratic rule under Zulfikar Ali Bhutto's PPP, General Muhammad Zia-ul-Haq imposed martial law and the expected elections were postponed. Zia changed Pakistan's constitution so that the democratically elected prime minister became subservient to the president. The most controversial power awarded to the office of the president was under Article 58(2)b, which gave the president the power to dissolve the National Assembly at his own discretion. Democratically elected governments resumed after Zia's death in 1988 for a decade, during which none of the four elected heads of state completed their legal term. General Pervez Musharraf took power in a coup in 1999. It was claimed that the army was forced to take this step to save the country from 'turmoil and uncertainty'. Today, even with a democratically elected government in place, the army is seen as the back-seat driver as the prime minister cannot decide on many domestic or foreign policy matters without the COAS's support (also see Shah 2019). Under Nawaz Sharif's government, there was no foreign minister, but an advisor to the prime minister on foreign relations, the portfolio remained directly under the prime minister's control. The COAS continues to make the important decisions related to foreign affairs, visiting important partners such as China and the United Arab Emirates.

All these fault lines are real and part of Pakistan's current issues. However, one consistent thread through all of them is the role played by the state in its treatment of its citizens, and how the citizens perceived the situation. This book argues that beyond these three typical explanations for Pakistan's political and economic woes lies a lack of 'citizenship' whereby Pakistanis, especially the youth, have neither a sense of rights and duties, nor an inclination for political participation. The issue of citizenship is linked to ethnic/provincial or sectarian identity when it comes to citizens' rights (or lack of rights for minorities) and lies at the heart of what kind of political participation is possible when the army has such a big stake in politics. This book therefore discusses different aspects of citizenship in light of the changing social and political circumstances that include terrorism and the rise of social media.

What is citizenship?

The idea of citizenship in this book focuses on the relationship between the individual and the state. Any understanding of this larger relationship has to encompass three different aspects as suggested by Joppke (2007, p. 38) – status, rights and identity. This definition also reflects Kivisto and Faist's (2007) understanding: they see citizenship as establishing the boundaries of the political community, defining who is in and who is out based on access to political life, as well as a sense of belonging through national identity.

The formal expansion of citizenship rights expanded over time from the civil to the political and further to the social sphere (Kivisto and Faist 2007). Going beyond the role and responsibilities of the state, philosophers have written about the ideal of self-governance that is based on the equality and equal liberty of all citizens. The concept of a mutually agreeable and reciprocal 'social contract' to which both the state and its citizens would adhere was born. This located citizenship squarely within democracy and largely Western literature has questioned if true citizenship can exist outside of a democratic system in the absence of political and participatory rights. This book takes the view that even in the absence of political participation there is a relationship between the state and the individual – albeit in a different form from democracies – and therefore the concept of citizenship remains relevant. This concept of citizenship in the context of Pakistan is linked to a 'security' state, where the traditional social contract has been greatly altered. The narratives in this book will highlight the nature of this altered social contract as the national narrative against extremism takes precedence over any ideals of 'rights and responsibilities' that may violate this state-sanctioned narrative. Furthermore, the book focuses on the macro relationship between the citizen and the state, not on the nature of citizenship at the level of the neighbourhood or city, which is also important in relation to the demands and expectations of citizens that might vary across neighbourhoods, cities and provinces related to 'everyday' existence (see Balibar 2010; Holston 2008).

In postcolonial countries, many of which are not necessarily democratic, the challenge of establishing a commonly agreed concept of citizenship has largely hinged on issues of defining national identity as opposed to rights, duties and political participation. Benhabib's definition of citizenship in the modern state as 'the collective identity of citizens along the lines of shared language, religion, ethnicity, common history and memories; the privileges of political membership in the sense of access to the rights of public autonomy; and the entitlement to social rights and privileges' (2005, p. 675) is more useful in postcolonial contexts as it engages with elements that emphasize the role identity plays as part of citizenship and acknowledges that these in themselves are diverse. In fact many postcolonial countries, especially in Asia, had as a political priority the establishment of a common national identity across ethnic, religious and linguistic boundaries, often using education as a political tool[4] to foster an often artificial unity based on imagined common bonds (Lall and Vickers 2009; Anderson 1983). Defining such a common identity allowed states to justify who could claim citizenship, and with it any rights, even if this was simply the right to live in a country.[5]

However, when it comes to defining citizenship, identity is often insufficient and rights, such as the right to political participation and freedom of expression and responsibilities, such as the duty to pay taxes, are still important, as is a general sense of legitimacy of the ruling government. In his work that examines how the concept of citizenship moved from West to East, Subrata Mitra expands on the relationship between citizenship and identity, arguing that only when both the legal and moral right to belong are combined, a legitimate sense of citizenship can develop. His point that the modern state has to work with traditional society is crucial in cases where in place of a nation there are diverse linguistic, ethnic and religious overlapping identities which existed well before the modern state was imposed:

> Just as the legal right to citizenship is accorded by the state, identity and following from it, the moral right to belong, is what people give to their claims to citizenship. When both converge in the same group, the result is a sense of legitimate citizenship where the individual feels both legally entitled and morally engaged. If not, the consequences are either legal citizenship devoid of a sense of identification with the soil, or a primordial identification with the land but no legal sanction of this. ... Orderly, legitimate citizenship is possible only if the concept is co-authored by the modern state and traditional society. (Mitra 2008, p. 348)

The relationship between national identity and citizenship is therefore a complex one, differing from country to country. According to the definitions above, identity is one of the elements of citizenship. However, citizenship goes beyond issues of identity as various groups within one state might have differing yet overlapping identities – ethnic, linguistic or religious – and should still be able to relate to an overarching concept of citizenship. For this, ethnic, linguistic and religious minorities need to be recognized by the state and in Pakistan there are tensions between historical realities, power and political will to accord equal citizenship to those who fall out of the mainstream definition of who is a Pakistani. Kymlicka and Norman (2000) have discussed the concepts of citizenship in diverse societies and have found that depending on the system, minorities sometimes are awarded special rights and sometimes have to play by the rules of the majority. Their work on multicultural citizenship discusses different possible paths of resolving conflicts – legal, social and political strategies for acknowledging and respecting the cultural or religious distinctiveness of minorities – and provides case studies of alternative policies that represent trade-offs among competing considerations. Their work shows that Pakistan is not the only country struggling to accommodate all its citizens.

The relationship of religion, national identity and citizenship in Pakistan

Allama Iqbal (1875–1938), who is credited with conceiving the idea of a separate Muslim nation on the subcontinent, believed that Islam could be a binding force between people of various ethnic and linguistic origins (Islam 1981). The father of the nation, Mohammed Ali Jinnah, however, had decreed that religion would have 'nothing to do with the business of the state'. Thus the aporia of creating a secular state for the Muslims in South Asia which has plagued the debates around Pakistani national identity ever since (Lall 2010).

> In hindsight one can say that Pakistan was born with a temporary sense of national identity, developed as a reaction to militant Hindu nationalism. Various Muslim groups in the subcontinent were able to suspend their regional, ethnic, and linguistic identities. Religion – a way of life – had become the predominant force as a basis for nationalism, other ethnic factors being temporarily pushed aside. (Islam 1981, p. 57)

So what is the role for Islam in Pakistani identity? At an official level using the word *Islamic* as a way of describing the state was debated for years. The 1956 Constitution called Pakistan an Islamic Republic; the 1962 Constitution removed that label; in 1973 it was reinstated. These were signs that right from the start the issue of Pakistan's national identity was in crisis. According to Hussain this led to a division between the ethno-nationalists and the ethno-Islamists. For the ethno-Islamists the identity oscillated between being a Muslim and being a Pakistani. For the ethno-nationalists the identity oscillated between their ethnicity – Punjabi, Baloch, Sindhi, Pakhtun, Mohajir or other – and being a Pakistani (Hussain 1976, p. 924). However, the transfer of citizenship from primordial to national levels proved difficult and there was no platform for negotiation to represent the views of ethno-nationalists, missing out on the 'moral dimension' of belonging that Mitra had outlined (Hussain 1976, p. 923).

Nasir Islam sees the development of the relationship between religion and national identity as changing across different stages of Pakistan's history. At independence the Western educated Pakistani elites were concerned with the creation of a state with a Muslim majority free from Hindu rule – yet not an Islamic state: 'The westernised leadership was modern and therefore capable of creating a viable state, but it was not religious and therefore incapable of creating an Islamic state' (Islam 1981, p. 58). During the Ayub era (1958–67) the military and bureaucratic elite shifted the focus from religion to economic growth, using 'bureaucratic mechanisms rather than ideological-political means for national integration' (Islam 1981, p. 59). Bhutto (1971–77) developed 'Islamic socialism' with a stress on popular conceptions of Islam. It was under General Zia that Islam was increasingly seen as a central tenet of Pakistani national identity, and religion became a means by which Pakistan not only justified its existence, but also used it as a tool for domestic unity as well as against perceived external threats such as India. Zia's policy of Islamization through the introduction of Islamic norms and laws radicalized Pakistani society between 1977 and 1988.[6] Sunni Islam became a central tenet of Pakistani identity. To the great consternation of Sunni communities, the introduction of Zakat and the Iranian revolution led to a radicalization of the Shi'a identity. This in turn also led to Sunni religious nationalism, especially among the Sunni urban middle classes, who were often Mohajirs, or the new middle class in the Punjab which grew due to the increased Gulf labour remittances of the 1970s. Radical sectarianism increasingly supported by the middle classes started to flourish and has over the years led to much bloodshed and the creation of radical sectarian groups such as the Sipah-e-Sahaba Pakistan (SSP) whose aim is to have Shi'as declared 'non-Muslim' under the Pakistani constitution. Zia's legacy of sectarian division as well as an Islamic curriculum across all state schools still affect society today.

From independence onwards issues of citizenship were confused with those of national identity. With national identity being so closely linked to religion it has meant that to this day all three concepts are often mixed up. The fact that national identity – and with it the role of religion – is only one tenet of citizenship has generally been lost. The 'other side' of citizenship, that is, rights and responsibilities and so on, has become a problem. Dean has argued that Pakistani children are not equipped at school with the tools to become participative citizens: '[W]hile Pakistani students acquire knowledge and learn some important values in school, they do not learn the skills (problem-solving, decision-making) and values (civic mindedness, critical consciousness) required for effective participation in democratic life' (Dean 2005, p. 35). Dean's study on citizenship in Pakistan showed that 'the organization and management of schools and most teaching and learning practices are not conducive to the preparation of democratic citizen' (2005, p. 51). The state failed to develop a clear understanding of the other, legal side of citizenship relating to rights, duties and political participation. This was not helped by thirty-plus years of military rule, where issues of citizens' rights were put on the back burner and political participation was restricted.

Citizenship in Pakistan

The issue of rights is particularly relevant for postcolonial societies such as Pakistan which are made up of various groups and whose state has the challenge not only of defining an overarching national identity, but also of fostering a concept of citizenship shared across various groups. Research has shown that in Pakistan, the overarching identity of being a Pakistani is often secondary to one or more ethnic, linguistic and religious/sectarian identities of the individual (see Lall 2012; Siddiqi 2010; Rahman 1998; Hussain 1976). This may be due partly to the fact that the new idea of Pakistan is in a way embattled with the regional identities that preceded the idea of Pakistan, the ethno-nationalists mentioned earlier. This becomes a problem when the state imposes a homogenous religious identity of being 'Pakistani'. Early leaders had expected that Islam would bind the new nation together and that previous fault lines would evaporate. The success of building the link between individuals and the state depends largely on how well the elites of a country have managed politically and through education to foster a common understanding of citizenship that goes beyond identity. However, as Pakistani political economist Akbar Zaidi has argued, in Pakistan the elites looked to the West, abandoning their country to be steered by those who had their own political and religious motivations.[7] As the state increasingly failed to provide the basics for ordinary Pakistanis, the rich either left or were able to buy what they needed from a parallel private sector world; this dynamic insulated the wealthy and their families from wider society. Given that elites are also those who make up the leadership of most political parties, the seeds for a disjuncture between the state and society had been sown.

Post-9/11 Pakistan

A major turning point in Pakistani politics was the terrorist attacks in the United States on 11 September 2001. General Musharraf, at the time in power, decided to stand with the United States in the 'war against terror', taking Pakistan into both an external war and an internal conflict. It is in these years that the seeds of today's terror attacks were sown and this time frame is also when our narrative in this book begins. Taking part in what was perceived to be a US war against a Muslim country and seeing the Pakistani state, despite being led by a general, push US programmes and policies to promote 'democratization', led to even deeper divisions across society. Radical Muslim groups used Pakistan's pro-Western foreign policy to question the legitimacy of the state. Musharraf's intent to reform the curriculum and the wider education system was swatted by local resistance as the state was seen as more and more out of touch with the day-to-day realities of the general populace.

Musharraf's policies ultimately engendered one of the most high profile political movements calling for citizenship rights and state responsibility, decoupled from the usual aspects of identity, in the form of the 2007 lawyers' movement that many credit with creating greater political awareness among young people. However, once Musharraf was removed, the movement died. More recently the rise of Pakistan Tehreek-e-Insaf (PTI) supported claims that young people are working towards a 'naya Pakistan' (new Pakistan), a claim further explored in this book.

In sum, citizenship as identity (in this case a common religious identity) was fostered while the legal aspects of citizenship relating in particular to rights, duties and political participation were neglected. This has created an important fault line in Pakistani society between individuals and the state as the state in effect operates in parallel with little or no connection to its citizens, unless citizens pose a threat to the 'national narrative', resulting in a 'security state' that makes its presence felt. Extensive fieldwork over nine years has shown increased alienation of the younger generation, who know their rights and duties but feel that political participation to change the system is all but useless.

Why a book on youth and citizenship?

Pakistan's youth population is one of the largest in the world. A recent United Nations Development Programme (UNDP) report (2017) focused on Pakistani youth offers the most comprehensive profile of the country's 54 million young people. The report estimates that Pakistanis under the age of 30 make up about 64 per cent of the country's population of 189 million, and 29 per cent – nearly a third (54 million) – are between the ages of 15 and 29.[8] The report says that human development can be achieved only through actively engaged citizens, while at the same time actively engaged citizens are an outcome of human development. The focus therefore is on three levers for change in Pakistani society:

1. education for knowledge and empowerment
2. gainful employment
3. engagement: voice, identity, inclusion and citizenship

The report, which is based on a large survey and focus group discussions with young people around Pakistan, defines the 'more intangible' third driver of change of citizenship as the youth's voice, identity, sociopolitical participation, marriage, societal inclusion and exclusion, radicalization and social attitudes. Without meaningful engagement, the report concludes, young people will not feel that there are opportunities for social, political and institutional integration into the fabric of society and its collective decisions (p. v). Reflecting the conclusions drawn in this book's chapter on political participation, the report explains why it is no surprise that there is little engagement with community and political affairs, and young people's aspirations, hopes, challenges and fears are not heard (pp. 7–8, 22). Pakistan is not a country that values its youth: 94 per cent of those taking part in the UNDP research do not have access to a library while 93 per cent do not have access to a sports facility. Seventy-seven per cent do not have any personal means of transportation, in a country with a dearth of public transport (p. 34). Despite all the social issues faced by the country's youth and increasing security concerns, the UNDP reports that an overwhelming number of young people are optimistic about Pakistan – of those surveyed, 70 per cent feel safe, 89 per cent feel happy, and 67 per cent feel that their life is better than their parents' (p. 34). These positive attitudes are reported notwithstanding Pakistan's large social disparities in terms of education, employment and income. While the report does not expand on the reasons for this optimism, there is nonetheless an element of hope that the report highlights, where such optimism can be harnessed towards progress and development for Pakistan.[9]

The problem with engagement

According to the UNDP report, providing young people with education and employment possibilities does not empower them unless they themselves feel that they can, in some capacity, influence or determine the decisions that shape their lives.

> Engagement is not simply an end itself but also the means to an end, towards an informed, engaged and responsible citizenry in control of the decisions that

> affect their lives. Meaningful engagement increases the chances that a young person's views are heard, respected and utilised. This in turn leads to young people feeling more connected to and developing a stake in a collective larger than themselves. (pp. 102–3)

The opposite of engagement, that is, marginalization, can drive the youth towards militant ideologies that carry false promises of certainty and reward. The lack of education and employment means that many young people cannot afford to get married and raise a family. 'It is no coincidence that most of those involved in militant attacks are young men who feel disenfranchised in one way or another and have never had the opportunity to develop a sense of their own potential in shaping a better future for themselves, their families and communities' (p. 106).

The report is particularly valuable in that it engages with youth representatives from all sections of society. Much research on politics in Pakistan has focused on youth as 'students' (as in higher education) and student politics (such as Nasr 1992; Nelson 2009; Nelson 2011; see also Jinnah Institute 2013). The majority of young people in Pakistan will never finish their education and will have dropped out somewhere along the way. It is therefore important to keep in mind the issues of class and education. It is for this reason that this book includes a range of voices from students in low-income areas who are unlikely to ever join a higher education institution.

Powell (2014) has argued that across the world marginality is now being experienced in a new and somewhat distinctive way by younger people. Writing on the youth allows us to contrast views collected between generations. While many young people do not seem to see the relevance of the state and its structures, teachers, parents and grandparents who took part in the study believed in the role of the state. Overall they spoke of their deep disappointment as the state has abrogated its responsibilities. Older people described how the state should be responsible for basic services, and at the very least provide security, but they acknowledged that in contemporary Pakistan the state had become elusive and they had to rely on family networks and civil society.

The data and our research

Four big field studies between 2009 and 2018 provided the material for this book. In 2009 a mixed-method survey was administered to more than 1,300 respondents across three provinces and supplemented with focus groups and interviews at schools and universities across the country. Data was not collected in KP in this phase due to the security situation at the time. However, the respondents included a large section of Pashtun[10] residents in Punjab, Sindh and Balochistan. Further qualitative data was collected again between November and December 2011 and in December 2012; that included focus groups with students, and interviews with teachers and parents. This follow-up work was conducted through a classroom exercise held with students, usually from Grades 9 and/or 10. The classroom exercise was conducted in 15 schools with around 370 students. Most of the data was collected in the Punjab, but the research took place in all four provinces and Azad Kashmir.

In total, data was collected in twelve private schools, twelve philanthropic schools, ten government schools and five colleges and universities in urban, semi-urban and rural areas in Karachi, Daharki, Tando Allahyar, Hub, Quetta, Bahawalpur, Dera Ghazi Khan, Sahiwal, Lahore, Islamabad, Abbottabad and Muzaffarabad.[11] Data was also collected at three madrassas (one for girls and two for boys), one Jamaat-e-Islami private school (serving the middle classes) as well as from various Lahore higher education colleges.

The 2015–16 survey was conducted in three government sector universities and two private sector universities in the provincial centres of Lahore and Karachi, where the largest universities in the country are located. Students were from Lahore, Karachi, Quetta, Hyderabad, Sargodha, Dera Ghazi Khan, Rajanpur, Kasur, Peshawar, Muridke, Faisalabad, Sialkot and Sheikhupura[12] who were studying at government sector universities or took part through the online survey. A total of 258 surveys were collected in 2015–16. While the majority of the students were enrolled in undergraduate programmes, there were also students from graduate schools across disciplines ranging from the humanities to the pure sciences and arts that were included in the sample. While the nature of the 2009 survey was more directly related to questions linked to meanings around being Pakistani, rights and duties of the state and citizens, as well as perceptions of belonging and alienation; the 2015–16 survey expanded on these, asking participants about political activism and awareness, social media and the function of state institutions. The 2015–16 survey, while building on a similar overarching theme related to citizenship, was nonetheless different, asking students about current events in Pakistan. Both male and female students participated in this research, but results were not disaggregated for gender. While the analysis explores tensions between ethnicity, sect and religion, it discusses overarching youth perspectives. In addition to these four periods of intense and focused fieldwork, the book is based on conversations and interviews with young people, that have been conducted over a decade regarding the changing Pakistani state.

Structure of the book

Chapter 1 discusses Pakistani youth's view on the social contract. Social contract theory posits that citizens and the state have an interdependent relationship with each other based on rights and responsibilities including the duty of political participation. This chapter questions how much this Western framework, which has underpinned Pakistan's postcolonial governments, is still relevant today. It further highlights how the social contract has increasingly been drawn into the security agenda with the NCEPG 2018 recognizing the importance of strengthening the state–citizen relationship through the delivery of basic services for the purposes of countering extremism at the community level. Many Pakistanis still feel the state ought to provide for their basic needs, especially with regard to employment. However, neither state nor government have delivered, resulting in civil society having to fend for itself. Since 2009, in light of growing numbers of terrorist attacks, the democratic state has increasingly turned into a security state – the rights of the citizens are protected on the condition that they do not challenge the writ of the 'security' state. The chapter explores the nature of this social contract, and young peoples' opinions about this state–citizen relationship.

Chapter 2 focuses on the nature of political activism among the youth. With the exception of ethno-nationalist movements that have support among young people from these ethnicities, political activism among students in educational institutions has gradually eroded over the past few decades. The chapter begins with an exploration of the historically located student activist and their role in the Pakistan movement, followed by an evaluation of the place of the student activist in the newly independent Pakistan. The first part focuses on important events linked to student activism on university campuses and their impact on larger provincial and national politics, highlighting a complex relationship of patronage as well as resistance between the state and its student activists. In contextualizing these narratives, the increasing use of violence by student groups within universities and the selective ban on union activities across the years is also explored, providing a context for the narratives of participants who are not members of such organizations. The chapter further highlights a problem with an understanding of political activism and what it means, as narratives of political awareness reveal the issue of political illiteracy among young people. This is especially important in light of the lawyers' movement against Musharraf and the emergence of the populist PTI, which claims to have the support of the 'youth of Pakistan' as well as the emergence of the PTM, that although based in ethnic grievances, transcends these. The discussion illustrates how the student activist, once celebrated by Quaid-i-Azam as 'an arsenal of Muslim India', has been predominantly depoliticized in today's Pakistan.

Chapter 3 gives the background on education in Pakistan. In order to understand the problem of political illiteracy among the youth in Pakistan, this chapter examines the nature of education and citizenship in relation to civic identity in Pakistan. It analyses Pakistan's education policy, curricula and young Pakistanis' opinions about the education system. The chapter argues that the Pakistani education system perpetuates an uncritical and often restrictive understanding of Islam and the Pakistani identity, teaching students to become loyal subjects rather than 'active citizens'. The chapter goes beyond the analysis of Zia-ul-Haq's Islamization drive of the 1980s, examining how even a reformed curriculum and a devolved education system after the Eighteenth Amendment has been unable to create 'active citizens' who feel they have a stake in the system.

Chapter 4 looks at terrorism. Terrorism is one of the biggest problems facing Pakistan today. From marketplaces being attacked by suicide bombers, to school children in Peshawar being targeted, terrorist threats are a part of everyday life for Pakistanis. This chapter explores the nature of this terrorist threat, especially the 'nontraditional' threats and the state's response to them, in particular the introduction of NCEPG 2018. The chapter examines what the security state has called a soft approach through a 'national narrative' on Pakistan that aims to challenge the ideology of terrorist groups, providing an alternative narrative for young people at risk of radicalization. The chapter further examines young people's views on terrorism, in particular their understanding of why terrorism exists in Pakistan. It also explores the pockets of resistance against the security state that exist in Pakistan but argues that the extent of this resistance and critique is limited. The students in this study in their assessment of the security apparatus have predominantly been in favour of the military and the state in its fight against terrorism, explaining the actions of the security state as a necessary response to the security situation that confronts Pakistan today.

Chapter 5 reviews the role of social media networks that are a more recent feature within the political landscape of Pakistan, and that have also become part of the security apparatus. This chapter examines the presence and policing of social media in Pakistan. It highlights how state policy towards preserving a 'national narrative' about the country that glorifies the army, criminalizes dissent and promotes an exclusive religious identity, is also reinforced on social media. Such criminalization of activity online is further problematic in a context where law enforcement authorities are ill equipped and lack training in dealing with 'online' crimes committed by individuals. Also problematic is the increasing level of fear and surveillance that such policies have reinforced among the country's citizens, as evident in cases of bloggers and activists being abducted for their online activity. The last part of the chapter explores young people's narratives to understand their use of social media, and the extent to which this medium of communication has the potential to promote political activism offline.

Notes

1 The discovery of illegal offshore accounts in Panama belonging to the prime minister and his family.
2 This was the third time Nawaz Sharif was unable to complete his term as elected head of state.
3 Enacted by Zulfikar Ali Bhutto to get the support of religious parties, not because most Pakistanis wanted it.
4 The use of education as a political tool is of course not confined to Asia. In Western industrialized societies education was also used to create what was in those days an 'artificial unity'. Generally today, however, education's role as a political tool is most visible in postcolonial countries where in a short span of time diverse ethnic, linguistic and religious communities had to be joined together under the banner of a new nation state.
5 See South and Lall (2017) and Lall et al. (2014) on Myanmar citizens focusing on the right to live in Myanmar.
6 Zia's policies created both radicalization and a powerful reaction across the civil society against it. The Women's Action Forum and Movement of Restoration of Democracy capitalized on the local cultural capital to militate against the project of radicalization.
7 See Zaidi (2013).
8 Pakistan's current population stands at 207.7 million according to the most recent census figures available (2017). Since age disaggregation had not been released at the time of writing, for the purpose of analysis the UNDP report uses data based on the 1998 census.
9 There is an important distinction to be made between hope translated into action, and patriotism that evokes sentiments of hope. In our work, for instance, the

participants continued to believe in the future of Pakistan, but the language used to express that belief echoed sentiments of patriotism, expressing how they would always serve their nation. This patriotism, as the chapters in this book illustrate, is the result of an education system that reinforces a nationalist ideology, inculcating a strong narrative of sacrifice for the country; this is reinforced through the media as well as political (or military) rhetoric.

10 The Pashtuns in the sample are not representative of KP in its entirety. Their points of view, especially in relation to their lived reality as citizens, is nonetheless important in highlighting regional disparities.

11 Karachi is the provincial centre of Sindh, and the financial capital of Pakistan; Daharki and Tando Allahyar are cities in Sindh; Hub is a city in Balochistan, and Quetta is the provincial centre of Balochistan; Bahawalpur, Dera Ghazi Khan and Sahiwal are cities in Punjab, with Lahore the provincial centre of Punjab; Abbottabad is a city located in eastern KP, Muzaffarabad is the capital of Azad Kashmir, and Islamabad is the capital of Pakistan.

12 Hyderabad is a city in Sindh; Sargodha, Rajanpur, Kasur, Muridke, Faisalabad, Sialkot and Sheikhupura are cities in Punjab; Peshawar is the provincial centre of KP.

1

Youth and the Social Contract

Introduction

I feel that generally people in Pakistan do not believe citizenship exists. ... If it does, it is a luxury open only to the elite and for them citizenship is only rights and not duties or responsibilities. As a concept it does not matter to the majority where basic human needs are not being met.

(Teacher, Female, Karachi)

Thar mei bachei mar rahei hain unkei liyei kuchh nahi karna par cricket match peh cheezei jilaani hain.[1] ... *We are willing to protest for not getting laptops but we won't do the same for the famine in Thar.*

(Focus Group, Government University[2])

These two observations, by a teacher in Karachi and an undergraduate student in Lahore, illustrate the fragmented nature of the social contract in Pakistan. Many postcolonial societies like Pakistan adopted a Western model of state–citizen relationship after independence. The social contract was almost a given for these newly independent countries in the advent of new state and institution building. After the Second World War, the decolonizing states were following in the democratic footsteps of their former Western colonial masters. As such the state was responsible for structural inputs – electricity, water and infrastructure – and services such as health and education as well as security, guaranteeing their citizens certain basic rights. Pakistan set up a state based on the social contract model, developing basic education, health and other public infrastructure for its citizens. From the start, however, Pakistan allowed for a parallel system to operate in the private sector, benefiting the richer sections of society. The poor, comprising the vast majority of the country, were reliant on the state to meet their basic needs. The response of the teacher from Karachi illustrates this fragmented nature of the social contract, with rights becoming a luxury guaranteed only to the rich or the upper middle classes, while the rest of the citizens struggle for basic amenities. The regional disparity in relation to rights and duties is evident in the response of the student from the focus group in Lahore, quoting the example of one of the most deprived areas in Pakistan, Thar, that is suffering from severe drought, resulting in the deaths of hundreds of children.[3] The lack of response or outrage from the population, particularly in Punjab, is indicative of the general divide across provinces and socio-economic groups in Pakistan. With Islam being mainstreamed into the state structure in the three decades after independence, the nature of the social contract for religious minorities and different sects also changed. In essence, this 'social contract' was different across socio-economic class and religious groups. Like most developing nations with a colonial legacy, Pakistan struggled to provide for its large and growing population. However, in the 1950s and 1960s, Pakistan was developing fast, and due to its market economy seemed poised to make the most of a growth trajectory.

Fast-forward to today and the picture looks rather different. There is an official recognition that the 'state by definition must be strong and effective with a monopoly over the possession and employment of force and the authority and obligation for providing basic socio-economic needs and good governance to its people' (NACTA 2018, p. 4). Yet, this recognition is in relation to a counterextremism strategy that attempts to examine how and why Pakistanis turn towards terrorism. There is a realization that the weakness of the state in governance and service delivery has created a vacuum exploited by extremist elements. It took over a decade of violence in the form of terrorist attacks for the Pakistani state to even acknowledge there was a failure on its part. But this recent acknowledgement is a long way from any concrete action. The state in Pakistan had become increasingly absent. State-provided services had been declining in quality and availability for several decades. Civil society and the private sector jumped in, but given Pakistan's size and population they were unable to replace the state. Increasing numbers of lower-middle-class people and even the poor turned to the low-fee private sector to fulfil their education and health needs. As electricity, gas and water supplies became irregular, those who could afford paid for generators and water tankers. Those who could not, continue to bear the bad infrastructural conditions.[4] From time to time there are protests reminding the government that the state structures have crumbled; however, most know that protests serve little purpose as officials are largely unable to do anything about the dismal state of affairs.[5] The state, while becoming increasingly ineffective, was still able to broadly provide domestic security until around 2005–6. However, this too changed as the effects of the war in Afghanistan, especially after 9/11, started to take their toll.[6] Until recently ordinary Pakistanis saw the role of the state not as one that necessarily provided basic amenities such as infrastructure, education and health, but one which at least provided security. As terrorist groups, both domestic and foreign, started to fight the Pakistani establishment, it was mostly ordinary citizens who suffered. Since 2008 the increased violence across the country in the form of suicide attacks and random bomb blasts has meant that the state is no longer fulfilling this role either, increasing the alienation across the country.

Over the seven decades since independence Pakistan has provided fewer and fewer basic social goods to its citizens and the political elites have failed to establish a relationship even in democratic times, reinforcing a stark class divide. Pakistan is ranked at 150 in the Human Development Index 2017 (UNDP 2018). According to a UNDP report, 'In 1987/88 the Gini coefficient, which measures income inequality, was 0.35; by 2013/14 it had risen to 0.41. Pakistan's richest 20 per cent now consume seven times more than the poorest 20%' (UNDP 2016b, p. 1). There is further regional disparity. In 2016 the Multidimensional Poverty Index 'found that 54.6% of rural Pakistanis experienced poverty compared to 9.3% in cities' (UNDP 2016b). Furthermore, 'multidimensional poverty stands at 31.5% in Punjab but rises to 73.7% in FATA' (UNDP 2016b). The level of disparity is evident in the fact that 'multidimensional poverty in Islamabad, Lahore, Karachi, and Rawalpindi is below 10%; it exceeds 90% in Killa Abdullah, Harnai, Barkhan, Sherani Kohistan' (UNDP 2016b). The Youth Development Index (YDI) that measures 'health, education, employment and civic and political participation' of youth between the ages of 15 and 29 for 183 countries, placed Pakistan at 154 in 2016, 'the only non-African country amongst the ten lowest-ranked Commonwealth countries' (UNDP 2017, p. 32). Regionally, Pakistan trails behind all other South Asian countries except Afghanistan in education indicators, 'with a youth literacy of barely 70.7%'. While many of the country's woes are often explained by the thirty-odd years of military dictatorships that plagued the country between 1958–69, 1977–88 and 1998–2008,[7] a closer look at these three decades shows that while citizens' rights were certainly abolished or violated, the social contract side of the state as a provider of services, that is, state responsibility, did continue, mostly unabated. Under military rule, the state was, if anything, more present in people's lives than it was during times of democratically elected governments.

In any case the youth of today have hardly known the kind of military rule that their parents lived under. The 'democratic decade' with alternating rules of Benazir Bhutto and Nawaz Sharif started in 1988. Musharraf's military rule was rather different than that of his military predecessors with his emphasis on 'Enlightened Moderation' quite a stark contrast to the last military dictator, Zia-ul-Haq, and his Islamization policy. Musharraf ensured that elections were held in 2002. So the understanding of Pakistan's youth is that of a country mostly led by democratically elected rulers and one pseudo despot.[8] Democratic rule, more than any other form of government, is what has shaped their view of state–citizen relations. Although they have grown up under more 'democratic governance', the young people of today have experienced less state responsibility towards citizens than previously. Consequently, there is a malaise across the youth; they have little or no understanding of the functions or 'use' of the state. Young people feel disconnected because the state is absent. While issues such as the energy crises and unemployment have triggered sporadic protests in urban centres, with calls for the state to take responsibility for the provision of basic amenities, the response of the state has been negligible. State responsibility only exists on paper, as families have to fend for themselves and rights, especially related to social goods, are largely nonexistent. Life across all sections of society is lived in parallel to the state structures. The state makes an occasional appearance, for example after natural disasters such as the floods in Sindh in 2010 and 2011, when limited aid was provided to certain communities (Siddiqi 2014); however, civil society also carries a large part of post-disaster burdens. Right-wing religious organizations are also known to intervene in post-disaster relief efforts, thereby gaining on the ground support (Bano 2009). Often the military is perceived as the only visible part of the state, from anti-terror operations to providing relief camps. With regard to rights, it seems to make little difference to ordinary people what kind of government is in power – military or democratically elected.[9]

Given this reality one can argue that there has been a historical failure by the political elites to make the state relevant to the wider population. Only now in 2018 has there been an acknowledgement of this failure albeit through a counterextremism strategy. The NCEPG 2018 clearly state:

> It is required to now restore further confidence in State as service provider particularly in conflict hit areas including Balochistan, Sindh and FATA. The basic unit of the administration in Pakistan is the revenue district with a population, outside the metropolises, of between one and three million people approximately. It is the center where people live, own land and property, earn

> their livelihood, interact with each other and get involved in disputes and conflicts. District is the meeting point between state and citizens and ought to be the most important unit in State hierarchy. Over the last forty years the District departments have gradually decayed due to under-strength operational departments, shortage of funds, centralizing placement and decision-making, inter alia. (NACTA 2018, p. 10)

Despite such an acknowledgement, this chapter illustrates the lack of confidence of young people in the state structure. It describes the nature of the social contract today, where citizens can no longer be appeased through such documents, jaded as they are by their experience of the state's failure to meet its responsibilities in the past.

The 'social contract' in Pakistan

> *Every man for himself. All of us are like that. In Pakistan only poor people, people at the bottom are punished, if you are higher up no sense of accountability. It is different in other countries like Japan. There is accountability.*
>
> (Focus Group, Private University[10])

Pakistan was never a welfare state, but due to its colonial roots and inheriting a British legal framework, the basis for a Western-style social contract was laid. The question that arises is whether a Western-style social contract system remains the appropriate model for Pakistan today – or, in other words, are Western political scientists and social contract theorists such as Hobbes, Rousseau and Rawls perceived to be relevant for Pakistan, by the Pakistanis themselves (Siddiqi 2013)?

Social contract theories tried to establish why citizens would and should accept authoritative governments and obey the law, laying the foundation for the contemporary understanding of the modern state. Today, however, social contract theories take the existence of the modern state as a given. Rawls is at the basis of the welfare state making the social contract a platform for the construction of rights and responsibilities. His interpretation, however, also requires a certain amount of agency on the part of the individual – citizens have to take part or be able to take part in public life. The contract rests on reciprocity and both sides have to take part for it to work. This reciprocity is also at the basis of the legitimacy of the modern state. The state has to justify its existence through what it should do with regard to meeting the needs of the individual citizens, and the state is only entitled to power if it meets the needs of its citizens. The state therefore has an obligation under the social contract to build institutions and to protect both private and public interests (Ritter and Bondanella 1988). It is an open question whether the Pakistani state has adequately built and maintained these institutions to safeguard Pakistani citizens, and as made clear from the observation by the student in the focus group, many perceive that these safeguards are not equally present for all citizens.

Globalization and state responsibility

At this point it is worth remembering that the relationship between the individual and the state is linked to the particular form of the nation state, which changes over time and is often related to social revolutions. State–citizen relations have not remained static, neither has the social contract. In low-income countries, citizenship is more likely to vary between democracies and military dictatorships. However, even when there is no democracy, and consequently a lack of rights (as opposed to duties), there is still a reduced form of citizenship as states can maintain some level of state responsibility and provide social goods to their citizens. Kirstein and Voigt write about the kinds of dictatorships that avoid a revolution and the risk of being overthrown (also called 'moderate exploitation') (Kirstein and Voigt 2006). These types of dictators do care about the state responsibility side of the social contract, thereby fulfilling a limited part of their citizens' rights.

Today globalization is credited with altering the concept of the state quite fundamentally across the globe (Kuisma 2008). In the era of globalization neoliberal policies have ensured the centrality of the market and this new order raises questions about the role of the state, especially since many hyperglobalists such as Francis Fukuyama and Thomas Friedman will insist that globalization actually entails a withering away of the state. Olssen and Peters (2005) have pointed out that globalization has not resulted in a reduction of state power, but rather in a shifting of such power to new areas whereby the state's role has moved from that of a provider of social and public services to one of a regulator. Consequently, neoliberalism is not about less state control but rather represents a new form of state involvement (Wrigley 2007). In Pakistan, neoliberalism has been further reinforced under the IMF and the World Bank's Structural Adjustment

Programmes (SAP). As the market logic is extended to the public sector, the state becomes a regulator rather than a provider of such services. This is further supported by the actions of the middle classes who have pulled out of communal responsibilities, often in part because state services are seen as inefficient and corrupt. As such the state uses the market as a new control mechanism. While there is a general withdrawal of the state it is not in the arena of control but rather in its position of responsibility for safeguarding all citizens, especially the weaker sections of society. The new economic realities have led to increased marketization across the public sector – commercialization of public services and the use of market proxies leading in turn to disaggregation, deregulation, commodification, an emphasis on measurable outputs, managerialism and accountability. This in turn delegitimizes the state. Neoliberalism is in effect the new 'common sense' that has replaced the social democracy of the post-war era (Giroux 2003). Globalization has allowed neoliberal market-oriented reforms to spread and it has become a Western hegemonic discourse that now dominates world economic relations, affecting state–society relations in developing countries.[11]

It was mentioned above that a reduction of the state is not unusual as globalization has changed the functions of the state. Gita Steiner Khamsi (2014) has written extensively about how aid politics and policy borrowing have brought the neoliberal model to countries like Pakistan. Today neoliberal theory literature looks less at citizens and more at consumers, and when it comes to rights it more often than not tends to operate on the basis of choice rather than rights. However, we do not argue here that neoliberalism is what has caused the increased absence of the state in Pakistan. Aid politics with a neoliberal agenda pushed in particular by Western development partners such as the International Monetary Fund (IMF) or the World Bank has reinforced and underpinned the absence of the state, but it did not cause it. This reinforcement is, however, crucial because it means that although Pakistan has embarked on a path where the social contract has lost its meaning and the social and political structures are being inexorably altered, the links between the state and today's young citizens will not be easy to reinstate.

> *The reality on the ground – the state is a parallel universe*
> *Subjugation, coercion and neglect. That is what the Pakistani state offers to its citizens.*
>
> (Student, Male, Lahore)

> *There is no concept of citizenship in Pakistan. The common man is helpless. He is not given basic rights. He is ridiculed and insulted. He is caught unawares by a stray bullet. He is a victim of the numerous bomb blasts and no one can save him.*
>
> (Madrassa Student, Male, Islamabad)

The state in Pakistan has failed to develop a clear understanding of the legal side of citizenship relating to rights, duties and political participation. This failure is compounded by issues of unemployment and poverty on the one hand, and violence and destruction on the other, depending on where the Pakistani citizen is located. For instance, the male madrassa student living in Islamabad quoted above is originally from a town in KP, and his experience of citizenship and the Pakistani state is informed by his lived realities in KP. There are degrees of state failure in the lives of Pakistanis, as narrated by participants in this book, depending on their locations, which range from the Hazaras in Quetta to the Pushtuns in Peshawar or the young people from the Muhajir community in Karachi. These failures fluctuate across class, ethnic and religious markers; gender is also an important indicator. A strong legal definition of citizenship could not have been developed during the thirty-odd years of military rule, during which issues of citizens' rights were put on the back burner and political participation was restricted. However, Pakistan has also had almost forty years of civilian leadership. In the most recent decade of civilian rule (2008 to the present) Pakistan has demonstrated slow progress in the World Economic Forum's Global Competitiveness Index (GCI)[12] as shown in Table 1.1 but continues to face challenges (see Table 1.2). It is still among the worst-performing nations on the index (World Economic Forum 2017–18) at 3.67 between Uganda (3.7) and Cameroon (3.65).

The key performance-determining factors for developing economies such as Pakistan's are the basic requirements which consist of four main pillars: institutions, infrastructure, macroeconomic stability and health and primary

Table 1.1 Global Competitiveness Index Rankings (2017–18)

Edition	2012–13	2013–14	2014–15	2015–16	2016–17	2017–18
Rank	124/144	133/148	129/144	126/140	122/138	115/137
Score	3.5	3.4	3.4	3.4	3.5	3.7

Note: https://www.weforum.org/reports/the-global-competitiveness-report-2017-2018

Source: p. 230.

Table 1.2 Global Competitiveness Index rankings (2017–18), p. 230

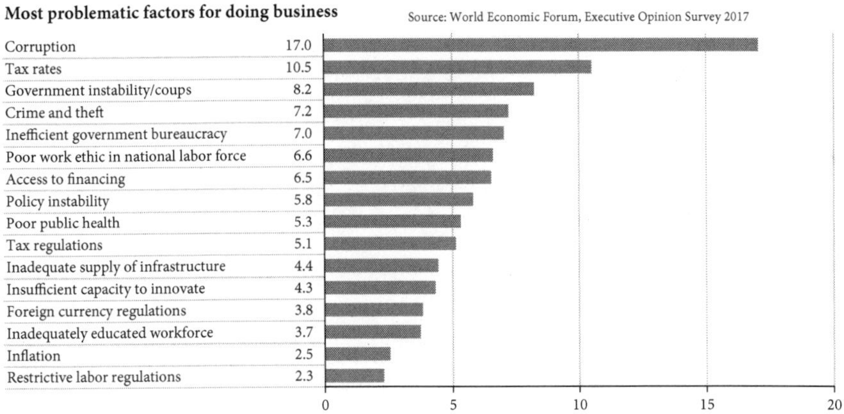

Notes: From the list of factors, respondents to the World Economic Forum's Executive Opinion Survey were asked to select the five most problematic factors for doing business in their country and to rank them between 1 (most problematic) and 5. The score corresponds to the responses weighted according to their rankings.

Table 1.3 Pakistan's HDI and Component Indicators for 2017 Relative to Selected Countries and Groups

	HDI Value	HDI Rank	Life Expectancy at Birth	Expected Years of Schooling	Mean Years of Schooling	GNI per Capita (PPP US$)
Pakistan	0.562	150	66.6	8.6	5.2	5,311
Bangladesh	0.608	136	72.8	11.4	5.8	3,677
India	0.640	130	68.8	12.3	6.4	6,353
South Asia	0.638	—	69.3	11.9	6.4	6,473
Median HDI	0.645	–	69.1	12.0	6.7	6,849

Note: HDI, human development indicators; GNI, gross national income; PPP Purchasing Power Parity

Source: United Nations Development Programme (UNDP) (2018), *Human Development Indices and Indicators: 2018 Statistical Update*. New York: UNDP; p. 3.

education. In comparison to its South Asian neighbours, Pakistan has been underperforming in human development indicators (HDI), as shown in Table 1.3 from the UNDP HDI report 2018 (UNDP, p. 3). The Pakistani state is not fulfilling its side of the bargain by failing to give what many consider basic rights to the common population.

Problems facing Pakistan

The current domestic and international challenges faced by the state include armed international conflict on its borders, domestic insurgency, a religiously radicalizing minority, and a corrupt government amidst 70 per cent urban and rural poor pitched against a small rich (and often feudal) elite. The state does not provide health and education for all; amenities such as water, gas and electricity are increasingly not available through public provision and have to be bought in the open market and are therefore only available to the middle classes.[13] Urban and rural infrastructure such as roads is often only built and maintained in elite areas, especially urban centres where the powerful can exert political pressure. In addition, poor economic conditions have led to rising prices and often shortages of basic foods such as rice, flour and sugar. The state also fails to collect taxes equitably for the improvement of public services. Another shortcoming in state duty is its failure to turn economic aspiration into reality. These failings leave a large part of the Pakistani population heavily deprived and decreases the state's legitimacy still further.[14] A largely corrupt police and judiciary compounds the lack of understanding of rights, especially for the poor.

When asked about Pakistan's problems the young people interviewed in 2015 reiterated many of the themes that came up in similar discussions between 2009 and 2012. The main issues highlighted included the energy crisis, bad governance, unemployment, terrorism, violence (such as target killings, muggings and sectarian killings especially in Sindh), corruption and the quality of the education system. Corruption, also the leading factor in Table 1.2, was recognized as a problem at all levels.

The participants connected the personal behaviour of individuals to a collective failure towards social responsibility by giving the example of citizen behaviour on the roads. It must be highlighted that this example also comes up in primary school textbooks in relation to following rules and regulations, one that was echoed across the participant population. They explained that the way citizens behaved in their personal lives, or even in the most mundane situations such as driving, where no one followed traffic regulations, reflected their lack of awareness for others and society at large. The problem of corruption and lack of accountability was prevalent across Pakistani society, from applying for jobs to accessing basic amenities such as electricity or clean water. There was no concept of honesty even at the ordinary person's level: '*From the rickshaw driver to the sweeper, everyone wants to take advantage of people, no concept of honesty*' (Student, Female, Quetta). This lack of a moral code was also believed to be one of the reasons for increased violence in the country.

When asked if this was only the fault of the politicians, or if others such as the army or the police were also involved, the same group of students explained: '*Of course they are also involved in all these killings. The Lashkar-e-Jhangvi took responsibility for the attacks but where is the government. Why doesn't it do something? It is a government failure*' (University teacher, Male, Quetta). Violence is a key variable in delegitimizing the state. The state not only is seen as unable to prevent the violence, but is actually blamed for initiating and sustaining it. Looking at the individual provinces, they all have different types of violence as a core part of the problem. Students pointed to the Muttahida Qaumi Movement (MQM),[15] political target killings in Karachi, the religiously inspired terrorism in Punjab, the sectarian and ethnic target killings in Balochistan and the terror groups in KP who mostly fight the Pakistani state. The radicalization of religious extremists feeds back into the violence, a theme echoed by students across this study, with one student pointing out that Pakistan is home to a large number of internationally banned groups who feed into the anti-state violent cycle. When discussing sectarian violence students highlighted the irony of Pakistan's origins: '*Besides the problem is which version of Islam are we trying to enforce in Pakistan*' (Focus Group, Private University[16]). However, most of the students also believed that these problems stemmed from a misunderstanding of Islam. '*We don't follow Islam. Religious awareness is given in masjids etc. but they sometimes express opinion that is not in Islam. Own limited knowledge, if we follow Islam our problems will be solved*' (Focus Group, Government University[17]); '*I think religious education needs to be reconsidered. We need to know what religion says. People say a lot but what is the true version*' (Focus Group, Private University[18]). In focus group discussions, there was no clear resolution as to what was the *right* Islam, with students highlighting differences between and within sects.

Alienation by the state

Alienation – a form of disconnect from the state – anger and frustration have been the result of a troubled relationship between citizens and their state. This is compounded by incompetence, corruption, pre-existing power structures and a feeling of powerlessness. Despite this fractured link with the state, the frustration and sense of powerlessness also points towards the state's inability to meet expectations concerning its responsibility to provide basic services such as electricity, gas and water; also at issue is the lack of employment for young people. The UNDP National Youth survey 2017 reminds us that young people aged 15–29 years make up 41.6 per cent of Pakistan's total labour force and that almost 4 million youth attain working age every year in Pakistan (p. 75). There is a need for more than 21 million additional jobs by 2030 (pp. 75–76).

The participants across the sample, while expressing their frustration with the state, also held little hope that the state would improve. Figure 1.1 highlights this sense of alienation. Of the 2009 sample 48 per cent said they were highly or very highly alienated.[19] In expanding on the meaning of this alienation the responses predominantly highlighted the failure or nonresponsiveness of the state in fulfilling its basic responsibility towards the provision of basic amenities.

It is generally assumed that anger and alienation are greater among the ethnic minorities who have suffered under Punjabi domination. Although this reduces the issue to ethnic grievances, it is true that the state has done even less for the non-Punjabis and Punjab remains the richest province with the best infrastructure, even if much of the natural resources come from other parts of Pakistan. As discussed in Chapter 4, the Balochistan rebellion has gathered pace as the Baloch feel deprived, accusing the state of not giving them their share of natural resources and distributing it to other provinces, in particular Punjab. In

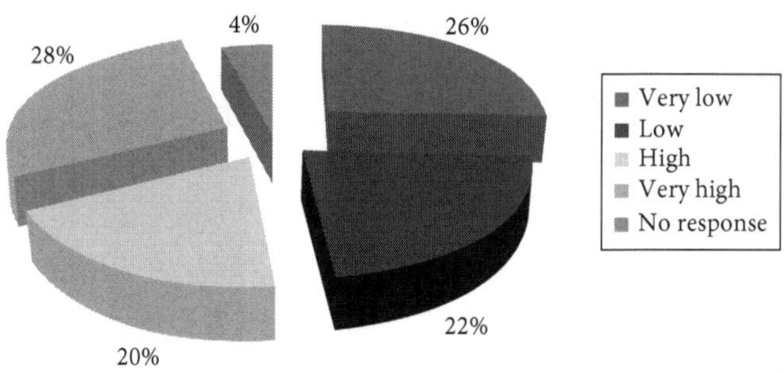

Figure 1.1 Sense of alienation across the 2009 sample.

Response	Sindh	Balochistan	Khyber Pakhtunkhwa	Punjab
Very low	21.6%	15.5%	18.7%	29.4%
Low	24.6%	20.7%	18.7%	22.0%
High	19.0%	8.6%	20.6%	20.3%
Very high	28.9%	53.4%	37.4%	24.7%
No response	5.9%	1.7%	4.7%	3.7%
Total	**100.0%**	**100.0%**	**100.0%**	**100.0%**

Figure 1.2 Responses to degree of 'alienation by the state', varying by province of origin.

Sindh ethnic grievances are known to be high as well. This is largely reflected in Figure 1.2, which captures data from 2009 (although there is enough anger felt by Punjabis as well). These frustrations were also reflected in data from the focus groups conducted in 2014–15.

The privileged elite

In examining the nature of the ruling elite in Pakistan and their influence on the state, Rais (2017) expands on LaPorte's argument illustrating how an 'elite' group comprised of high-level military and 'central administrative' officers and big landlords and their families from across the country has dominated politics in Pakistan. It was this relationship between the army and the bureaucracy that further weakened political institutions of the country (2017). Hussain (2018) in his work presents a 'model of an elitist economy' (1999) that comprised '1–2 per cent of the population' that enjoyed 'accumulation of wealth amidst widespread poverty and squalor'. In highlighting this inequality he argues that 'the state, which has to ensure equitable distribution of gains of economic growth, is also controlled by the same elite who evade taxes and appropriate the public expenditure for their own benefits' (p. 17). The study participants were aware of this corruption, which was often associated with the state and the elite who had privileges because of their socio-economic status.

> *In my view, rich people are less aware of their rights and duties as compared to poor because rich look down upon the poor and do not perform their duties. Rich are given preference in our society. For instance, if a rich [person] indulges into a wrongdoing he can easily escape from the punishment with the power of money. Poor are punished for what they have never done. This difference is causing deterioration in the society.*
>
> (Student, Female, Hub)

The increasing gap between the rich and poor and the resulting class differences also contributes to an increased sense of alienation. Poverty is a real problem as the elites are seen to benefit from the system while no one ensures that the poor get a better life: '*In my view, the concept of citizenship in Pakistan among the "high" class is living in luxury with lots of servants around*' (Teacher, Female, Karachi); '*When the people have enough to eat then come to me and ask about citizenship*' (Focus Group, Private University[20]); '*The rich do not consider their or anyone else's rights seriously. Because they are rich they are more individualistic, they have an attitude of being unconcerned about most of the things around them. In addition to it, nobody really criticizes them for that too*' (Madrassa Student, Male, Islamabad).

Students across higher educational institutions in 2009 expressed anger and discontent, and their frustration about how the elites benefited at the expense of the commoners. The lower strata were perceived to be bogged down with the weight of their day-to-day existence such as earning an income and sustaining a livelihood. This recognition of socio-economic inequality was considered a part of the status quo, where students, especially from the more elite institutions, did not question their own position within that status quo. There was a lack of self-awareness among the students in these elite institutions who often (though not all) belonged to business-class families but did not recognize their position as the elite. Their discussion of poverty and inequality within Pakistani society highlighted a sense of resignation and heightened alienation, both with the state and with their own ability to go against 'the system'. The students came across as pessimistic, not believing that a transformation of the system was even possible. There was a sense of helplessness, with the students believing that they cannot change the existing political structure because nothing can change in this country. The majority of the participants across the sample lost interest in politics: '*Don't feel passionate about politics*' (Student, Female, Karachi); '*I don't think that anything I can do could possibly make a difference*' (Student, Female, Karachi) was a common refrain. One student expressed the way they saw Pakistani society succinctly:

> *'Elite: unthinking landlords*
> *Upper Middle Class: unthinking burglars (party people)*
> *Middle Class: unthinking slaves at offices*
> *Lower Class: unthinking majority'*
>
> (Student, Male, Karachi)

While the quotes above reveal how the youth felt about the state at the end of 2009, a time characterized by violence, corrupt governance and insurgency, the sense of alienation the wider Pakistani population feels towards the state is nothing recent.[21] Weinbaum (1996) has argued that Ayub's Basic Democracy[22] was designed 'to keep the ordinary citizen out of politics' (p. 642). This denial of the right for political participation undermined the citizens by declaring them 'not ready' for democracy. This historical legacy also fostered alienation and lack of belief in a political system. The feudal political system based on patronage networks, still widespread among landowners in Sindh and Balochistan, works on a similar premise: those who own land should be elected as they know what is best for the uneducated and poorer peasants – who are often seen as 'not ready' for a proper democratic system. This not only results in little or no support for the state structures across the broader population – it also results in less political participation since no one believes that involvement in politics can really change things.[23]

In 2015, six years after our research had started, attitudes had not changed significantly. Alienation and anger ran high when young people spoke about the state: '*The government needs to get its priorities right. We don't need roads, [we] need to solve more the energy and unemployment crisis*' (Focus Group, Private University[24]). Some did not even recognize the state: '*We are not aware of things like the state*' (Focus Group, Private University[25]), while for others it was a '*symbol of strength*' yet '*not fulfilling its role*' (Academic, Female, Faisalabad[26]). Most young people across Pakistan had little or no understanding of the nature of the state. In explaining the definition of a state, some linked it to Islam: '*Islam ka kila aur uska mustakbil*'[27] (Focus Group, Government University[28]); '*Aik Islami Riyaasat hai jo keh ab barai naaam hee islami hai*'[29] (Focus Group, Government University[30]); '*Popularly: "To provide a homeland for Muslims of India and to help establish Islam in the world*"' (Focus Group, Private University[31]). Most confused the roles of the state, the government, political parties, and the army: '*I doubt we really have a state now. It's just political parties and the army taking turns at playing king*' (Focus Group, Private University[32]); '*Pakistan state is just the training ground for the army*' (Student, Male, Karachi[33]). Given the role of the military in Pakistani politics and the running of the state, in particular its direct influence on foreign relations and internal security, such conflation between the state and the military only highlights the nature of the 'security' state in Pakistan.

Consequently, there is no confidence in public institutions. However, for the social contract to work, institution building and trust in institutions is key. Yusuf in his work (2011) highlights the lack of young Pakistanis' confidence in public institutions; 60 per cent have confidence in the army, 40 per cent in religious institutions and less than 10 per cent in the national government. 'Perhaps the most alarming is how averse Pakistani youth are to direct political activity' (Yusuf 2011, p. 266). This is despite the creation of a youth parliament in 2007.[34] The engagement of political parties with young people in the run-up to the 2013 elections was largely superficial despite political rhetoric around jobs, education and inflation. Only the PTI and the PML(N) promised seats to young people in their programmes[35] (Jinnah Institute 2013).

In-depth research[36] conducted by the British Council (BC) about how the young generation felt about the 2013 elections found that on aggregate young people in Pakistan were very pessimistic. The main issues remained inflation, lack of employment opportunities and issues pertaining to security and violence. Most importantly the youth reported very low confidence in the official institutions, in particular the government, parliament and political parties. According to the BC research 71 per cent of the young respondents rated the national government unfavourably, 67 per cent rated the National Assembly unfavourably and 69 per cent rated political parties unfavourably.[37]

In July 2018, with upcoming elections, the Institute of Development and Economic Alternatives (IDEAS) undertook a political attitudes survey in Lahore that included a total sample of 2,127 respondents from 'four provincial assembly constituencies (PP 146, 147, 148 and 149)[38] in three national assembly constituencies' (NA 121, 122 and 124).[39] 'Close to two-thirds' of the participants indicated 'purchasing power or kuwat-e-kharid', that is, economic issues, as the most important concern, followed by one-third who were concerned about unemployment, and a little more than one-third concerned about corruption (Cheema and Liaqat 2017, p. 4). While this survey cannot be generalized to the whole of Pakistan, let alone Punjab or even Lahore, it does highlight issues that took centre stage in the previous elections as well.

Rights and responsibilities

In examining the meaning of the state–citizen relationship for young Pakistanis, the participants were also asked their opinion about rights and responsibilities. In 2009, the responses highlighted that none of the young adults thought that the basic tenets of the social contract were functioning. '*The concept of citizenship in Pakistan is not according to what it should be. A citizen is not receiving his rights and duties the way it should be. Unemployment is at the peak and educated young ones are irritated with it*' (Teacher, Female, Faisalabad); '*I believe there is a great difference between the concept and implementation of citizenship. Citizens in Pakistan have rights but hardly any of them are available to us*' (Teacher, Female, Karachi); '*In Pakistan there is no concept of citizenship. People do not know about their rights as citizens, they are being exploited by people who are supposed to serve them as public servants. For example, if you are an ordinary man, you can not dare get your FIR[40] registered in a police station*' (Academic, Male, Lahore). The 'ordinary man', normally from a less privileged background, would not have the same rights as the rich. However, even young educated Pakistanis in private and government universities expressed their lack of knowledge about their rights as citizens, while for others citizenship and the rights that followed seemed irrelevant in Pakistan: '*Apparently every citizen has equal and basic rights but sometimes these rights seem to be abolished*' (Teacher, Female, Hub).

The views expressed across the sample also pointed to not just the rights but also the responsibilities of citizens. They were responsible as well for the breakdown of the state–citizen contract: '*It is kind of vague there in Pakistan, as people are more concerned of their rights and negligent of their duties, blaming the state for all miseries and troubles ignoring the fact that they also somehow [are] responsible for it*' (Focus Group, Private University[41]).

In the 2015 survey the mindset had hardly changed, as students continued to give similar responses. Rights and duties, the basis of the social contract, are enshrined in Pakistan's constitution. Hardly anyone taking part in the focus groups had actually read the document. One of the students that had read it said: '*It is important. How can you talk about politics or argue if you have not read the constitution?*' Others, however, agreed with the student who said: '*I don't think I need to read the constitution. It is the duty of our legal representatives to read the constitution. Not us*' (Focus Group, Private University[42]).

In another focus group in Lahore only one student had read the constitution. She said that reading it had made her realize that the promises politicians make are already rights given to the citizens under the constitution. '*They take credit for something that is already given*' (Focus Group, Government University[43]). However, the student population across the provinces acknowledged their lack of understanding about the Pakistani constitution. While a few expressed their embarrassment at not having read their own country's constitution, for most young people there was no point in knowing what was in the constitution, as nothing would happen: '*No faida*'[44] (Focus Group, Government University[45]); or that it is too long and complicated: '*I think it is long and complicated on purpose.*' Another said that he had thought about reading the constitution but had not done it yet: '*In a country like Pakistan ignorance is bliss … But we are supposed to know what it says.*' However, it was felt that reading it would cause more stress and frustration. The same group of students were clear that citizenship meant 'understanding your rights and responsibilities', but it remained unclear how they would be able to do this without bothering with the constitution (Focus Group, Private University[46]).

The issue of corrupt and inauthentic politicians came up at several institutions. For the participants, politics was essentially considered a dirty word, for the morally corrupt. This was evident in the response of participants to the cricketer turned philanthropist turned politician Imran Khan, where his entry into politics was considered to be dangerous for him precisely because of its immoral nature, and the possibility that it would taint his reputation. The discussion also turned to expectations and responsibilities. While the majority view was of politicians as power-hungry opportunists who made false promises, there were students who pointed out that citizens also expect a lot: '*[We] expect too much for politicians. ... We ourselves are corrupt. [We] don't queue when we need to, break traffic signals. ... We should also take responsibility*' (Focus Group, Government University[47]).

While politicians failed in upholding their responsibilities, and continued to be a disappointment for young people, the discussion on rights and responsibilities also brought in the 'problem of sectarianism' and provincialism: '*The problem of sectarianism goes back to the constitution. The separation clause for Muslims and non-Muslims. That is where it begins*' (Focus Group, Private University[48]). The failure of the state to guarantee equal opportunities and protect all citizens across Pakistan was evident not only in the continued persecution of different sects and non-Muslims, but also in the unequal representation of provinces in the army and bureaucracy, as well as the inequitable distribution of resources across the provinces. This sentiment was most clearly expressed by students in Karachi, as well as students from the Hazara community. Students gave several explanations for these disparities between provinces and communities: '*The army has always been Punjabi dominated. I think after the separation of East Pakistan the army has been afraid of other such movements so keeps it Punjabi dominated*'; '*No I think it is because of the population, because they are larger in number [in Punjab]*'; '*They say whoever wins Punjab wins Pakistan*' (Focus Group, Private University[49]). The inequalities between provinces struck a chord across a number of discussions: '*It is the same as Karachi. Karachi generates 70% of Pakistan's budget but is given very little. KP generates energy but is given very little.' Q.: Where does it go? 'To Punjab.' Q.: Why? 'It is the biggest province in terms of population. Also the bureaucracy and army are dominated by Punjabis*' (Focus Group, Private University[50]). In the focus groups in Karachi only one student disagreed: '*I think Punjabi domination is also a narrative created to an extent by the Balochi and Sindhi bureaucrats. They use this narrative to cover their own failure and the fact that under them no development has taken place within our own provinces*' (Focus Group, Private University[51]).

However, the discussion of inequality across provinces also came up in focus groups in Lahore. In talking about Sindh, students believed that '*they hate Punjabis. Say Punjab has taken everything*,' while for Balochistan there was a recognition that '*the other three provinces*' had '*ganged up against them*' (Focus

Group, Private University[52]). Yet, other students also pointed to the inefficiency of provincial governments in fulfilling their responsibilities.

The discussion on rights and responsibility often veered towards micro and macro issues around sectarianism, provincialism and political corruption, where the importance of the constitution and the duties and responsibilities of the citizen, while acknowledged, were not considered significant enough to challenge the issues facing Pakistan. Hence, for the majority of young Pakistanis in this study, the constitution of Pakistan, while in principle was important, held no practical value for them as citizens.

Views on democracy: The role of the state and the army

When discussing the social contract in Pakistan, the related issue of democracy is never far away. The lack of democracy and the involvement of the army are often used to explain the problems in Pakistan today, including the apathy of the young. Jinnah wanted Pakistan to be a constitutional, parliamentary democracy informed by Muslim values. From independence he assumed control of all key levers of power in Pakistan: governor general, president of the Muslim League, head of the Constituent Assembly; even ardent supporters would concede that the concentration of power set an unfortunate precedent, and when Jinnah died thirteen months later there was no one to fill his shoes. Governance of the country continued to be concentrated in the hands of the elite.

The army became involved in domestic politics early on after independence and Pakistan suffered from three long periods of army rule starting with General Ayub Khan in 1958, when the parliamentary system came to an end for the first time. Corruption had become so widespread within the national and civic systems of administration that Ayub Khan was welcomed as a national hero by the people. He handed over power in 1969 to General Muhammad Yahya Khan, who then oversaw the 1970 elections and the secession of Bangladesh. After six years of democratic rule under Bhutto's PPP, General Muhammad Zia-ul-Haq imposed martial law and the expected elections were postponed. Zia changed Pakistan's constitution so that the democratically elected prime minister became subservient to the president. Democratically elected governments resumed at his death in 1988 and continued for a decade, but none of the four completed their legal term until 2013. General Pervez Musharraf took power in a coup in 1999, claiming that the army was forced to take this step to save the country from 'turmoil and uncertainty'. Given the army's involvement in policing the country and the long periods of army rule with subsequent heavy involvement in Pakistan's economy (Siddiqa 2007), another common fault line through which Pakistan's troubles are explained is the opposition between the army and the rest of the population. Many scholars (Talbot 1998 and Lieven 2011 among others) have looked at the army's role in denying Pakistan a sustained democratic development; they argue that even in times of democratic rule, the army continued to rule the country from the 'back seat'. According to Rais (2017) the Pakistan military 'adopted three strategies to build the Pakistani state … de-politicization, centralization, and modernization of the economy' (p. 65). In particular, in order to achieve 'de-politicization' the military 'produced a politics of their own brand with the character of patronage, cultivation of groups that would serve as its "democratic" or political façade, and restructuring of political and state institutions to ensure its domination of the state' (p. 65). Today Pakistan again has a civilian government but the army remains a major stakeholder in politics.

In their article 'The Democracy Barometers, Surveying South Asia', De Souza et al. (2008) argue that those in Pakistan supporting democracy as a form of government (identified here as 'strong democrats') are down to 10 per cent of the population and 48 per cent are defined as 'weak democrats' (p. 90). Forty-one per cent of the population self-define as non-democrats, and the support-for-democracy ratio is 0.24 (p. 91). As such Pakistan is different from all the other South Asian countries where democrats outnumber non-democrats in much higher numbers (p. 89). De Souza et al. also contend that those who are more educated tend to support democracy more than those who are less educated (p. 92) and that having experienced democracy also had a positive correlation with being supportive of democracy. As a result of Pakistan's many years under military rule, today's youth has had less exposure to democracy than young people in other South Asian countries, and according to De Souza this matters when it comes to how they describe their political leanings.

Kugelman (2012) sees the role that patronage plays, reiterating Lyon's (2002) and Lieven's (2011) ideas that many would hesitate to change the political order in ways that could threaten the structure they depend on for future influence. Although young people did not mention this explicitly, their families would caution about too radical a change. In fact, one can argue that Nawaz Sharif's win in the May 2013 elections underlined this point. Many wanted change but were equally reluctant to give it to the PTI, who they saw as inexperienced in 2013. Neither does Kugelman (2012) believe that anger and alienation could translate into a youth-led, religion-based political movement, despite many young people being in general anti-government and anti-American, with a majority favouring an Islamic style of governance.

Yet, the question of what young Pakistanis want as a system of governance is not a simple one to answer. 'Polling in recent years finds that nearly two-thirds of young Pakistanis favour an Islamic state; more than 80% are at least moderately religious; and a full third support Sharia-style punishments such as floggings and the severing of limbs. Overwhelming numbers identify themselves as Muslims rather than as Pakistanis' (Kugelman 2012, p. 4). Yet, what is meant by an 'Islamic rule' remains unclear. Such sentiments are not restricted to the poorer, less educated classes. However, a more in-depth analysis of Pakistani society, in particular young Pakistanis, reveals how Pakistan's religious fault lines are as stark as the ethnic ones. The Islamic revolution promised by Munawar Hassan's Jamaat-e-Islami (JI) party has not brought in support at the polls, and Islamic rule such as that of Maulvi Fazlullah, who ruled Swat when that region was subjected to Sharia law, was characterized by the kind of brutality that has cost him public support.

Yet, BC research has shown that democracy does not seem to be the system of choice for many – 38 per cent expressed a preference for Islamic rule and 32 per cent would opt for military rule, while only 29 per cent thought that democracy was the best system for Pakistan (BC NGBB[53] Data Pack National, slide 24). While disillusionment with the last five years certainly played a part in these opinions, one could also argue that the lack of understanding as to how the system works is largely at fault. It is important to see what the youth has to say about democracy, 'Islamic rule' and the role of the army in Pakistani politics.

In the discussion that follows, young Pakistanis express their lack of faith in state institutions and a functioning democracy, with most having no understanding of the social contract. However, many do trust the army, not only for providing security but also for dispensing justice through military courts. In a country where young people lack confidence in state institutions, the future of democracy is in question.

The army continues to occupy a position of reverence for the majority of young Pakistanis in this study. Across all groups most, although not all, seemed to think that the army was a key player in the Pakistani system and the most visible and able part of the state apparatus:

> *'[The] army is everything here. The link between state and army is so vague. Foreign policy is run by the army'; 'Army is the only stable institution we have'; 'With bureaucrats there is a bond between them and the army. Come on – in every family one brother is in the army and the other in the bureaucracy. That is how it works.'*
>
> (Focus Group, Private University[54])

The army and the state were therefore always interconnected in the minds of the majority. The opinion about the army taking over given the current climate was often split, though supporters for both the army and democracy were found in all focus groups.

The political leadership is not able to handle the current situation.[55]

> *We are not politically stable. People are not politically aware, not educated to elect the right lot. Would've opted for democracy for a country that was educated. The masses here are uneducated.*
>
> (Focus Group, Private University[56])

Those who support army rule say that they are '*better organized; [there is] no corruption; one rank to the next [is] based on ability – baap ki jaagird nahi*' *[it's not based on your father's inheritance]* (Focus Group, Private University[57]). Some support the army because their parents do or some because the army is visible in times of need, and the rest of the state is not: '*Whenever there is a natural disaster, earthquake or floods only the army goes in*' (Academic, Male, Quetta; Student, Female, Quetta[58]). Others point out that '*the reason the army is doing everything is because of the enormous budget that goes directly to the army. They are doing it because they can*' (Focus Group, Private University[59]). However, while the army's larger budget (in comparison to other government departments such as education and health) is considered a factor in its efficiency, there continued to be little faith in state institutions to perform, no matter how large their budget, because of corruption and lack of accountability. There are also those who point out that being anti-state or anti-army is not a choice: '*You can't go against the state narrative, or critique the army*'; '*People who critique the army are labelled anti-patriotic. It is like "political suicide"*' (Focus Group, Private University[60]). Many also give reasons as to why the army is or should be running the show: some point to a weak democracy, where the political parties are unable to run the country. Hence the army is compelled to intervene politically. '*The army does not want to be in power but is being forced because the government is not standing. Look at the Sindh government. The army is running the whole show because the Sindh government is not doing it*' (Focus Group, Private University[61]) Others point to an uneducated and poor majority, that is incapable of practising their rights as voters:

> *In a country like Pakistan democracy does not work. There is so much poverty. You give people a little money and they will vote for you for the rest of their lives.' An example is given: 'They voted out of sympathy for [Asif*

> *Ali] Zardari after Benazir [Bhutto]'s death, and elected him. People don't know how to vote.*
>
> (Focus Group, Private University[62])

Others say that the army is necessary because of the deteriorating security situation: '*It brings up the argument of security versus freedom. How much of our freedom are we willing to give up for that security?*' (Focus Group, Private University[63]). And given the levels of violence, few can argue with that logic. The army has been fighting terrorism at all fronts in Pakistan, from the Zarb-e-Azb operation in Waziristan, to targeting terrorist outfits within urban centres. The support for the army as the only functioning institution is therefore quite strong.

Since the participants in this study had witnessed General Pervez Musharraf's rule, there were participants who expressed outright support for the general. Students, especially those in private universities, gave Musharraf's rule as an example of 'good governance': '*Local government under Musharraf when we had a local nazim [it's a local organiser/district representative – part of the administrative system] worked. ... It is interesting how under a military dictatorship we had nazims; streets and roads were changed but no nazims under a democracy*' (Focus Group, Private University[64]); '*Musharraf represented us. The dollar was 60 rupees then, petrol was 30–35 rupees/litre. In his time Pakistan was in the limelight, Musharraf is the only brave leader that Pakistan has ever had. With the line of control, and Kargil, he was the (COAS[65]), and on his orders did the army move into the Kargil territory ... Musharraf [was the] only leader after Bhutto bold enough to take steps needed to show other countries*' (Focus Group, Private University[66]). '*Musharraf is the lesser evil*'; '*Things were so much better when he was in government. He took action against the Taliban*'; '*Martial law is more efficient*' (Focus Group, Private University[67]).

However, many of those who disagree with army rule also point to the problems with the democratic system they have been living under. Interestingly none of the respondents came out clearly in favour of democracy, rather focusing on the issues that the democratic system in Pakistan faced: '*If democracy changed anything, it'd be illegal. For me, democracy is an illusion, a capitalist agenda which could never work in a country like Pakistan*' (Focus Group, Private University[68]); '*No ... but military dictatorship brings in a different set of problems, while democracy brings in another set of problems*' (Focus Group, Private University[69]); '*We are so confused and divided which is why democracy does not work. Look at our group, confused about what it is, whether the army should come in or not*' (Focus Group, Private University[70]). Others argue that for democracy to take root and to work, time is needed: '*Democracy needs time and it cannot be constantly interrupted. We are not allowing democracy to work*'; '*We also believe that agar jamhooriat aajai gee tu humarei saarei maslei theek ho jain gei [if we get democracy all our problems will be solved] but it does not work that way. It needs time*' (Focus Group, Private University[71]).

Despite the fact that in 2015 Pakistan already had had eight years of uninterrupted democratic rule, the students felt that more time was needed. They also believed that the regular coups of the army in the past had affected the function of a democratic system in Pakistan: '*The army has never really given space to democracy. We have never witnessed democracy in Pakistan, so we can't say democracy doesn't work when we haven't seen it*' (Focus Group, Private University[72]).

In contrast with the anger expressed by many about the state, there is less resentment towards the army: '*I think the army has done fantastic work in the past but if you want to succeed as a state you can't give power to one institution*' (Focus Group, Private University[73]). The normalization of the military not only in Pakistan's history and sociopolitical existence but also within the everyday lives of Pakistanis is evident with the inauguration of the Army Museum in Lahore that aims to celebrate and recognize the history of the army including its struggle and sacrifices for Kashmir.[74]

The role of the army and issues of security also brings up the role of military courts and how the army is dealing with terrorism and justice. Even those respondents who did not support army rule saw the use and logic of military courts: '*[They are] not the solution but [there is] no alternative. [It is] useful in specific cases.*' None of the students questioned whether military courts could be detrimental to the functioning of democracy in Pakistan. Most students agree that '*the alternative is not functioning too well. So for a limited period military courts make sense*' (Focus Group, Private University[75]). After all, the army is there to protect them and they 'don't trust the political powers'. Since the '*Government can't even provide basic right to justice, that is why military courts [are] needed*' (Focus Group, Government University[76]). Military courts were also described as '*more efficient*', having '*more accountability*' and being '*more stubborn. Question: Stubborn? You know they just do it. They get the job done*' (Focus Group, Private University[77]).

The army for young Pakistanis is an institution that not only provides security but also guarantees swift justice. The success of military courts and the kind of confidence they inspire among young Pakistanis was often pitted against civilian institutions and their inability to provide justice. This was all the more surprising especially in the aftermath of the lawyers' movement, which brought together lawyers, judges, students and the civil society in a struggle to restore the chief justice of Pakistan; the movement became an important factor in the downfall of the Musharraf regime.

However, the role of the military courts is primarily to deal with terrorism and impose the death penalty, despite the fact that there is no clarity about the identity of the individuals who have been executed by these courts. Yet, many of those interviewed in this research support the death penalty and had complete confidence in the military courts: '*If you are the mother of one of the children killed in the Peshawar attack, you would want to see them hanged*'; '*Avenge the family*'; '*Not just vengeance, it is about the law. Keep fear in those people*' (Focus Group, Private University[78]). '*Khoon ka badla khoon hai*[79] *according to Islam. Complete trust in the military courts*' (Focus Group, Government University[80]).

In one focus group, for example, out of forty respondents only three did not believe in the military courts (Focus Group, Government University[81]). A few pointed out that there is '*selective justice even in military courts*' or that it was '*Not really justice. Don't really serve for justice, since they are also political but better than nothing*' (Focus Group, Private University[82]). However, across the focus groups the majority of students believed that the military courts were useful, and that the death penalty was just and effective in combating terrorism in Pakistan.

The relationship between democracy and the army in Pakistan is more complex given the strength of the military and its involvement and influence over the Pakistani state. Despite Pakistan having had a democratic transfer to the PML(N) after the PPP completed a full term in office, one student points out that '*problems are still there. Violence, terrorism, electricity shortage, water shortage, gas shortage.*' The state is not visible. '*People have basic needs. They do not want terrorism. Everyone blames the last party in power. We have had democracy for eight years. It has not done anything*' (Focus Group, Private University[83]).

The non-Muslim citizens

While the relationship between citizens and the state varies along lines of class and ethnicity, religion is also an important factor, especially when it is clearly written in the constitution of Pakistan that the head of state can only be a Muslim. In March 2018 a 'Pakistani court ruled … that all citizens must declare their religion when applying for identity documents, a move human rights advocates say is another blow for the country's persecuted minority communities' (Sayeed 2018). Religious minorities have also been targeted repeatedly under the blasphemy laws. Accusations of blasphemy in Pakistan have proved lethal, where an estimated '62 men and women were killed on mere suspicion of blasphemy' in Pakistan between 1987 and 2016 (HRCP 2016, p. 96, citing the Centre for Social Justice). While laws related to 'offences' against religion date back to the British era, it was during the time of General Zia-ul-Haq in the 1980s that 'additional laws were introduced against blasphemy that were specific to Islam, including laws explicitly targeting the minority Ahmadiyya Muslim community' (Amnesty International 2016, p. 10). According to Amnesty International (2016) 'the most frequently invoked blasphemy laws in Pakistan's Penal Code' include section 295-A 'outraging religious feelings', 295-B 'desecrating the Quran', 295-C 'defiling the name' of the Prophet of Islam and 298-A 'defiling the names of the family of the Prophet' or 'his companion or any of the caliphs' (p. 10). Around '1,472 people ... have been accused under the blasphemy laws between 1987 and 2016, specifically under sections 295-B, 295-C and 298' (HRCP 2016, p. 96). A blasphemous allegation against an individual in Pakistan is akin to a death sentence as evident in the case of Governor Salman Taseer who was assassinated by his security guard when he was accused of having committed blasphemy through his efforts to amend the existing blasphemy law, or in the case of 'Shama Masih and her husband Shahzad Masih' who were lynched by a mob when accused of blasphemy (Amnesty International 2016). Discrimination against religious minorities also exists in education and employment (UNDP 2016b[84]).

The issue of religious minorities was seldom raised by the participants in this study. It did not make the list of the most urgent issues facing Pakistan today. It was largely absent, with the exception of a few outliers who recognized the unfair position of religious minorities in Pakistan, including a member of the Hazara community: '*The basis for Pakistan was that security will be provided to minorities of all religions, as Muslims were a minority in the Indian subcontinent. But now it is the opposite*' (Academic, Male, Quetta). In a focus group in Lahore, when the students were asked about the meaning of Pakistan, the following discussion ensued:

> *A.: 'purity', 'haven for minorities'*
>
> *Q.: Haven?*
>
> *A.: 'That is what it was supposed to be. This is why it was made.' [Everyone agrees] 'The oppressed became the oppressors in Pakistan.'*
>
> (Focus Group, Private University[85])

As the proceeding chapters will illustrate, individuals who do not belong to the dominant Sunni Islam (where fault lines are further drawn between the Deobandi and Barelvi schools) are often lower in the line of service delivery and protection offered by the state. The state–citizen relationship is not the same for all Pakistanis, where discrimination on the basis of religion has become part of the status quo.

So whither the social contract? The state–citizen relationship in Pakistan is constrained by problems of terrorism, sectarianism, provincialism, infrastructural inadequacies, in other words the state's struggle and often failure to provide physical, social, political and economic security and stability for its citizens. The more direct interference of the army in the past, and its crucial role in combating terrorism in present day Pakistan, not to mention its continued influence (if not control) over foreign affairs in the country and its access to a large chunk of the budget, has further strengthened the army. Therefore, any discussion about the state and democracy in Pakistan is incomplete without understanding the place of the Pakistani army. This is also reflected in the findings of this study.

Young Pakistanis may have doubts about the democratic system, may be ignorant or dismissive about their rights and responsibilities as citizens, and may lack confidence in state institutions, but they have complete faith in the functioning of the army. They are more confident in the army's ability to provide justice and security than they are in any other institution in the country. While the Pakistani state exists, it is largely irrelevant in the lives of ordinary Pakistanis, having been unable to provide any economic or social security and repeatedly accused of corruption and negligence. The social contract between the state and the citizens in Pakistan is therefore broken, not only because of the lack of responsibility on the part of the state, but also because of the citizens' lack of involvement in strengthening this relationship. While the NCEPG (2018) plans to fix this broken relationship, highlighting how 'better governance and service delivery through public inclusion and effectiveness of state institutions at district and tehsil level' is important 'to regain citizen trust and engagement with State' (NACTA 2018, p. 9), this realization may be a little too late, especially when that social contract is now about strengthening the relationship between the 'security state' and its citizens. The entry of the PTM in 2018 might present an opportunity for the state to show this commitment to fixing its broken relationship with its citizens. Among PTM's demands are basic rights as guaranteed under the constitution of Pakistan, including the rights of Pashtuns (and other ethnic minorities, evident in the support given to their grievances in the PTM rallies) to be protected against abductions and 'disappearances' by the security state; 'dignity' of existence (this refers especially to dehumanizing treatment at security checkpoints); de-mining of their homes and villages; and the establishment of a Truth and Reconciliation Commission to provide justice to families whose loved ones have been 'picked up' or killed in military operations. Manzoor Pashteen, the twenty-five-year-old leader of the movement, has repeatedly cited the constitution when making these demands, clearly providing an opportunity for the state to demonstrate its commitment to its citizens. The movement has been critical of the military's role in promoting a culture of racial profiling and violating the rights of Pashtuns as Pakistani citizens. However, far from engaging with this movement, the response of the security state has been one of censorship and intimidation, with supporters being harassed and picked up by security personnel, with Pashteen being denied the right to freely move around in Pakistan to travel to his rallies. Policies such as NCEPG 2018 clearly illustrate that the state is aware of the weaknesses of state–citizen relations (albeit through a security lens), where its failure to respond to a peaceful movement demanding rights under the constitution is all the more revealing of the nature of the security state that will only allow narratives of national identity and belonging that are defined within its security contract with its Pakistani subjects.

Notes

1 Translation: '*We will not do anything for children who are dying in Thar, but for a cricket match we will even burn things.*'

2 This focus group included participants from Lahore, Kasur, Kanganpur, Dera Ghazi Khan, Rajanpur and Rawalpindi.

3 The Thar desert is a drought prone area but has particularly witnessed worsening conditions since 2013 (https://reliefweb.int/report/pakistan/pakistan-life-grip-drought-thar-desert).

4 See for example the water racket in Karachi that keeps residents without water for weeks at a time (Hashim 2017b).

5 A reduction of the state is not unusual as globalization has changed the functions of the state from provider to regulator across the developed world. Aid politics and policy borrowing have brought the neoliberal model to Pakistan. Today neoliberal theory literature looks less at citizens and more at consumers, and when it comes to rights it more often than not tends to operate on the basis of choice rather than rights. However, we do not argue here that Pakistan has chosen a neoliberal path

and that this is what has caused the increased absence of the state. Aid politics with a neoliberal agenda has certainly reinforced the absence of the state, but it did not cause it.

6 See Tankel (2016); Lieven (2011); Fair (2008).

7 Not mentioning the two-year rule of Yahya Khan here.

8 Where the pseudo despot was more interested in providing social goods than his democratic counterparts.

9 One could argue that the government under Musharraf was closer to a social contract model than the democratically elected governments before and after. This is explored later in this chapter.

10 This focus group included participants from Lahore.

11 For more on how globalization changes the nature of the state in South Asia see Lall and Nambissan (2011).

12 World Economic Forum (2017).

13 In Pakistan a middle class as such does not exist. This is why the term 'middle *classes*' is preferred as it allows the inclusion of a wide variety of groups that range from urban white-collar workers to rural land-owning families (not including the feudal lords who own large parts of Sindh and the Southern Punjab). The term is used here to refer to the classes who can provide the basic necessities, from education to health, for their own families without recourse to the state and whose children do not need to work.

14 Poverty in Pakistan is not easily measured as even the Gini index data varies between various official websites. Increasingly the Multidimensional Poverty Index is used (as in the 2010 UNDP Human Development Report) and details found in Naveed and Islam's RECOUP paper give some details on the various and combined depravations faced by ordinary Pakistanis (http://recoup.educ.cam.ac.uk/publications/WP28_Arif.pdf). Another problem is that of transitory poor – where families are living under the poverty line for just a part of the year. According to a study conducted by the Centre for Research on Poverty and Income Distribution (CRPID), '63 per cent of poor in Pakistan fall in the category of "transitory poor". The remaining 32 per cent and five per cent of the population that subsist below the poverty line are "chronic" and "extremely poor", respectively.'

15 A political party.

16 This focus group included participants from Hyderabad, Sukkur and Karachi.

17 This focus group included participants from Lahore, Sheikhupura, Muridke, Dera Ghazi Khan and Sargodha.

18 This focus group included participants from Hyderabad, Sukkur and Karachi.

19 This direct form of asking was chosen deliberately by the research team after a pilot study conducted with more general questions about the state resulted in surprise that anyone wanted to discuss the state at all. In discussion and in the qualitative

part, alienation and anger were both expressed and it was therefore decided to ask participants directly. The Urdu word used, *naraz*, can be translated both as 'anger' and as 'alienation'.

20 This focus group included participants from Lahore.

21 It has not improved either as the UNDP National Youth survey published in 2017 clearly states, 'The overwhelming belief is that *chance of birth or geography* or fate determines out-comes, and that powerful others control their lives' (p. 108).

22 Ayub introduced the system of "basic democracies" in 1960. It consisted of a network of local self-governing bodies to provide a link between the government and the people. Primary governing units were set up to conduct local affairs; their members were elected by constituencies of 800–1,000 adults.

23 See Anatol Lieve, *Pakistan a Hard Country*, as well as work by Peter Lyon on patronage politics in Pakistan.

24 This focus group included participants from Hyderabad, Sukkur and Karachi.

25 This focus group included participants from Hyderabad, Sukkur and Karachi.

26 Online survey.

27 Islam's forte and its future.

28 This focus group included participants from Lahore, Kasur, Kanganpur, Dera Ghazi Khan, Rajanpur and Rawalpindi.

29 An Islamic state which is now only Islamic in name.

30 This focus group included participants from Lahore, Sheikhupura, Muridke, Dera Ghazi Khan and Sargodha.

31 This focus group included participants from Hyderabad, Sukkur and Karachi.

32 This focus group included participants from Hyderabad, Sukkur and Karachi.

33 Online survey.

34 The Youth Parliament (www.youthparliament.pk) was created 'to engage youth in Pakistan in healthy discourse and expose them to the democratic process and practices'. PILDAT (Pakistan Institute of Legislative Development and Transparency) launched the project of first-ever Youth Parliament Pakistan in 2007. Members of Youth Parliament Pakistan are selected for duration of a year at a time. The first batch of Youth Parliament Pakistan was selected in 2007 and since then Youth Parliament has had three batches, including the 2007 batch, the 2008–2009 batch and the 2009–2010 batch. This is not the only Youth Parliament – see www.pkhope.com/youth-ambassador-of-geo-jang-sms-registration-ali-moeen-nawazish/.

35 The PTI promised 25 per cent of all parliamentary tickets at national and provincial level to the youth – which is also why it is seen as the most pro-youth party.

36 The British Council study included a sample of over 5,000 young Pakistanis through a survey undertaken by the Nielsen Corporation.

37 British Council NGBB Data Pack National, slide 13.

38 These are constituencies of the Provincial Assembly of Punjab.
39 These are constituencies of the National Assembly.
40 First Information Report (when a crime is registered with the police for the first time).
41 This focus group included participants from Lahore.
42 This focus group included participants from Hyderabad, Sukkur and Karachi.
43 This focus group included participants from Lahore, Sheikhupura, Muridke, Dera Ghazi Khan and Sargodha.
44 Translation: '*No use*'.
45 This focus group included participants from Lahore, Sheikhupura, Muridke, Dera Ghazi Khan and Sargodha.
46 This focus group included participants from Hyderabad, Sukkur and Karachi.
47 This focus group included participants from Lahore, Sheikhupura, Muridke, Dera Ghazi Khan and Sargodha.
48 This focus group included participants from Hyderabad, Sukkur and Karachi.
49 This focus group included participants from Hyderabad, Sukkur and Karachi.
50 This focus group included participants from Hyderabad, Sukkur and Karachi.
51 This focus group included participants from Hyderabad, Sukkur and Karachi.
52 This focus group included participants from Lahore.
53 British Council report, (2013) The Next Generation Goes to the Ballot Box.
54 This focus group included participants from Hyderabad, Sukkur and Karachi.
55 Also this is the point in time when 1,400 people have died in Karachi because of the heat and the government is nowhere to be seen.
56 This focus group included participants from Hyderabad, Sukkur and Karachi.
57 This focus group included participants from Hyderabad, Sukkur and Karachi.
58 The participants from Quetta were part of the Hazara community.
59 This focus group included participants from Hyderabad, Sukkur and Karachi.
60 This focus group included participants from Hyderabad, Sukkur and Karachi.
61 This focus group included participants from Hyderabad, Sukkur and Karachi.
62 This focus group included participants from Lahore.
63 This focus group included participants from Hyderabad, Sukkur and Karachi.
64 This focus group included participants from Hyderabad, Sukkur and Karachi.
65 Chief of Army Staff (COAS).
66 This focus group included participants from Lahore.
67 This focus group included participants from Hyderabad, Sukkur and Karachi.
68 This focus group included participants from Lahore.
69 This focus group included participants from Hyderabad, Sukkur and Karachi.
70 This focus group included participants from Hyderabad, Sukkur and Karachi.
71 This focus group included participants from Hyderabad, Sukkur and Karachi.
72 This focus group included participants from Hyderabad, Sukkur and Karachi.

73 This focus group included participants from Hyderabad, Sukkur and Karachi.

74 Express Tribune (2017a): https://tribune.com.pk/story/1502658/army-museum-opens-doors-public-lahore/.

75 This focus group included participants from Hyderabad, Sukkur and Karachi.

76 This focus group included participants from Lahore, Kasur, Kanganpur, Dera Ghazi Khan, Rajanpur and Rawalpindi.

77 This focus group included participants from Lahore.

78 This focus group included participants from Lahore.

79 In essence referring to the ideal of an eye for an eye.

80 This focus group included participants from Lahore, Kasur, Kanganpur, Dera Ghazi Khan, Rajanpur and Rawalpindi.

81 This focus group included participants from Lahore, Kasur, Kanganpur, Dera Ghazi Khan, Rajanpur and Rawalpindi.

82 This focus group included participants from Hyderabad, Sukkur and Karachi.

83 This focus group included participants from Hyderabad, Sukkur and Karachi.

84 Political representation or opportunities are also a problem; according to UNDP since 'the entire community within the country or province is considered a constituency … the elected representatives of minorities do not have a geographical constituency in which to locate a development project; thus, depriving the minority communities of development opportunities that other communities benefit from' (UNDP 2016b, p. 15). These in-built sociopolitical structures lead to the disengagement of whole minority communities (UNDP 2016a).

85 This focus group included participants from Hyderabad, Sukkur and Karachi.

2

Youth and the Changing Political Activist

Introduction

> *I think our parents' generation was more into street politics. Our generation is more politically aware but we have more opinions rather than actually going through it.*
>
> (Focus Group, Private University[1])

> *NO [not politically active] I am currently a student and during my studies I don't consider this as a healthy activity to be [involved] in.*
>
> (Madrassa Student, Male, Islamabad)

> *No one interested in politics. Can't change politics. In Islam woman cannot be allowed to take part in politics. We've observed.*
>
> (Focus Group, Government University[2])

The nature of political activism among young Pakistanis has changed over generations, the result of a state crackdown on student politics juxtaposed with an education curriculum that curtails possible expressions of dissent. These student quotes from three different groups of students testify to the extent to which students are disconnected from political action. As this chapter illustrates, political awareness is often confused with political activism, and interest in politics in general has decreased across generations, as stated by the student in the focus group at a private university in Karachi. Also, the idea of student politics is perceived to be antithetical to the idea of education, evident in the second quote of a student from KP who was studying at a madrassa in Islamabad. And a lack of interest in politics, combined with a particular understanding of Islam, especially in relation to female political activism, is another factor that has normalized apathy among students. This does not take away from the fact that in the past five years student movements have emerged, particularly in urban centres, such as the Progressive Students Collective or the Women's Collective that promote student political activism related to issues of social justice and rights. However, as this chapter illustrates, the extent of apathy or lack of political literacy is much more extensive among the younger generation.

The nature of student politics has historically been linked to political parties and state patronage, where religious and secular student groups use university campuses as spaces to fight ideological battles, often resulting in violence and death (Nasr 1992; Llyod 1999). Student political activism, especially in public sector universities in Pakistan, is closely linked to politics within the provincial or national arena, where the extent of patronage provided to any one group is dependent on which political party is in power. Officially, student union activism has been banned time and again by various governments,[3] but the implementation of this ban has been selective, again linked to the dominant governing political party. The power of certain student groups is evident in the control these groups have on not only students but also faculty and administration, all of whom, either through intimidation or through ideological affiliation to the parent political party, tend to side with one student group against the other (see Nasr 1992; Nelson 2009; Akhtar 2018). Nelson's research in particular highlights 'the *growing irrelevance* of 'politics' as we know it – in effect, politics as a pattern of contestation, conflict and (ultimately) compromise' (Nelson 2009, p. 94; emphasis in original). It is this 'growing irrelevance of politics' that this chapter explores, by examining the neglected narratives of students who are not members of student societies.

The chapter begins with an exploration of historically located student activists and their role in the Pakistan movement, followed by an evaluation of the place of student activists in the newly independent Pakistan. The first part focuses on important events linked to student activism on university campuses and its impact on larger provincial and national politics, highlighting a complex relationship of patronage, and resistance between the state and its student activists. The increasing use of violence by student groups within universities and the selective ban on union activities across the years are also explored, providing a context for the narratives of students who are not members of such organizations. The nature of such students' political activism is also problematic, where narratives of political awareness reveal a limited understanding of political literacy. This is especially important in light of the lawyers' movement against Musharraf and the emergence of the populist PTI, which claims to have the support of the 'youth of Pakistan'. The discussion illustrates how the student activist, once celebrated by the Quaid-i-Azam as 'an arsenal of Muslim India'

(Liaqat Ali Khan quoting Jinnah in Mirza 1989, p. 178), has been predominantly depoliticized in today's Pakistan. The chapter also looks at young people's views on political participation just before the elections in 2013, illustrating a lack of trust in the electoral process, with opinions about political parties and the structure of democracy in Pakistan ranging from apathy to animosity and disappointment.

Citizenship, democracy and student political activism

How does one gauge the effectiveness of a democratic system? Welzel and Inglehart's (2008) research on democracies uses a 'Human-Empowerment Model' which defines 'self-expression' as one of the factors linked to an 'effective democracy'. They argue that 'interpersonal trust, tolerance of other groups, and political activism' are 'the core components of self-expression values' which 'are far more important to the emergence and survival of democratic institutions than is mere lip service' (2008, p. 132). Sant's (2014) study of political participation in the context of Spain underlines two main paradigms in defining political participation: the 'old paradigm' that is limited to 'voting, joining a political party or becoming a candidate', and the 'new paradigm' that moves beyond the conventional and includes 'boycotting, network campaigning etc.' (2014, p. 12). This in some ways is also similar to Welzel and Inglehart's (2008) discussion of electoral and liberal democracies, and their argument that democratization increasingly includes the 'orientations of ordinary citizens' that moves beyond electoral votes. Hoskins et al. in engaging with the concept of 'active citizenship' include both 'knowledge and skills, and positive attitudes towards participation', as crucial factors where 'positive attitudes' are linked 'to participation in the community, in school and in politics' that 'tap both traditional (e.g. voting) and non-traditional forms of participation' (2012, p. 423). This understanding of democracy could further translate into what Bernard Crick calls 'political literacy' that includes 'not only knowledge of political and social institutions and ideas, but the skills, values and attitudes' essential 'for the practice of good citizenship' (1998, p. 64).

In Pakistan though, as Chapter 1 has illustrated, the level of trust citizens have in the democratic system, in the political system, is highly problematic. The space ordinary citizens have to 'protest' against the state has increasingly shrunk over the years as evident in the treatment of nonviolent movements such as PTM. Yusuf (2011) and De Souza's (2008) discussion (see Chapter 1) further highlights a lack of political engagement on the part of young people.

Such lack of engagement from the youth can be explained by exploring Ryan's (2011) research that draws on the work of Henri Lefebvre, conceptualizing the importance of 'lived space' in the day-to-day lives of young students, and their expression of resistance and activism. For Ryan (2011) 'lived space is a space to resist, subvert and re-imagine', creating 'new possibilities and imaginings of how things could be, a space of transgression and symbolism' (Ryan 2011, p. 1021). The 'space' a student has to be politically active or engaged is defined at different levels of 'perceived, conceived and lived spaces of representation' (Ryan 2011, p. 1019 discussing Henri Lefebvre 1991), where all these levels intersect with each other in defining/confining the space for political thought or action for young students. The question of why some students are politically active and others are not can also be linked to perceptions of space, but may also be influenced by other indicators. Braungart (1971) in his study links the nature of student activism and protest to socialization through one's family, where 'family politics, argumentation, religion, and social class' all 'affected student political identification' (p. 127). In the case of Pakistan though, Lall (2012) has argued that while 'family' or 'school' are both important, other factors such as ethnicity, religious ideology and class may also become important factors in determining the nature of political activism.

The Pakistani case becomes problematic where historically the student political activist occupies an important 'space' within the Pakistan movement. Yet the patronage of student political groups by political parties, and by the military, with violence dominating the 'space' of political activism especially in the 1980s and 1990s, the activist, far from upholding democratic principles and values, often became a tool of political repression within university campuses. The next section highlights this evolution of the student activist, and provides a context to the narratives of nonpolitical or apolitical youth in this study who have become disillusioned by the corruption and violence of the student political activist.

The Pakistani student political activist

The role of the student political activist was clearly defined in a speech by Muhammad Ali Jinnah at the Muslim University Union, Aligarh, on 2 November 1941: 'I am not going to repeat hackneyed phrases like the youth of today will be the leaders of tomorrow. But as a practical man I tell you that great responsibility rests on you. The youth will have to bear the brunt of the struggle in the very near future' (as quoted in Mirza 1989, p. 147). The All India Muslim Students' Federation (AIMSF) was established in 1937. In its initial years the AIMSF faced opposition from the All India Student Federation (AISF) as well as other Muslim student groups, but through their lobbying the AIMSF was able to get wider support. While the initial objective of the federation was to lobby for the rights of Muslim minorities, it soon became involved in the Pakistan cause, actively supporting the All India Muslim League (AIML) (Altbach 1970). While other regional student groups had emerged across India, the Punjab Muslim Students Federation (PMSF) was further instrumental in supporting the Pakistan movement. PMSF support was considered to be one of the main factors that led to the victory of the AIML in the 1946 elections in Punjab; AIML defeated the once dominant Unionist party (Mirza 1991).

The role of student unions in supporting mainstream political parties had already been defined in the years before partition. 'Students who played an important part in the League's election campaign, had in particular been trained to appeal to the electorate along religious lines' (Talbot 1980, p. 77). These included 'Aligarh students' who came to the Punjab to support the AIML. The extent of this support can be gauged from the fact that 'during the peak of student activity, the 1945 Christmas vacation, there were 1550 members of the Punjab Muslim Students' Federation and 250 Aligarh students working on the League's behalf' (Talbot 1980, p. 78). The 1946 victory was important in furthering the agenda of the AIML, and strengthening the Pakistan cause.

After independence, the AIMSF like the AIML fell victim to internal politics that resulted in these organizations breaking apart into factions, and the emergence of other student political groups. However, the links between student groups and political parties outside the university continued to develop where ideological battles among national or provincial players were also reflected on university campuses through rivalries and strategic coalitions. Nelson (2011) highlights how after independence the emergence of the Democratic Students Federation (DSF) linked to the Communist Party of Pakistan was perceived to be a threat by the ruling Pakistan Muslim League which created a new 'state sponsored student union' the National Students Federation (NSF) to counter this threat. However, by the early 1950s the DSF members had overtaken the NSF, making it another leftist party. Bajwa in her discussion of the DSF highlights its popularity in Karachi when it swept 'most of the college union elections in Karachi and initiated the Inter-Collegiate Body (ICB) to unify the student unions under one banner' (Bajwa 2015, p. 12). The extent of the threat of the DSF was evident in the eventual ban in 1954 of the Communist Party of Pakistan and the DSF (Nelson 2011). The political debates on campus were increasingly reflective of the wider social debates concerning the place of religious ideology in Pakistan. This was clearly evident in the rivalry between the Islami Jamiat-e-Tuleba (known as the Jamiat), which was linked to Maulana Mawdudi's Jamaat-e-Islami and the DSF (see also Akhtar 2018). However, Nelson in his study illustrates how other identities had also persisted from the 'sectarian' nature of the 'Imamia Student's Organization', and the 'regional' nature of the 'Baloch Students Organization and the Pakhtun Students Federation' (2011, p. 567). The Ministry of Education in 1966 in fact had its own categorization of the student societies, distinguishing between the East and West Pakistan student organizations. These included both 'recognized' organizations that were clearly affiliated with a university and 'unrecognized' organizations that were believed to be independent, in which the DSF, the now largely leftist NSF and the Jamiat were also implicated.[4] The 'unrecognized' organizations were blamed for the violence and chaos that erupted on student campuses (Ministry of Education 1966). The DSF in particular through the ICB was instrumental in organizing what was called the '8th of January movement' (Bajwa 2015, p. 12).

Student violence: Demands Day – 7–9 January 1953

Student political organizations had a complicated relationship with the state, with some under the patronage of the state depending on the ruling party and others often at loggerheads. The threat posed by opposing student groups to the ruling elite is evident in the strong-armed tactics of the police in repressing the Demands Day movement of 1953, which incited greater resentment and violence. The 8 January movement involves one of the earliest student clashes with the police; it resulted in the death and injury of students and protestors in 1953. The students had local education grievances which continued to be ignored by the university administration despite constant appeals.[5] The students further appealed to Education Minister Fazlur Rahman, who also did not respond to their requests, resulting in a resolution being passed by university unions 'demanding their basic rights and asking Minister to meet the ICB members' (Herald Student, 1953). The students decided to hold a 'Demands Day' on 7 January, leading a peaceful procession to meet the education minister. In the events that followed between 7 and 9 January, the police clashed with student protestors, using live ammunition on students and killing seven and injuring several others (Bajwa 2015). As news of the police brutality spread, 'several processions were taken out by students across Pakistan, with solidarity protests' across 'cities of West and East Pakistan throughout the year 1953'

(Bajwa 2015, p. 12). According to Bajwa, the student movement became bigger, 'engaging' with questions around 'citizenship rights, democracy and national culture in a state that was in the process of establishing a coherent national narrative' (pp. 12–13).

This debate on rights and democracy is evident in the education policy documents that were published in later years, that kept referring to the problematic place of student unions and student protests. The *Report of the Commission on National Education January–August 1959* published by the Ministry of Education (1961) highlights this problematic position of the student protestor. The report recognizes the sacrifices and contributions of the 'academic community' to the freedom struggle for Pakistan, but also highlights how students were being manipulated by politicians, where 'the influence of the teacher' was destroyed, and the 'moral of the academic community' undermined (1961, p. 39). As the report states:

> It is imperative that colleges and universities rid themselves of those who serve the ignoble interests of groups outside the academic community. The future of Pakistan will be poorly served by dissension, agitation, and political activity on the part of the academic community. (p. 40)

The *Report of the Commission on Student Problems and Welfare*[6] in examining the rise of student agitation concluded that the growing unrest among the student population was a result of universities being under-resourced. There were three main universities – in Karachi, Dacca and Lahore – which had lost their predominantly Hindu teachers and staff to India, and were largely unable to accommodate a growing student population. Despite 'new Universities' being set up in 'Peshawar, Karachi and Rajshahi, mostly by making make-shift or temporary arrangements' the grievances of the students were largely ignored. It was only after these grievances culminated in 'demonstrations and agitation' that 'the authorities became conscious of their chronic difficulties and redressed some of them' (Ministry of Education 1966, p. 11). For the commission then, the response of the authorities to such student agitation set a precedent for students who believed they could only be heard if they demonstrated or agitated. The commission attempted to present a balanced account of student demands and the problematic response of state actors that ignored these demands, pointing to the fact that students had to agitate out of desperation (Ministry of Education 1966, p. 11).

The problematic place of student unions for the Pakistani state was further evident in the student-led movement against Ayub Khan's regime that began as a resistance to the imposition of the University Ordinance. Under this Ordinance 'students could be rusticated; student unions were abolished; graduates could lose their degrees, and faculty fired without due process for a variety of reasons' (Kornson 1974, p. 126).

Even though they shared many grievances, student groups on campuses continued their rivalries. Nelson in his analysis of student union activism noted how in certain cases despite having similar goals, student groups who came from different ideological positions still continued to clash (2009), based on a rigid ideal of 'one state, one party, one way' (2011, p. 570). The NSF during the 1960s was further divided into factions, with the Jamiat strengthening its hold on student politics and winning campus-based elections at both the University of Karachi and the University of Punjab in the late 1960s, only to end up breaking into factions itself (Nelson 2011). Ironically, Ayub Khan, to counter the threat of the NSF and the Jamiat, patronized another student group, the transnational Tabligh-i-Jamaat, which claimed to be both apolitical and nonviolent, with Ayub employing the same tactics as his predecessors (Nelson 2011). The student unions, despite these setbacks, were nonetheless successful in leading a movement against Ayub Khan. In fact, Humaira Iqtidar in her work argues that the PPP only later got involved in a movement that had already gained momentum because of student action in bringing down Ayub Khan's government (2011).

The 1970s saw what Paracha terms 'one of the most democratic periods in the history of student politics' during which the government promoted student politics. The 1974 Student Union Ordinance allowed political activity on university and college campuses. Zulfikar Ali Bhutto's victory not only rid the country of Ayub's dictatorship, but also deepened the fault lines on the campuses between the Islami Jamiat-e-Talaba (IJT), that Jamaat-e-Islami (JI) had used for anti-Bhutto propaganda, and leftist groups. IJT started to organize study circles that appealed to students who came from more conservative rural areas and who according to Paracha could not relate to the radical left philosophy of groups such as the NSF. However, far from engaging with the student left, Bhutto started his own agenda of purging the left of individuals who were critical of his policies and alliances with the right-wing elite (Nelson 2011). NSF accused Bhutto of rolling back his original socialist manifesto and they were angry with him for sending the army to Balochistan.

Another student group that emerged in 1978, that would dominate student politics especially in the urban city of Karachi through violence and intimidation, was the All Pakistan Mohajir Students' Organisation (APMSO). Richards (1993) in her doctoral work traces the emergence and evolution of the APMSO and its ties to the Muhajir Qaumi Movement, not to mention the historic rivalry between the People's Student Federation (PSF), another student group that had emerged in affiliation with the PPP. In fact, APMSO has also been linked to the 'militarization' of campuses in the late 1970s. The predominant grievances that led to the emergence of the APMSO were based on ethnic lines, reinforced through the introduction of a quota system for university seats under Bhutto that was perceived to limit opportunity for the Urdu-speaking Mohajir community, with preference given to less educated Sindhis and in certain cases Pashtuns (Richards 1993). The nature of this confrontation between the PSF and APMSO at different points in the 1980s resulted in the kidnapping and in certain cases killing of students; in 1989 after Benazir Bhutto's government lifted the student ban the Karachi Rangers were called to the university by the vice chancellor, as violence got out of control (Richards 1993; see also Nelson 2011). As far as state patronage is concerned, Richard argues that there have been suggestions, though mostly 'speculative', that the government of Zia-ul-Haq, which had imposed a ban on student unions with the exception of the Jamiat, eventually had a falling out with the Jamiat who were critical of the 'pace' at which Islamization was taking place. To counter the power of the Jamiat (and possibly the PSF), MQM received indirect 'funds' from the military (Richards 1993). Richards further points to tensions between the parent political party and the student wing for both the MQM and the PPP, a strained relationship that would be true for other student political organizations as well, especially in times of violence where the parent political party pretended to distance or dissociate itself from the troublesome student group. The Jinnah Institute's research highlights how the 'tension' between the 'youth wing' and the parent political party might have been the result of the 'youth wing's' predilection for change or reform, while older senior party members were more inclined to the 'preservation of the status quo' (Jinnah Institute 2013, p. 15). However, there were also instances where the parent political party responded in support of its student groups, as was the case of the MQM. The MQM in response to the killing of its students withdrew from the PPP coalition, with the government eventually dissolved by the president for incompetency. The PML(N) government came into power with the Muslim Student Federation (MSF) linked to the PML(N) gaining power in Punjab, and in particular the Punjab University. However, as the Jamaat-e-Islami accused the PML(N) of ignoring the Sharia, with the MSF and Jamiat clashing, the Jamaat-e-Islami eventually left the PML(N) government's coalition, weakening its support which again eventually dissolved.

The power of these student unions linked to the political parties, receiving patronage from the political parties and manipulated by the political parties but also at times resisting the political parties, shows how important such student organizations have been to the political elite. Such political activism, though, does not necessarily strengthen democracy, as Welzel and Inglehart (2008) and Hoskins et al. (2012) have argued. Far from it; this activism reinforces the status quo, and is one of the factors that has led to a larger dissociation and depoliticization of the broader student body. Nelson traces the reactions of parents to the violence that their children were subject to on university campuses, many of whom (those who could afford to do so) placed their children in private universities. However, Nelson's work also highlights how both in public sector and especially in private sector universities the dominance of religiously linked student movements did not dissipate, though the attraction was more to organizations that were nonviolent and often apolitical. He traces the emergence and success of the Tablighi Jamaat, a largely Deobandi organization that does not believe in political action but associated itself with the larger Ummah; the Dawat-e-Islami, a largely Barelvi organization that is also apolitical though ideologically different from the Deobandis and linked to a transnational cause; and Hizb ut-Tahrir (HT) that predominantly targets the elite in private universities (2011). Under Musharraf especially, with his involvement in the global war on terror, and the HT declared an extremist organization in the United Kingdom, Musharraf also banned the HT in Pakistan, which far from disappearing went underground, like other campus-based societies before it. The danger of the nonpolitical, apolitical or transnational nature of these organizations is creating a further disconnect from local politics and the state, where political activism again is perceived as a problematic and corrupt phenomenon.

The lawyers' movement and PTI

On 9 March 2007, President General Pervez Musharraf suspended the chief justice of the Supreme Court, Iftikhar Muhammad Chaudhry. This engendered a peaceful resistance movement, largely termed 'the lawyers' movement'. The suspension of the CJ led Aitzaz Ahsan, the president of the Supreme Court Bar Association, to call on the Pakistani population to observe 'black flag week'. A rally was launched from Ahsan's residence in Lahore by the Lahore High Court Bar Association and the Lahore District Bar Association. During the next week protestors carrying black flags, banners and posters demonstrated in major cities throughout the country. In addition, groups of lawyers began to organize Thursday strikes at district and high courts, which were stacked with judges that most lawyers accused of being regime acolytes. By this time other judges who refused to heed Musharraf's orders had been suspended as well. Civil society provided support and soon the opposition parties joined the movement, all calling for Chaudhry and the other judges to be reinstated. In early November 2007 martial law was declared and the lawyers announced the launch of the Adliya Bachao Tehreek (Save the Judiciary Movement) to protest against it.

According to Ahmed and Stephan (2010, p. 497):

> Pakistani students, who were prohibited from forming unions during Musharraf's rule, surprised everyone by turning out in sizeable numbers to demonstrate against emergency rule. Students from the elite schools of Islamabad and the Lahore University of Management Sciences (LUMS), University of the Punjab, Karachi University, Quaid-i-Azam University, FAST University, Hamdard University, and colleges in major cities took to the streets along with their teachers to rally in support of the judiciary. Their banners read '*Adliya kee azaadi tak, jang karain ge*' (We will fight until the judiciary is free) and prominent student slogans were: 'We will decide our own future', 'Justice now', 'Give justice to the judiciary', and 'Stop playing with the law'. As a price for their activism, hundreds of students, many of whom were active in various opposition parties, were badly beaten and imprisoned along with their teachers in Islamabad, Rawalpindi, Lahore, and Karachi.

The student movement included students from the elite university Lahore University of Management Science (LUMS), whose activities were documented by Martha Bolognani.[7] She notes how the elite student movement did not join the mainstream protests outside of the LUMS gates for fear of repercussions and arrests. The contribution of these elite students was more in terms of how they were able to push the debate into the international media and create an international audience for Musharraf's emergency.[8] Many young people started to engage in politics during this campaign, which saw more than 100,000 people on the street.

The lawyers' movement paved the way to a decisive opposition victory in the 2008 general elections, after which Musharraf was forced to step down from power. Later, after the civilian government led by President Asif Ali Zardari reneged on its earlier promise to restore the deposed judges, a new movement by lawyers, rights activists, media and civil society, backed by Nawaz Sharif's opposition party, put relentless pressure on the Zardari government until it was forced to yield on 9 March 2009, agreeing to reinstate the deposed judges.

However, while students had been politically very active during the lawyers' movement, the political engagement quickly died down after the 2008 elections, despite the media hype around the rise of PTI and their leader's popularity among young people.

Politics beyond the lawyers' movement and the hype of the youth vote in the 2013 Elections

The hype around the 'youth vote' started with PTI's direct engagement with the youth after 2009. The main argument had been that in the 2013 elections a new generation of young Pakistani voters would emerge that had never been to the polls before and that they wanted change. Imran Khan was already popular among Pakistanis, a national hero for having led the Pakistan cricket team to victory in the 1992 World Cup. He was also a well-known philanthropist. He was therefore the ideal leader to attract especially young Pakistanis to politics. PTI's agenda was simple, to combat corruption, which was perceived to be the main reason for Pakistan's domestic and international failures. The strategy for combating corruption, though, lacked focus, with PTI often undermining the fundamentals of democracy and the Parliament in its quest to defeat corruption. Imran Khan's[9] PTI targeted youth participation by 'aiding them in their procurement of the party's membership' (Express Tribune 2012). The Insaf Student Federation (ISF) was set up as the official student wing of PTI with youth representatives from all five provinces.[10] Forums were set up on social networking sites such as Facebook and Twitter in order to encourage youth to use social media to participate and express their views. They raised debates on issues such as 'Rental Power Plants, the shortcomings in the education system and the environmental and medical hazards in the country'[11] at the Youth Parliament. In the autumn of 2011, a rally in Lahore attracted 100,000 supporters, most of them young. This turnout, in the stronghold of Pakistan's chief opposition party the PML(N), stunned politicians and analysts alike. The PTI's next rally in Karachi attracted a similar number of supporters. Since then the PTI has been credited with re-engaging the youth in politics, and much of the media hype before and around the elections focused on the youth vote, and what role social media played in this re-engagement process.[12] However, according to Zaidi (2013) the media hype around the role of social media has been vastly overplayed and most of the debate on change took place within a social media bubble that bore little resemblance to reality.

The British Council research on how the young generation felt before the 2013 elections found that on aggregate young people in Pakistan were very pessimistic. The main issues remained inflation, lack of employment opportunities and issues pertaining to security and violence. Most importantly the youth reported very low confidence in official institutions, in particular the government, parliament and political parties, reflecting research by Lall (2012) and Yusuf (2011) and showing that attitudes had not changed much when it comes to government institutions.[13] While disillusionment with the previous five years certainly played a part in these opinions, one could also argue that the lack of understanding as to how the system works is largely at fault. This is reflected in the crux of the problem, which remains voter registration. The pre-election survey by the BC showed that only around 40 per cent of the young definitely planned to vote on the day.[14] Of those who definitely did not plan to vote, 29 per cent were not registered and 5 per cent did not have a national identity card. Another 19 per cent did not believe that the elections would make a difference and 13 per cent did not like the political parties or candidates.[15] Overall in the BC survey there is little difference between urban and rural responses, except that in rural areas the number of those not voting because they are not registered or do not have a national identity card goes up to 41 per cent and 7 per cent respectively.[16] This is despite the fact that the CNIC (computerized national identity card) process has made voter registration so much easier.[17] On the day of the elections 16.88 million of the 85.42 million registered voters were aged under 26, and 12.73 million were aged under 30, that is, the total number of young people voting represented 34 per cent of registered voters (Haider 2013).[18] Actual voter turnout was 55.02 per cent (i.e. 44.8 million voters). According to the Gallup exit polls (2013) 11.2 million voters (25 per cent) were from the 18–29 age group; however, we do not know exactly how many young people actually cast their vote. It looks like their turnout was proportionately smaller than that of other age groups, defying the media hype.[19]

Even if (according to the BC research) there are few differences between the attitudes of urban and rural youths, it is likely that there are stark differences between social classes. A random selection of thirty-three youths from working class and poor backgrounds in a Karachi slum and in a poor area in semi-urban/rural Punjab in December 2012 had shown that although all who took part in the focus group to discuss citizenship were excited about Imran Khan and the PTI, none were actually registered to vote, less than six months before the elections. This illustrates that many of those who would have possibly voted for Imran Khan were not registered voters, underlining that the system is not recognized or understood, placing political participation in the realm of media debates, away from true political participation. This could possibly be due to the fact that the lawyers' movement in which the youth was engaged simply petered out. However, there were still bouts of public anger, such as the fury in 2010 about the government's slow response to the catastrophic floods across Pakistan. Between 2011 and 2012 due to frequent power outages and breakdowns there were protests in different cities across Pakistan. These, however, do not translate into larger political activity – not even into anti-state movements.[20] Kugelman (2012) has written on the role that patronage plays, reiterating Lyon (2002) and Lieven's (2011) ideas that many, including the younger generation, would hesitate to change the political order in a way that could threaten the structure they depend on for future influence. Although the young people did not mention this explicitly, their families would caution about too radical a change.[21] Neither does Kugelman (2012) believe that anger and alienation could translate into a youth-led, religion-based political movement, despite many young people being in general anti-government and anti-American, with a majority favouring an Islamic government.

Given the history depicted so far in this chapter, it is not surprising to find a disconnect between the wider student population and politics in Pakistan. However, the extent of this disconnect, where political illiteracy[22] is the norm, where political activism, especially in government universities, is associated with violence, is highly problematic. Added to this is of course the problem of terrorism (see Chapter 4) that further creates a fear of public protest. This section unpacks all of these problems associated with political activism and participation among the youth, beginning with an analysis of the meaning and understanding of political activism by young students, their understanding of political awareness and level of political activism, and their perception about politics and political parties in Pakistan.

Politics and the Pakistani youth

Across the various interview and focus groups, corruption and lack of trust were one of the main reasons cited by young people for not getting involved in politics. Other reasons cited included the need for family connections, the fear of violence, the lack of role models and the fact that many saw their most important responsibility as being towards their own family, rather than the wider country (Lall 2012): '*I would never go into politics, too many double standards*' (Student, Female, Quetta); '*Political parties just work on their interests*' (Student, Male, Kanganpur); '*No one will go into politics. Make your character dirty*' (Focus Group, Government University[23]); '*In present day politics is all about corruption. Anyone who becomes a politician robs and cheats the country that causes misery for the public whereas we should work for the welfare of our country*' (Student, Female, Lahore). Similar sentiments were expressed across the student sample.

The anathema towards politics is a constant theme across the narratives. The findings that politicians are considered 'untrustworthy', only looking out for their own interests, with most of them corrupt and indifferent to the plight of the common man, was not surprising. This was a theme across all institutions from madrassas to government schools, from private to public sector universities. There is a collective abhorrence towards politics, in line with the findings of the Jinnah Institute's work on political activism and the youth (2013). Politicians were perceived to be obsessed with the '*kursi*', the seat of political power which usurps the rights of the people. '*Aaj kal tu buss koi siyaasi kaam keiliyei jamaat nahi buss kursi kei hasul keiliyei aur barei barei ohdei hasil karnei kei liyei hai*'[24] (Student, Female, Lahore).

Others were clear about their perception of political parties, saying they were '*made for the destruction of the country*' (Student, Female, Quetta). The teachers interviewed also did not look fondly at the political structures and political parties that exist: '*Mulk mei afra tafreeh aur muashrati tabaahi ki wajuhaat*'[25] (Academic, Female, Lahore).

Generally, there were responses that attempted to provide a more nuanced definition of political parties, '*[t]o ensure that a country is stably run, and to provide people of equal rights*' (Student, Female, Lahore), but on further probing it was found that the respondents were often referring to the ideal of a political party, not the reality of it in Pakistan. While politics and politicians were regarded with loathing and suspicion, the study further examined young people's understanding of politics, of political activism and political awareness.

Political awareness and activism: A definition

Political awareness, an understanding of the rights and responsibilities of both the citizenry and the state that in turn would lead to political action, for young people was limited to the idea that it simply meant knowledge about political parties and the political system of Pakistan. The lack of understanding of political awareness was clearly indicative of the failure of the education system in inculcating civic values and responsibilities (see Chapter 4). However, the participants also did not link political awareness to university-level politics. The main focus of their discussion on awareness linked to politics was the mainstream political parties and the rhetoric employed by these politicians. The first narrative takes this political awareness 'across the border', highlighting the significance of geopolitics in defining the political reality of Pakistan. Chapter 4 discusses the problematic narratives associated with countries 'across the border' that are held responsible, often solely responsible for internal threats and issues around terrorism: '*To be aware of the current political context/scenario of the state and also across the border*' (Student, Female, Lahore); '*Khoobsurat alfaaz ka mujmuah jiss par amal nahi hota*'[26] (Academic, Female, Lahore). While 'across the border' reality is an important aspect of political awareness, religion is also part of this understanding. Political awareness has to be within the context of Islam, since '*this is a religious state*'. The existence of the arch-enemy across the border (read: India), and the significance of Islam in defining our sense of political awareness, reveals the extent to which the discourse on Pakistan linked to Islam has been normalized: '*As we know this is a religious state, so every work according to Islam. If we know this state then work according to it*' (Student, Female, Kasur).

However, among the shared definitions were also meanings that stood out, where the '*know how about politics*' (Student, Female, Lahore) was connected to the hope that by better understanding the political structure one will be able to improve it. This kind of optimism, though, was more an exception to the narratives than the norm: '*Siyaasi shaaur sei hum mulk ko behtar tareequei sei chala saktei hain*'[27] (Student, Female, Lahore).

Political activism was further understood as moving beyond awareness and taking part in formal politics at the national and provincial levels. '*Activism is the next step after awareness. The knowledge you actually have in which you believe*' (Focus Group, Private University[28]). However, again as was the case with the term 'political' the responses often included value judgements about the nature of politics in Pakistan, and activism linked to it. One participant dismissed it as a '*publicity stunt*' (Student, Female, Lahore), while another described it simply as '*chaos*' (Student, Female, Lahore). Academics from a government sector university also had similar negative connotations attached to political activism, but what was revealing for these academics in particular was that they belonged to the Islamiyat department of a university in Lahore which Nelson (2011) in his study had already indicated was a stronghold of the Jamaat-i-Islami. A focus group was conducted in this department with faculty members who sat in a segregated classroom. Their response to the question of which political party they supported was that it depended on who did good work, and insisted that they had '*no allegiance to any one party*'. Political activism then was '*not considered "good*"' (Academic, Male, Lahore), while another described it as '*Muasharati tabaahi aur afra tafri*'[29] (Academic, Female, Lahore). However, in other narratives participants did attempt to provide a balanced definition with some highlighting how '*political activism is very essential to survive in a state like Pakistan*' but also problematized this statement by asking '*what politics is?*' (Student, Male, Lahore); '*To take a part in different parties and to be aware of political current issues*' (Female, Student, Lahore); '*means used to gain favor of the people*' (Female, Student, Lahore); '*Siyaasi soch ki bedaari*'[30] (Female, Student, Karachi); '*A person or campaign work through various activities of political parties and management of that party*' (Academic, Male, Quetta).

While these definitions provided a generic understanding of political activism, participants also shared the extent to which they themselves were both politically aware and politically active. The narratives around political awareness predominantly evoked a passive level of political awareness. Again from getting news through the internet, to being '*aware of the ups and downs in the politics of our country*', to watching 'media', talk shows and 'news channels'. However, young people also used being 'a student' as an excuse for not being politically aware, while for others their source of information was their parents: '*Not that much. As I am a student so I don't get time*' (Student, Female, Quetta); '*Yeah because my father is politically active*' (Student, Female, Lahore).

The disconnect between being a student and political activism goes against the tradition of political activism that had been prevalent in universities in the past, more so with student groups associated with political parties. However, this also highlights the changing nature of the university where students are burdened with work to such an extent that other issues around rights and politics become irrelevant (see Jinnah Institute 2013; Nelson 2011). For others the link to politics came through their fathers who they believed to be politically aware so would inform them about the political situation in the country. The difference between the parents' generation who were students during the period described in the preceding section, and their own generation's level of political activism was also a subject of discussion. The responses from the focus groups were mixed, with some arguing that their parents were politically active while others arguing that they were less so than them. Figure 2.1a and 2.1b highlights the trends in these

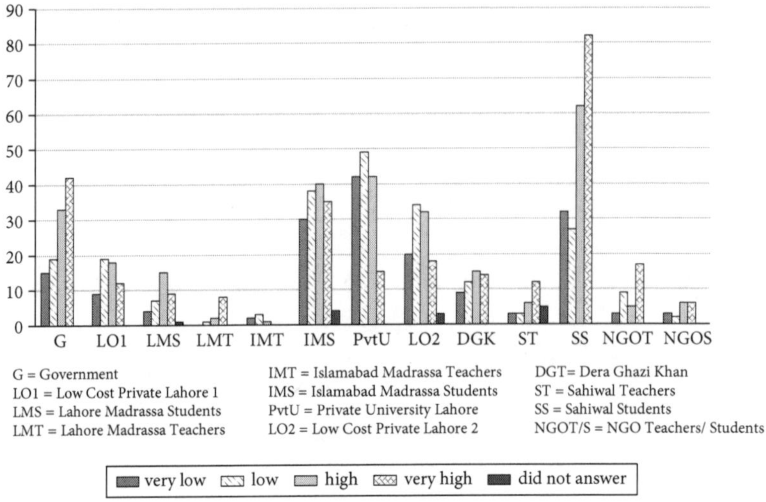

Figure 2.1a Punjab: Is your parents' generation more aware of its rights and duties towards the state as compared to your generation?

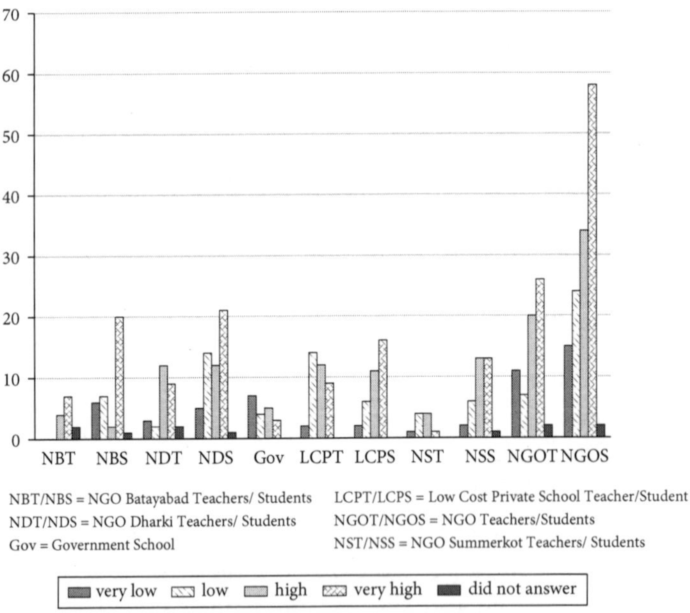

Figure 2.1b Sindh: Is your parents' generation more aware of its rights and duties towards the state as compared to your generation?

responses, where the exception of students who believed their parents were less politically active was in the case of a private university in Lahore, where children predominantly came from an elite background. The sample from Sindh also predominantly agreed with the statement that their parents were more politically active than their own generation, a sentiment that was echoed in the 2014–15 focus group at a university in Sindh.

That this difference is a result of their social and political class is a possibility, highlighting Hasan's (2002) analysis of how the 'elite' has politically disengaged. In the focus group with a private university in Karachi students expressed differences of opinion: '*No, I think we are less politically aware because of a plurality of opinions that we are exposed to through the news. Don't know what to believe*' (Focus Group, Private University[31]).

The discussion with students also highlighted how parents today discouraged their children from engaging in political action linked to protests. Emblematic of the parents discussed in Nelson's study, there is a fear that the students might be at risk, not only from other student groups (often dependent on which city or university) but also from the added threat of terrorism (discussed in Chapter 4). One student explained that there was a '*lack of support and motivation from parents because they find it unsafe and somewhat useless*' (Student, Female, Lahore), while others simply stated that they were not allowed. The fact that students need permission for political activism is also indicative of the lack of understanding students have towards politics and what it means to be politically active.

A disconnect with politics was quite evident in the narratives, especially with some honestly admitting that they did '*not understand the political structure of Pakistan*' (Student, Female, Lahore), and others dismissing '*Pakistani politics*' as completely '*worthless*', and hence a waste of time.

The response on their level of political activism also yielded similar results. Figures 2.2a and 2.2b shows the distribution of political activism across institutions, and highlights how predominantly students described themselves as being politically inactive. In Punjab, the exceptions are negligible but include the Islamabad madrassa staff and the students going to NGO/civil society-run schools. For the madrassa staff again their activism was linked to their religious obligations, which seldom translated into political duties and responsibilities, but the NGO students were taught in a community-based school that attempted to create a sense of civic identity. Yet as the graph illustrates the major trend is lack of political activism as described by the participants. In Sindh a similar trend is visible in Figure 2.2b where politics was perceived to be too corrupt a profession for the honest citizen.

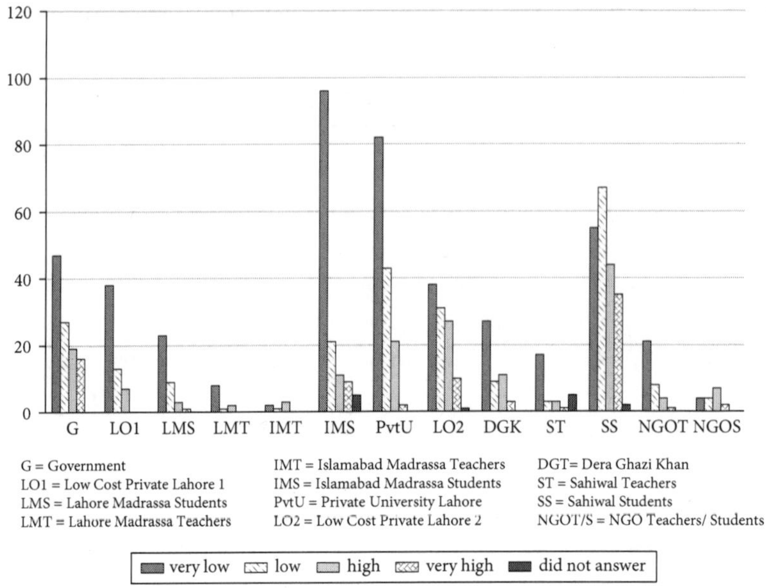

Figure 2.2a Punjab: How politically 'active' are you?

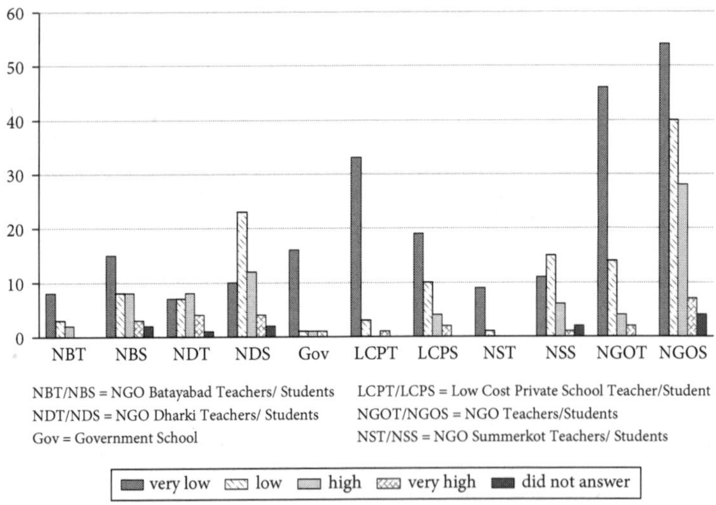

Figure 2.2b Sindh: How politically 'active' are you?

Exploring the data across rural areas and smaller and larger cities suggests that people in rural and smaller localities were more involved in politics as compared to the big cities. Young people in a small city in Southern Punjab, for example, said they were actively involved in various campaigns. However, participants also included individuals who belonged to political families, therefore were part of a privileged socio-economic class, which also meant that they had a greater inclination towards politics, acquiring this aptitude as part of their grooming within the family. In other instances students from these localities mentioned how they were active as part of a forum or an NGO, while others cited social work as a political activity: '*Yes, I love politics, actually I am aware of the current affairs of a number of countries but I just love Pakistani politics because they are so much you know attractive*' (Student, Male, DG Khan). This attraction, though, seldom translated into actual action.

A minority of students do take part in political campaigns. With regard to university students it was those who take political science courses who were the ones with more political awareness and were generally perceived as the 'politically active' lot. Students who are politically active are also the ones who are part of political or law societies or Amnesty International university chapters.

However, this begs the question of what political activity actually means for those who do profess to 'participate' beyond university clubs and societies. Most of those who classified themselves as politically active said that they are active because they watch political shows on TV and discuss it with their family or friends. They keep track of current affairs through electronic and print media, take part in political discussions or chose it as a subject for a degree programme. For most, being aware (through electronic or print media) of the country's politics is tantamount to being 'politically active'. '*Yes, I'm very much into politics. I watch political shows and am also interested in newspaper. I also discuss politics with my parents and colleagues*' (Student, Male, Lahore).

This would not be classified as active if one goes by the definition offered by Verba et al., as it does not try to affect or influence the behaviour of the government. However, as mentioned in the beginning of this chapter, there are student groups such as the Democratic Student Alliance, the Progressive Students Collective, the Feminist Collective, the Women's Collective, Girls at Dhabas – groups that have been formed by young people often promoting leftists or feminist ideals across educational institutions by using social media to organize and coordinate. While such groups have support and large numbers of members on social media pages, only a small number of young people physically take part in their events. Social media, however, does become a platform to raise awareness (see Chapter 5).

The role of media is also clearly important. Pakistan today has hundreds of channels and many broadcast political debates. However, in this case political awareness (through the media) is confused with political activity, which also highlights the extent of political disengagement where interfacing with political parties and structures was not an option for our participants when answering the question of political engagement. Again hardly anyone mentioned political institutions in their responses; political activity is reduced to the passive act of watching TV and having an opinion (and possibly discussing it with someone else). This problem was linked to a lack of trust and belief in the possibility of change through political action: '*No, there would be no point as I could bring no change*' (Student, Female, Lahore); '*No, because it is of no use. Corruption is so evident here nothing can be done here*' (Student, Female, Lahore); '*No. Because politics is all about removing someone and getting their place. Welfare of people is not given any priority*' (Student, Female, Lahore); '*No, kyon keh iss ka koi faida nahi. Agar aisi jamaat ya rehnuma mila jo mulk aur kaum keh saath mukhliss ho tu zaroor shamooliyat ikhtiyaar ki jai gi*'[32] (Academic, Female, Lahore). This lack of political activism on the part of the academic community was also evident with male academics, with one dismissing political activism on the basis of having 'a different field', where the underlying assumption was that only students and faculty of political fields would get involved with such idle pursuits as political activism. For others watching the news or having dinner table conversations with family amounted to a form of political activism.

Gender and Islam in the case of an all-female university in Punjab was considered a reason as to why women would not be politically active, as indicative in the quote at the beginning of this chapter. This was also reflected in the one female graduate madrassa that was visited. In one class of forty-seven female students in the university studying biochemistry, only three were willing to join politics, while the general sentiment was that women should not go into politics since it was not allowed in Islam. The discussion that ensued included examples of female leaders such as the Mughal ruler Razia Sultana and the Pakistani prime minister Benazir Bhutto but the class predominantly believed that they were wrong in running for political office. '*While women could become heads of businesses, "running a country", "becoming the leader of a nation", "the head of a state" was "not allowed in Islam"*'. Given the way religion has been used within schools to create the submissive subject, it also reinforced a gendered notion of the politically inactive youth. The narrative in this class of forty-seven students became particularly problematic when the argument given for why Islam did not allow women to be state leaders was given as '*auratoon ki psyche*',[33] the fact that psychologically and biologically they were not equipped to lead and hence could not be politically active. After all, as some students argued none of the Caliphs of Islam were female, thereby illustrating that it was not allowed in Islam. In the same university, in the biotechnology class the students also shared similar opinions. Their views about political activism ranged from '"*lack of interest*" *to their inability to* "*change politics*" *and finally to the fact that it was not allowed in Islam because* "*women are emotionally weak, and emotional women can't make decisions*"'. The irony of these focus groups in this government university is that being one of the oldest all women's educational institution (that only recently obtained a university status) it produced activists who were the pioneers of the feminist and leftist movements in Pakistan. Their students today were far from being politically active, let alone politically aware. However, given the history of state crackdowns on student politics (as the preceding discussion illustrates), such political apathy or disconnect was also not surprising.

Yet, there were exceptions to the norm. Participants belonging to a minority sect or ethnicity had actively protested for their cause, though these protestors were limited in number. '*Went to a protest against Shia killing. I come from a Shia family so I went to protest against such killings. Went with friends and family and yes we did have an effect but I think if more people had joined, and they do join it can make a difference*' (Focus Group, Private University[34]); '*Yes I have taken part in many protests because I am Hazara and I am facing target killing*' (Student, Female, Quetta). There was this belief that as the affected community they had a responsibility and therefore had to hold the state accountable. The involvement of young Pakistanis, especially those from the Pashtun community in the PTM, but also its appeal to other ethnic groups that have been unjustly treated by the Pakistani state, further highlights the nature of political participation. Organization along ethnic categories is the result of increasing discrimination of particular communities such as the Pashtun and the Baloch by the security state.

Other exceptions towards political participation included those who had been involved in the Tehreek-i-Insaf, having taken part in their dharna, though on further probing through focus groups the extent of their involvement and their belief in the leadership of the PTI was becoming exceedingly problematic. '*Imran Khan makes a lot of silly statements but he also says a lot more than other politicians. I watched a documentary called Pakistan's Shame about child abuse in Pakistan, and there he was seriously addressing the problem. At least he does that*'; '*Sceptical about PTI now but do support Imran Khan*' (Focus Group, Private University[35]).

In one focus group of forty students, thirteen supported PTI, four PML(N) and four PPP, while the majority refrained from acknowledging any political party. Everyone unanimously agreed that they hated politics, with one giving the example of Imran Khan and how her '*hero's character*' had been targeted because he got involved in politics. For others the dharna that was organized again and again caused too much 'damage' while other supporters felt that he had been a disappointment. In fact, the failure of the dharna was another factor given by students that showed that political protests did not work. In focus groups in Karachi there were students who had previously voted for MQM, but the rationale for such voting was based on their family's commitment to MQM, thereby continuing the tradition. There were those who also struggled with voting, MQM supporters who had voted for PTI but had already decided that they would vote for an independent, since PTI was a disappointment: '*Dil abhi bhee Mutaahida ka hai*[36] *but you just can't support them because things around you are such*'; '*I would vote because in my ilaaka bachpan sei hum MQM ko vote daaltei hain.*[37] *MQM is a progressive party. It has Muhajjir representation*'; '*Actually my grandma was an active MQM supporter and went to protests in the 70s. She says they used to be peaceful in the past but she does not vote for them anymore. She went through the 1990s and saw her friends getting killed and saw what MQM did*' (Focus Group, Private University[38]). In the focus groups held in Karachi and Lahore, the students in Karachi were more expressive of their political views, and more aware of broader provincial and national politics. In Lahore, the majority of supporters still belonged to the PML(N), while PTI had managed to gain the support of some. The PPP had least support among the students, as one observed '*Apna bhee nahi hai.*[39] *Will see what Bilawal does*' (Focus Group, Private University[40]).

Another exception was an active supporter of the Jamaat-e-Islami who highlighted her role in the party and considered the Jamaat-e-Islami to be '*[a] good party to give Islamic rules for Islamic state*', but the same person also recognized that '*I am not interested in political activities too much because work of political parties to give garbage on one another*' (Student, Female, Kasur).

In another case in a private university, one student admitted that she would consider getting involved in politics, but was already convinced that she would not be able to 'make a difference' for the simple reason that she did not have enough money to succeed at politics. '*I would but it wouldn't make a difference. There is lack of sincerity. You need a big car, big house and lots of money to succeed in politics. I will not survive*'; '*You can't be an honest person as a politician in Pakistan*' (Focus Group, Private University[41]). Another student mentioned how she had been politically active online by engaging in discussion forums related to politics on social media, but she stopped after the murder of Sabeen Mahmud, the political activist who was murdered on the night she hosted Baloch activist Mama Qadeer's talk on 'The Missing Baloch'. While her murderer was caught and confessed to killing her for her liberal views, it had been perceived as a warning sign for many young people in this study. There were students in Karachi who had gone to a protest condemning the murder of Sabeen Mahmud, but as one participant commented '*it was a tough decision to make*' since she was '*scared to go*'. Mahmud's murder was further connected to her openly celebrating Valentine's Day, which offended the religious sensibilities of her murderer. Such differences in opinion also reflect the kind of debates that religious versus leftist or nonreligious student unions have been engaged in on campuses. In Nelson's study of the University of Peshawar, violence erupted on campus following Valentine's Day because of the Jamiat's stance against Valentine's Day as being un-Islamic. Jamiat at the Punjab University has also engaged in violence against Valentine's Day, preventing couples from sitting together, to the point of beating up the men. The ideological battle for Pakistan, for what is permissible and what is 'haram' as defined by men still continues, and the violence it breeds clearly acts as a deterrent for young Pakistanis. '*I think the main problem in Pakistan is that people like us will not join politics, so nothing will change*' (Focus Group, Private University[42]). There have also been examples like Mashal Khan, a student who had been politically active, and had taken on the university administration for its corruption, but ended up being lynched by fellow students after false accusations of blasphemy were made against him (Akbar 2017). Further investigations exposed the university's connection with his murder. The freedom to be politically active, to even be taught about politics or civic values within schools and universities, is almost nonexistent today. While there have been exceptions of university professors attempting to create an atmosphere to promote political awareness and activism, such professors have been pushed out from universities.[43] There is an increasing call for universities to follow the state narrative on security, becoming part of the security agenda as evident in the seminar organized by the ISPR at the army auditorium entitled 'Role of Youth in Rejecting Extremism'. The ISPR has also been active in giving talks at universities about the challenges facing Pakistan, and inviting students to interact with soldiers. Talks on PTM or Baloch rights have been shut down not just in government universities, but also in elite private universities, either through warnings or through intimidation by the security state.

The nature of political activism across different generations in Pakistan has clearly changed, with young people less politically active than their parents' and, one could argue, their grandparents' generation. From the student activists involved in the Pakistan movement, to students who believe that politics and education are antithetical to each other, the present generation of students is more likely to uphold the status quo. Ironically, one student from KP studying in a madrassa in Islamabad quotes Muhammad Ali Jinnah to make a case for why he is not politically active: '*Work, work and work – Quaid-e-Azam. And I am a full time student*' (Madrassa Student, Male, Islamabad). In the sample only 5 per cent of the participants provided an exception to the general narrative, and these were young people from either ethnic minorities or the Shi'a population, with very few allies across the student body.

Furthermore, in Pakistan today there is an active attempt by the security state to thwart any possibility of political activity by young Pakistanis, especially on university campuses. The Pakistani state ever since its inception has had a troubled relationship with student activism, despite the active role of students in the independence struggle. The history of student activism post independence is marred with episodes of violence that led to student unions being banned (see Mullick 2008; Paracha 2000). This ban is part of the reason that today young people do not identify with politics. Since the majority of the Pakistani youth who are now of voting age were born in the 1980s or later, they would not have experienced student politics and seen the link between student and national politics (Jinnah Institute 2013), except for the occasional ethnic-based campus violence often led by the Jamiat.

However, as we will establish in Chapter 3 the education system in Pakistan inculcates values of discipline to the point of curtailing any form of critical reflection or questioning by the students. It was therefore not surprising to find that the majority of the young people in this study were either apolitical or antipolitical. Even academics in universities and school teachers described any form of politics as being unworthy and corrupt.

The Pakistani government is aware of the youth's apathy. The report published by the Centre of Civic Education (CCE) (2009) makes a number of suggestions to improve political participation by the youth. They include first that students' unions need to serve as a training ground for young people to learn the art of politics by working on solutions to academic and administrative problems on campuses. While student politics on campus is not meant to engage in national politics, political parties have a responsibility to engage the students through their youth wings and should device a strategy to build their confidence in political institutions.[44] The report also addresses the fact that politicians should lead by example and as public figures should be seen as serving the nation rather than for their personal gain. In this way the report hopes the image of politics could be improved. Yet it is clear from the data collected and the preceding discussion that young people are not getting involved in politics for a number of reasons, which are not really related to the issues thrown up by the CCE report and which go beyond student politics, that after all only affect those who access higher education.[45] Rather 'many transition to citizenship without developing an understanding of their rights as citizens or the responsibilities that citizenship entails. Thus, they view politics mostly in terms of political office, rather than as a comprehensive set of relations where voting and participating in public life are as important as successfully contesting elections' (UNDP 2017, p. 106). Furthermore, the security state is increasingly creating an atmosphere of self-censorship, where students and academics are discouraged from engaging in any form of activism that might challenge the national narrative of the state.

Notes

1 This focus group included participants from Hyderabad, Sukkur and Karachi.

2 This focus group included participants from Lahore, Sheikhupura, Muridke, Dera Ghazi Khan and Sargodha.

3 A detailed history of student politics and the various bans is detailed by Paracha (2000). Two notable bans when Pakistan was under military rule were in 1958 when the NSF (as well as student politics) was banned when Field Marshal Ayub Khan imposed the country's first martial law. This included a fresh crackdown on student radicals. On 15 February 1984, General Zia-ul-Haq imposed a ban on student unions in all colleges throughout the country.

4 The other 'unrecognized' organizations in West Pakistan included The Inter-Collegiate Body (ICB), The All-Pakistan Students' Organization (APSO), The Karachi Students' Federation (KSF), The Girl Students' Congress, The National Students' Organization (NSO), and The West Pakistan Students' League (Ministry of Education 1966, p. 8).

5 'Three Days That Shook the Country' (https://drsarwar.wordpress.com/2009/11/16/three-days-that-shook-the-country-students-herald-jan-19-1953/). (see Herald Student, 1953).

6 Set up after the student agitations in the 1960s.

7 Visiting lecturer at the time at LUMS.

8 Also see Bolognani and Lyons 2011.

9 Imran Khan, Pakistan's former cricket captain, comes from outside the traditional political establishment; however, he is part of the elite. He is seen as having delivered on two counts: cricket and building a cancer hospital in his mother's memory; this has given him credibility on the political scene.

10 However, the student president of the ISF was killed in an act of target killing so this only confirms the fears of the youth that being a part of politics is risky business. Accessed on 22 May 2012. www.defence.pk/forums/national-political-issues/12 9729-waseem-baloch-killed-pti-isf.html
11 PTI's official website. Accessed on 22 May 2012. www.insaf.pk/Forum/tabid/53/fo rumid/42/tpage/1/view/topic/postid/83416/Default.aspx#83416
12 See, for example, Iqbal 2013; Sattar 2013; Al Jazeera 2013.
13 National government – 71 per cent rated unfavourably; National Assembly – 67 per cent rated unfavourably; political parties – 69 per cent rated unfavourably (British Council NGBB Data Pack, slide 13).
14 NGBB Data Pack National, slide 32.
15 NGBB Data Pack National, slide 34.
16 NGBB Data Pack Rural, slide 34.
17 A CNIC applicant is required to produce the following documents at the time of application: birth certificate or old NIC or matriculation certificate or CNICs of immediate/blood relative's citizenship certificate issued by MOI (www.nadra.gov.pk/index.php?option=com_content&view=article&id=6&Itemid=9).
18 The UNDP Human Development Report 2017 has slightly different figures. 'The 2013 general elections in Pakistan marked a shift in perceptions about the youth, who emerged as a significant political constituency. Numbering about 55 million, nearly one out of two registered voters (48 percent) were between 18 to 30-years old – half of them from the urban middle class – against the national turnout of 55 percent' (p. 116). However, despite the number of registered young voters there is no data that can show if on the day these young voters went to the polls, making the comparison with the national turnout of 55 per cent a moot point.
19 Voting data by age is not consolidated centrally. Age-specific data is kept in each district separately.
20 Because these are not organized protests as such and people, mostly poorer, gather on their own with no one leading them.
21 One can argue that Nawaz Sharif's win in the May 2013 elections underlines this point. Many wanted change, but were equally reluctant to give it to the PTI who they see as inexperienced.
22 Crick develops the concept of political literacy that is imparted through education but is 'more than a school educational subject' (2000, p. 110). He discusses political participation as an essential element of citizenship. He describes political literacy as a combination of knowledge, skills and attitudes, developing alongside each other, each one enforcing the other two. Davies (2008) also believes there are reasons why political literacy should be promoted: 'Politics has to connect with young people: it must be taught and learned in ways that are congruent with the essential nature of political education' (Davies 2008, p. 381). Dean (2004 and 2007) has argued that in Pakistan political literacy is low as there is a lack of dedicated citizenship education.

This is not unusual in societies that have a history of military dictatorships. But today, although no longer ruled by a military dictator and having reverted to a multi-party democracy, political literacy in Pakistan remains very low – even in urban centres and among the educated middle classes' (Lall 2014).

23 This focus group included participants from Lahore, Sheikhupura, Muridke, Dera Ghazi Khan and Sargodha.

24 Translation: '*Today political parties are not here for politics but for the "kursi" (seat) or to grab high influential posts.*'

25 Translation: '*The reason for chaos and social destruction.*'

26 Translation: '*Beautiful collection of words which are never followed.*'

27 Translation: '*Through political awareness we can run our country in a better way.*'

28 This focus group included participants from Hyderabad, Sukkur and Karachi.

29 Translation: '*Social destruction and chaos.*'

30 Translation: '*Consciousness or awareness of political thought.*'

31 This focus group included participants from Hyderabad, Sukkur and Karachi.

32 Translation: '*No, because there is no point to it. If I find a party or leader who is sincere with the country and nation, then I will definitely get involved.*'

33 Translation: '*Women's psyche.*'

34 This focus group included participants from Hyderabad, Sukkur and Karachi.

35 This focus group included participants from Hyderabad, Sukkur and Karachi.

36 Translation: '*Heart still belongs to Mutahida.*'

37 Translation: '*In my area, we've been voting for MQM since my childhood.*'

38 This focus group included participants from Hyderabad, Sukkur and Karachi.

39 Translation: '*Does not even belong to itself.*'

40 This focus group included participants from Hyderabad, Sukkur and Karachi.

41 This focus group included participants from Lahore.

42 This focus group included participants from Hyderabad, Sukkur and Karachi.

43 The case of Ammar Ali Jan, an academic fired from Punjab University for his political views, in particular his support of PTM (Warsi 2018); seminars linked to PTM have been forced to be cancelled at private and government universities after organizers and university management received warnings from individuals claiming to be part of the security state.

44 Political parties engaging students have completely misused them in the past, destroying academic culture by creating issues of discipline in colleges and universities.

45 There is a difference between rural and urban youth which the fieldwork revealed and is discussed later. It seems that the data Khan refers to is largely taken from urban areas as the youth in the rural areas are actively involved in politics, pursuing local MPs, getting involved in mobilization and demonstrations.

3

Youth, Education and Citizenship

Introduction

I was born in my beloved homeland Pakistan wherein Islamic traditions hold forth. We can live our lives according to our religion here, it is our home and our religion is Islam. To me Pakistan means that there is 'No God but Allah'.

(Student, Female, Sahiwal)

Education should use national interest, historical heritage, religion or multi-culturalism as tools to engender a sense of belonging with the country. Historically our educational system has selectively or collectively used the above mentioned factors to create national cohesion.

(Student, Male, Karachi)

The education system is instrumental in pushing the national narrative of the security state, as the ideological struggle over citizenship in Pakistan continues into the twenty-first century. What is the meaning of Pakistan? Was it established in the name of Islam to be an Islamic state following Sharia law, or a homeland for Muslims and religious minorities under secular rule? These questions continue to be debated by media analysts, scholars and political actors (Yasmeen 2013; Zaidi 2011; Nelson 2008; Rais 2007; Dean 2005; Ahmed 2002; Whaites 1998), yet the definition of citizenship moves beyond a simplistic dichotomous framework as both religious and secular political actors have used Islam to promote and legitimize their political objectives. It is this (ab)use of religion for political gain that has cemented the place of Islam within the Pakistani citizenship discourse.

Islam gained a legitimate place in the national narrative of an independent Pakistan as early as the Objectives Resolution of 1949, only to take on a state of permanence under the Constitution of Pakistan 1956, which declared Pakistan an Islamic Republic. Islam was meant to weave together an ethnically diverse nation, but instead promoted greater discord through a hegemonic Islamic discourse that undermined ethnic identities, with different state and non-state actors seeking to provide the 'true' meaning of Islam for the Islamic Republic of Pakistan (Nelson 2009; Rahman 2004). With Pakistan's increasing involvement in the Middle East and the influx of petro dollars in the 1970s and 1980s as Pakistani migrants travelled back and forth to the Gulf, the 'true' meaning of Islam in Pakistan started to take on a more puritanical version of Sunni Islam. Pakistan, the homeland of Muslims, the Land of the Pure, was linked to a larger Muslim Ummah located primarily in the Middle East, a connection that had major repercussions for domestic politics and notions of Pakistani citizenship. This puritanical version of Islam as a defining feature of Pakistani citizenship was reinforced through the education system of the country. While the role of madrassas increased in the 1980s under the patronage of the Saudis and Americans to support Pakistan's war against the Soviet infidel, such Islamic schools were only a fraction of the education system (Winthrop and Graff 2010; Rahman 2004). Instead it was the mainstream education system, and the subsequent Islamization of the national curriculum, that paved the way for a concept of Pakistani citizenship that is immersed in Islamic dogma, where patriotism and loyalty are laced with religious fervour, where the enemy of Pakistan is often seen as an enemy of Islam. After 9/11, and Pakistan's involvement in the 'war on terror', the Musharraf regime under its 'Enlightened Moderation' agenda sought to de-Islamize the education curriculum by focusing on a more inclusive interpretation of Islamic values through the National Curriculum 2006, while mainstreaming madrassas, despite facing opposition, with the aim of fighting extremism under pressure from the United States and its allies. Even though the Musharraf period was followed by democratic rule under the PPP and the PML(N), this chapter illustrates how the de-Islamization of education, especially citizenship education, was far from successful, with young Pakistanis' notion of identity immersed in religious ideology.

The chapter explores the nature of such citizenship for young Pakistanis in modern-day Pakistan. It begins by examining how the education system has been used to promote a discourse of Pakistani citizenship defined by Islam. The first part therefore provides the backdrop to the narratives of young Pakistanis today, by exploring significant policies and curricular reforms that have had a direct impact on citizenship education. The chapter does not provide a historical timeline of events but only highlights policies that were instrumental in the Islamization of the education system, in particular the curriculum for subjects such as Social Studies/Pakistan Studies and Islamiyat. This context is important in understanding the narratives that follow in the second part of the chapter, where participant responses highlight how the Pakistani education system perpetuates an uncritical and often restrictive understanding of Islam and the Pakistani identity, teaching students to become loyal subjects rather than active citizens.

Education: A political tool

Education in its very essence of educating individuals or communities is value laden, propagating a philosophy or point of view through the learning experience. Dewey (1910) in his exploration of the role of education in democratic societies emphasized its importance in inculcating democratic values that promote critical reflection for societies to progress. For the critical pedagogues like Paulo Freire (1972), or bell hooks (1994), the role of education was to challenge existing systems of oppression, with education becoming a means of liberation and progress for society. Yet, the same philosophers were also wary of the ability of education systems to produce uncritical automatons to preserve the status quo. The formal education system of Pakistan has proved to be just that, a tool used by the Pakistani state to promote its nationalist agenda of an Islamic Republic, reinforcing the struggle for Pakistan within an Islamic ideological framework, with Pakistan emerging not only as a Muslim homeland but also as a country built on Islamic principles and way of life. The problem with using religion as a means of legitimizing one's citizenship is that religion becomes an exclusive domain of clerics and political actors, removing any possibility of dialogue, where only those deemed acceptable by the religious and political elite become an acceptable part of the national narrative. In religious terms the non-Muslims and the Ahmadiyya communities become second-class citizens in a context where being Pakistani is equated with being Muslim as defined by the state. Given the rise of sectarian and ethnic violence in Pakistan over recent years, the definition of an acceptable Pakistani continues to shrink, and this is reflected in the education system, and the young people that are emerging from these educational institutions.

At its inception, the Pakistani education system, far from celebrating the diversity of the new state, tried to impose a uniform identity by making Urdu, the language of a minority, the national language, and by using Islam to promote a Muslim ideology to unite Pakistan (International Crisis Group 2004; Rahman 2004). In the first education conference the government of Pakistan reflects on the role of religion in education: 'What should be the ideological basis of education? Whether the Islamic conception of universal brotherhood of man, social democracy and social justice should constitute this ideological basis – cultivation of democratic virtues, i.e. tolerance, self help, self-sacrifice, human kindliness etc and the consciousness of common citizenship as opposed to provincial exclusiveness' (Government of Pakistan 1947). This is an early portrayal of how Islam is to act as the glue to a nation made up of diverse provincial and regional characteristics. Religion however is not enough and the role of Urdu as common language, propagated through the schools, is also seen as a way of binding the nation together. Rahman (2004), in his analysis of the education policies of Pakistan at its independence, highlights how the education system through its imposition of language and religion attempted to counter 'ethnic and religious divisions' but never challenged the 'socio-economic class divides' which went in favour of the ruling elite (2004, p. 9). English therefore retained its precolonial position as the language of the educated elite despite the imposition of Urdu as the national language, thereby creating an education hierarchy from the time of independence.

Under the rule of the first military dictator, General Ayub Khan, the Commission on National Education was convened in 1959 with the aim of redefining 'the philosophy of education', emphasizing its importance in developing the 'national character' of Pakistan (Hayes 1987, p. 45).[1] Two priorities characterize Khan's education policy: national integration/homogenization and modernization. The national integration part is discussed in a chapter on the role of education in character building, with the latter notion centred on good citizenship. According to Rubina Saigol patriotism was to be inculcated through the schools and policymakers recommended that primary schools should open each day with the national anthem in the assembly, accompanied by the hoisting of the national flag and short talks emphasizing patriotism and character building. Saigol goes on to describe that 'A very strong emphasis should be placed on the national language at the primary stage and reading should build "desirable attitudes", "good character traits" and "industrious habits". Religious instruction should be compulsory at this stage' (Saigol 2003, p. 11). In order for Pakistan to develop, premodern identities rooted in regional and communal consciousness had to be shed. Saigol explains how religious difference and otherness were not central components of this form of nationalism and that

> religious tolerance and diversity of faiths were among the values espoused in Ayub's period as part of becoming a modern and secular polity. In a history

> textbook produced for Class III in 1963, a separate chapter was devoted each to Jesus, the Hindu God Ram and Buddha, along with chapters on the holy Prophet of the Muslims. Jesus, Ram and Buddha, who were later excised from social studies textbooks, and their religions denigrated as false, appear in the Ayub era textbook as positive characters who represented peace, justice, humanity, generosity, kindness and truth. (2003, p. 26)

However, the role of Islam was key in promoting the 'right values' (Saigol 2003, p. 11). The emphasis on Islam is clearly highlighted in the following excerpt from the Commission report:

> National unity and religious values have to be translated into deeds in a manner that all our citizens can accept them and join in the common effort. Islam teaches honesty in thought, in deed and in purpose. It lays emphasis on social justice and active participation in the removal of distress and poverty. In short it seeks the identification of those who know with those who do not know, of those who have with those who do not have, of those who are powerful with those who have no power. These are tasks which can unite all of us, and it is through identification of all our problems and all our citizens that we shall find real unity. (Ministry of Education 1992, p. 2, quoting from the Commission on National Education 1959)

The promotion of this Islamic unity was propagated through the education system. A 'uniform school curriculum' was introduced to promote 'national unity', and 'religious education' was made 'compulsory at elementary school', with 'social studies' teaching about 'rights and responsibilities', 'problems facing Pakistan' and the importance of being 'useful and loyal citizens' (Dean 2005, p. 37). However, under Ayub Khan the use of religion in schools remained 'symbolic', similar to his successor Yahya Khan who again paid 'lip service to Islam' (Rahman 2004, pp. 14–16). Whether or not these rulers were simply paying 'lip service' to Islam for the purpose of promoting national unity, or appeasing the religious elite, the use of religion in education by so-called secular leaders was instrumental in normalizing a citizenship discourse that equated national identity with religion. This problem was also evident under Z. A. Bhutto's education policies. At a time when the separation of East Pakistan had challenged the 'two nation theory' and the idea of the Islamic Republic, Bhutto, to both appease the Islamic conservatives and push forth his agenda of 'Islamic socialism', made the education curriculum more Islam centric (Mohammad-Arif 2005; Rahman 1998), introducing compulsory *Islamiyat* in all schools. To further appease the religious lobby, Bhutto declared Friday as a national holiday, and established the Federal Ulama

Academy (Talbani 1996). However, unlike his predecessors and following the agenda of Islamic socialism Bhutto nationalized the educational institutions of the country (Rahman 2004). It was also under Bhutto that *Pakistan Studies* was promoted as a subject. The Pakistani identity and citizenship as propagated by the education system gradually began to be framed within the context of Islam, only to be permanently sealed during the Zia era.

Under Zia-ul-Haq's regime the education curriculum was revised in line with 'Islamic ideology' to create a 'society' that was in accordance with 'Islamic tenets' (Ministry of Education 1979, p. 2, as discussed in Dean 2005, p. 37). The National Education Policy and Implementation Programme 1979 focused on an Islamization agenda of all subjects 'including the sciences and mathematics' (Lall 2009, p. 184). This was further supported in higher educational institutions, where 'Islamiat and Pakistan Studies were made compulsory at the undergraduate level', with an 'Education of the Citizen' chapter included to 'impart the teachings of Islam', to help the citizens lead 'a clean, purposeful and productive life' (Ministry of Education 1979, p. 30, as discussed in Dean 2005, p. 37). Students who had 'memorised the Quran' were given additional marks in 'professional studies' (Lall 2009, p. 184), something leading to discrimination against non-Muslim students.[2] A female-focused curriculum aligned to the 'distinctive role' of Muslim 'women in Islamic society' was also developed (Ministry of Education 1979, p. 3, as discussed in Dean 2005, p. 37). The private school sector nonetheless flourished under Zia's regime thereby retaining the status quo of the English-speaking elites (Rahman 2004). With Pakistan entering the Cold War as an ally of the United States, the madrassa system received a boost from the government, perpetuating the narrative of the true Muslim against the God-hating communist. Salim and Khan (2004) exploring the legacy of Zia-ul-Haq's military regime note that his primary legacy can be seen in an intolerant curriculum that continues to promote Hindu–Muslim differences, reinforces the idea of a separate Islamic state, the dispute in Kashmir, India's constant threat and the urgent need to defend Pakistan against its enemies, thereby reinforcing the role of the military for Pakistan's survival.

The 'democratic interlude' that followed Zia's government did little to challenge Zia's legacy of Islamization, continuing with the 'emphasis on the two-nation theory with its concomitant hatred for India, glorification of war and the military, subservience of teachers to administrators, increased control of the military and the private sector over elite education' (Rahman 2004, p. 18). According to Rahman (2004) the 'lip service' was only 'to democracy' (p. 19). The Musharraf era that followed proposed educational amendments in line with a policy of 'Enlightened moderation' and in keeping with its role in the 'war against terror' to root out intolerance and radicalization from Pakistani society. A madrassa regulation board was also established for the regulation of the madrassa system (Lall 2009). A National Curriculum Policy 2006 as discussed in the next section was formulated to encourage critical thinking, and the responsibility of managing and monitoring schools was devolved to the districts (International Crisis Group 2004). Yet, Musharraf was forced to backtrack on many qualitative changes that aimed at de-Islamizing the curriculum to appease the religious right (International Crisis Group 2014a).

The PPP that emerged victorious in the 2008 elections continued with the reform efforts, introducing the National Education Policy 2009 that was being developed under Musharraf. The policy reemphasized the importance of Islam informing the 'social, cultural and moral values' that are inculcated through the education system, but also the need to 'ensure equal educational opportunities to all the citizens of Pakistan and to provide minorities with adequate facilities for their cultural and religious development, enabling them to participate effectively in the overall national effort' (Ministry of Education 2009, pp. 9, 18). However, such policies were far from being implemented in the education system. In 2010, the Eighteenth Amendment was introduced that devolved the authority to provide education from the federal to provincial governments.[3] Under the Sharif government the changes introduced by the provincial governments have varied, with most provinces following the National Curriculum of 2006, especially for citizenship education, that is, Social Studies and Pakistan Studies. The next section examines the curriculum for these subjects, and the changes that have been introduced to further contextualize the student narratives that follow.

Citizenship education, curriculum and the Pakistani youth

The role of citizenship education in promoting civic mindedness and responsibility towards the nation state, in facilitating social cohesion and multiculturalism is evident in countries from the United Kingdom to Canada, Australia and South Africa (see Keating et al. 2010; Whitely 2012; Niens and Chastenay 2008; Print 2005). In their study on citizenship education in Quebec and Northern Ireland, Niens and Chastenay (2008) highlight its importance in challenging social and religious divisions within society, but also its limitations in cases where the curriculum does not address the social, cultural and historical realities of its society (p. 535). Finkel and Ernst (2005) concluded that 'under the right pedagogical and "classroom climate" conditions, civic education can be an effective agent not only for increasing democratic values and skills, but also for facilitating the integration of these orientations into a more general democratic belief system' (2005, p. 335). Print in her study on youth political participation in Australia noted the importance of both the 'formal' and 'informal' curriculum on citizenship education, that included 'participatory pedagogy', through a more inclusive classroom, 'participatory approaches' that encouraged 'group learning' and engagement outside the classroom, and participatory practices such as 'critical discussion with non/bi-partisan teachers' as key elements in encouraging civic mindedness among the youth (2005, pp. 337–8). However, the citizenship curriculum in Pakistan, far from promoting civic mindedness, has created a narrative of exclusion, emphasizing the importance of the Muslim identity, the superiority of the military in protecting the Islamic Republic, and the role of citizens in supporting the Islamic ideology of the country (Dean 2005; Saigol 2005). As Nelson (2008) in his study of religious education in Pakistan observes, conflating 'Islam' with 'citizenship' as part of school 'syllabi' has resulted in 'religion itself' becoming 'a proxy for a specific construction of religious nationalism' which 'emerges as a relentless push for religious and sectarian homogeneity' (p. 283). Instead of accepting and celebrating a diversity of cultural and religious practices, the citizenship curriculum has imposed a puritanical version of Islamic nationalism in defining the meaning of a Pakistani citizen.[4]

'The role of education in the preservation and inculcation of Islamic values as an instrument of national unity and progress' (Education Policy 1972, as discussed in Khan 1997, p. 650) is a consistent theme across all education policies in Pakistan reinforced through the curriculum, with the Islamization drive of General Zia-ul-Haq making Islam and the notion of a 'good' Muslim a central feature of citizenship as taught in schools. However, there was little or no change made to this central feature of education after the Zia era. According to the Ministry of Education's 1992 report the 'guiding principles' for the National Education Policy 1992 included the following:

> A Muslim population consistently exposed to almost a value-definition western scientific, political and economic thought must be made to imbibe the true spirit of Islam. This brings the educational system into sharp focus. It is through school system alone that human mind can be educated to understand, accept and practice the worldview of Islam. This would require new Islamic curricula for building up the ideological base. (Ministry of Education 1992, p. 5)

Far from promoting a critical worldview, the education system, the curriculum, the textbooks, pedagogy and school ethos all contribute towards citizens who obey those in power without question, where religion in particular is beyond the domain of discussion or dialogue. This is especially problematic when religion becomes the basis of the citizen's identity. While the goals of the 1992 education policy included encouraging 'a spirit of appreciation for religious and cultural activities and festivals of all communities', the emphasis was on a particular ideology as linked to the Pakistani identity, a form of indoctrination that began from primary school (UNESCO 1997, p. 4). With Social Studies introduced in Grade 4 the 'basic rights and duties of a citizen' and the 'Pakistani ideology' was part of the curriculum, but Social Studies also taught the importance of 'understanding … Islamic values of social justice' (UNESCO 1997, pp. 23–4). Islamiyat for Grade 5 promoted 'love for Pakistan and its citizens' (UNESCO 1997, p. 28). The ideological intersection between different subjects with an emphasis on Islam was taking place in a post-Zia era, at the time of Rahman's 'democratic interlude' of the 1990s, where the education system, far from challenging an exclusive religious citizenship curriculum, reinforced it. Another prominent feature of the education curriculum was the glorification of the military as an important aspect of citizenship in Pakistan, one that was repeatedly highlighted in the Social Studies and Pakistan Studies textbooks, often supported by historical factual errors as examined by K. K. Aziz (2010) in his aptly titled book *The Murder of History. A Critique of History Textbooks Used in Pakistan.*

The 1998–2010 education policy also emphasized the role of Islam as a central feature of education, promoting the idea of Pakistani citizenship in relation to the notion of a good Muslim (see Zaidi 2011; Dean 2005). Nayyar and Salim in their analysis of the 2002 education curriculum revised by the Ministry of Education found that the curriculum continued to 'distort' historical events to serve its own citizenship agenda, incited 'militancy and violence', promoted 'prejudice' and 'insensitivity' against women and minorities, glorified war, and continued to promote an uncritical understanding of history and identity (2003, p. v). However, with Pakistan becoming more involved in the war on terror, and fighting militancy on its own soil, there was a recognition of the need to rethink the education curriculum, evident in the National Education Curriculum 2006. Yet, there remained a stark difference between rethinking policy and actually enacting it through reforms to textbooks and teaching across educational institutions in Pakistan. For example, the Pakistan Studies 2006 curriculum highlighted the importance of promoting 'an understanding of the ideology of Pakistan, the Muslim struggle for independence and endeavours for establishing a modern welfare Islamic state', as well as inculcating 'awareness about the multi-cultural heritage of Pakistan … to enable the students to better appreciate the socio-cultural diversity of Pakistani society and get used to the idea of unity in diversity in our national context' (Ministry of Education 2006, p. 1). The National Education Policy 2009 also reemphasized the need to 'promote equity in education with the aim of eliminating social exclusion and promoting national cohesion' (Ministry of Education 2009, p. 19), yet the fundamental core of the education system was still Islam:

> Pakistan is currently engaged in the process of reviewing, updating and reforming school curriculum from Early Childhood Education up to Higher Secondary School levels keeping in view the Islamic teachings and ideology of Pakistan, cultural and religious sensitivities in the country and modern emerging trends to make the whole education purposeful and to create a just civil society that respects diversity of views, beliefs and faiths. (Ministry of Education 2009, p. 32).

This commitment to an Islamic ideology informing the education curriculum while recognizing the importance of respecting 'diversity of views' was also reflected in the Pakistan Studies curriculum under the section titled, the 'role of minorities in Pakistan with specific reference to Quaid-i-Azam's speech of 11 August 1947, defining their status'[5] (Ministry of Education 2006, p. 13). Despite these policy objectives and commitments, the National Commission for Justice and Peace's (NCJP) 2013 study found that hateful and biased material against religious and ethnic minorities had in fact increased in books published after the 2006 and 2009 policy changes (p. 12). Such material was present in textbooks not only for Social Studies and Pakistan Studies but also for Urdu. Examples included statements such as 'Hindus got enraged and started genocide of Muslims' in Grades 9 and 10 Urdu Grammar and Composition textbooks; 'Hindus left the Muslims alone representing their narrow-mindedness' or 'In East Pakistan, education sector was completely under the control of Hindus. They prepared Bengalis against Pakistan and provoked their sentiments' in Grade 10 Pakistan Studies textbook; 'Because Christian rulers were led by fanatic priests; that war with Muslims is necessary for the protection of Cross' in Grade 7 Social Studies textbook; 'Hindus can never become true friends of Muslims' in Grade 5 Social Studies textbook (NCJP 2013, pp. 13, 14, 17, 18). The divisiveness and intolerance promoted through textbooks continues to be a problem irrespective of policy commitments.

Textbooks, Pakistani identity and the Eighteenth Amendment

After the introduction of the Eighteenth Amendment with educational responsibilities devolved to the provinces, provincial governments have taken on the role of reforming the education system, though the process of educational reform varies across provinces. This is particularly true of curricular reform and the objective of promoting tolerance and removing discriminatory content from textbooks. The Punjab Curriculum Implementation Framework (School Education Department 2014) for instance clearly highlights the importance of the curriculum in promoting 'values for peaceful co-existence, unity in diversity, and development of positive attitudes towards fellow human beings through respect and tolerance' (p. 4). Yet the Peace and Education Foundation (2016) has reported that while some 'objectionable content' has been removed from textbooks by the Punjab and KP textbook boards, new discriminatory content has instead been added. The textbook boards for Sindh and Balochistan have yet to undertake effective reforms in 'removing objectionable content' (pp. 2–3). According to the Peace and Education Foundation (2016) examples of new 'objectionable content' includes the following: 'The Governor of Rome remained neutral as he knew the deceitfulness of Jews. He left the decision [of Jesus' punishment] on religious scholars of Jews. Upon the decision of the Crucifixion of Jesus, the Jews became happy. They tortured Jesus badly. Jesus was surrounded by a crowd of Jewish enemies' in Grade 5 Islamic Studies textbook by the Balochistan Textbook Board (p. 24); 'The Urdu-Hindi dispute and the division of Bengal unleashed the evil aims of the Hindus. With the passage of time, their anti-Muslim activities reached a peak' in Grade 7 Social Studies textbook by the Balochistan Textbook Board (p. 26); 'in the last half of the twentieth century, the Muslim world was free from Western oppression, but the West continued its conspiracies to keep Muslims disempowered so that Muslims could never become a super power of the world again. ... In 1949, the Jews tried to set fire to the occupied Al-Aqsa mosque', in Grade 6 Urdu textbook by the KP Textbook Board (p. 29); 'there were two enemies of Muslims, the Englishmen and Hindus. Both of these were against the formation of Pakistan. On one hand, the Englishmen renounced the division plan of Hindustan, while on the other hand, Hindus were planning to occupy the entire Hindustan and enslave Muslims', in Grade 7 Urdu textbook by the Sindh Textbook Board (p. 33); 'Jihad in Islam means making efforts for pre-eminence of truth by all means of sacrificing one's financial, physical and mental capabilities for the sake of Allah, Even one should not hesitate to sacrifice lives of their family, relatives, and friends,' in Islamic Studies Grades 9/10 for Sindh Textbook Board (p. 34); 'Hindus tried to extinguish the Muslim dominated province of East Bengal and Assam in order to squeeze/hurt Muslims through a conspiracy,' in Grade 10 Urdu textbook by the Punjab Textbook Board (p. 37). Whether a textbook for Urdu, Islamic Studies, Pakistan Studies or Social Studies the content is consistent in promoting hostility towards non-Muslims, especially Hindus and a Hindu India, Christians and the British missionaries, and even Jews as the tormentors of Muslims.

This ideological intersection that reinforces a form of Islamic nationalism as the defining feature of the Pakistani identity has also been found in the textbooks published in 2014–15, 2015–16 and 2016–17, despite the commitment to reforming the curriculum. For example, the Punjab Curriculum and Textbook Board (PCTB) and the KP Textbook Board both include chapters on Muhammad Bin Qasim and Shah Wali Ullah in their Islamiyat textbooks for Grade 8, with the KP Islamiyat textbook highlighting the role of the Islamic scholar Shah Wali Ullah in laying the foundation of the 'two nation theory' in the Indian subcontinent that reinforced the notion that Hindus and Muslims were two separate entities ('Islamiyat' KP Textbook Board 2015–16a, p. 123).

English is another subject which is often overlooked in studies on identity in Pakistan. The PCTB is clear on its objectives of promoting an Islamic ideology even through English textbooks with most beginning with the saying 'In the Name of Allah, the most Gracious and Merciful' that appears either in the beginning of the Table of Contents or in the first chapter. Furthermore, the English textbooks for Grades 5, 8 and 10 begin with a chapter on the 'Prophet Muhammad (p.b.u.h.)'.[6] The reason for such Islam-centred content is related both to the PCTB's own focus on promoting Islamic ideology and to the influence of the Council of Islamic Ideology on curriculum and textbooks. All Urdu textbooks begin with a 'Hamd' – a piece written in praise of God, and a 'Naat' – a piece written in praise of the Prophet Muhammad (p.b.u.h.). The ideological connection between being Pakistani and Muslim is further reiterated through other narratives in the Urdu textbook. For example, the Urdu textbook for Grades 9–10 by the Punjab Textbook Board has a chapter explaining how to write a dialogue, where one of the examples includes a conversation between a student and teacher on the history of Pakistan that begins with the 'Islamic rule' of Muhammad Bin Qasim, and ends with Quaid-e-Azam defeating the combined forces of Hindus and the British to gain Pakistan (see p. 77, 'Urdu Quaid o Insha' Grades 9–10 2015–16).

The Urdu textbooks produced by the Sindh Textbook Board begin with either a 'Hamd' followed by a 'Naat' or a chapter describing the life of the Prophet Muhammad (p.b.u.h.), or includes them in the section on poems. The Urdu textbook for Grades 9 and 10 has chapters on prominent historical figures that were part of the Pakistan movement, including one chapter on 'Nazariya Pakistan' or the ideology of Pakistan which focuses again on Islamic ideology, starting with the Mughals while emphasizing the differences between Hindus and Muslims ('Urdu Lazmi' 9 and 10 Grades, Sindh Textbook Board 2016).

Furthermore, the history section of Grade 5's Social Studies textbook printed by all three textbook boards begins with a chapter comparing the 'Gregorian and Islamic Calendar', emblematic of the ideological emphasis on the distinction between Pakistan (read: Muslims) and the West. For the KP (2015–16b) and Sindh textbooks, this is followed by the 1857 War of Independence as the beginning of Pakistan's history, whereas the Punjab Textbook Board has opted to begin with Muhammad Bin Qasim, with a photograph of the Muslim ruler wearing the Arab 'keffiye'. While all three textbook boards emphasize the Islamic nature of the Pakistani identity, the Punjab Textbook Board is more prominent in locating the Pakistan identity within the Arabian Peninsula with its emphasis on Muhammad Bin Qasim. Hence, the Pakistani identity and the notion of a Pakistani citizen as defined by the education curriculum is limited not only to subjects that directly deal with identity and citizenship, such as Pakistan Studies, and Social Studies, but also to subjects that ought to be neutral in teaching a language like English or Urdu, and these are just as likely to propagate a nationalist Islamic discourse.

This is the kind of knowledge and education that the participants in this study were exposed to during their time in school – their narratives of citizenship therefore reflect much of the ideology that such textbooks and education systems promote in Pakistan. While this was particularly true for those who followed the government curriculum, the research engaged with students across the system.

Previous research (Lall 2012) shows that the type of school in which young people are educated is closely associated with views on citizenship and the state. It is difficult to infer that the type of school is solely responsible for the attitude of the children, since particular family views and/or a perceived school ethos might determine school choice. For example when middle-class parents choose a graduate madrassa for their children they will expect the teaching to reflect a religious vision, possibly even a belief that religion should be determining in how the state is run. However, when it comes to other school types it is unclear if parents factor in ethos when making their choice, or if the practical considerations (distance, infrastructure, cost, etc.) play the paramount role.

Different types of schools, however, do impart different visions and views of the state through how and what they teach.[7] With higher education and madrassas this is obvious as students in colleges or universities are exposed to a diversity of views and increased critical thinking; in madrassas mostly the opposite holds true. Private schools catering to the elite almost always bring in upper-middle-class parental background, foreign trained teachers and alternative textbooks, as well as education in English. Government schools on the other hand often have badly trained teachers and are limited by narrow (sometimes outdated) government textbooks with students studying only in Urdu. The philanthropic alternative will differ depending on the type of organization that runs the school. All these factors influence how the students learn about the state and how they will view their position.

But it is also important to note that the issue of class and school choice is no longer as clear-cut as it used to be with the elite and the middle classes sending their children to private schools and others going to either government schools or madrassas.[8] This is partly due to the explosion of low-fee private schools catering to the lower middle classes and the poorer sections of society. As the middle classes have diversified in income and ability to pay, new schools catering to them emerged. In parallel, philanthropic schools have started to offer alternatives to poorer sections of society as well. The middle classes always had a choice – and that choice from very early on was to buy out of the state sector. In doing so the middle classes weakened the citizenship bond and ensured that the quality of public education plummeted. Today an interesting development shows middle-class families also opting for secondary madrassas, which beyond the national curriculum offer a very restrictive view of the state, focusing rather on Pakistan's religious identity. Choice now has come to poorer sections of society as well with International Non-Governmental Organization (INGO)-supported schools, low-fee (sometimes low-quality) private schools and philanthropic provision on offer. In following the lead of the middle classes the move made by the poor has further weakened the link between the state and society. Not much is known about what drives choice for the poor, barring the obvious (school close/walking distance from home, especially important for girls in rural areas; good reputation, teachers being present etc.). Middle-class school choice has always been driven by wanting to give children a head start and being 'different' from others (Ball 2003; Vincent and Ball 2007). What is interesting is the consequences of this choice both in terms of the differing attitudes and the severance of the bond with the state.

Young people's voices

Participants in this study were asked questions about their understanding of what it means to be a Pakistani, the meaning of citizenship in Pakistan, and the role of education in defining the meaning of citizenship. Given that the sample focused on students, studying in either schools or universities, the majority of the participants believed that the education system was instrumental in defining their meaning and understanding of citizenship in Pakistan. For a nineteen-year-old female in Hub, education '*played a great role in determining the conception of citizenship*' developing '*discipline and self-control in one's life*', providing a sense of organization to one's life, and teaching the '*difference between good and bad*' (Student, Female, Hub). Education was also instrumental in making students both '*aware*' of their '*history*' and take '*pride*' in their identity (Teacher, Female, Karachi), while motivating them '*to do something for*' their '*country*'. '*As a "Pakistani" we must strive to make Pakistan a better place and to contribute to its well-being*' (Student, Female, Lahore). This sense of responsibility towards Pakistan was for many students a result of their education system, but the question that arises is what does it mean to be a Pakistani citizen for young Pakistanis today? This is especially important to explore in a context where the education system propagates Islamic nationalism as the defining feature of being Pakistani.

The meaning of citizenship for most is linked to an uncritical notion of nationalism and loyalty to an Islamic Republic, with limited understanding of civic duties and responsibilities. Given what is promoted through textbooks in schools, it was not surprising to find students from government schools or universities highlight the importance of Islam for their Pakistani identity. However, this was also true for the majority of students belonging to private sector universities and schools, especially private universities catering to the more privileged sections of society in Lahore and Karachi, where only a small percentage of students questioned the possibility of an alternative history and the place of religion in defining their Pakistani identity. The overall responses of participants were predominantly divided into citizenship as linked with nationalism and Islam, as anti-Indian or a sentiment that connected them to the sacrifices of their forefathers. However, these responses were not mutually exclusive, but were rather interconnected thereby reinforcing the Pakistani-Muslim connection. For those who were critical of the notion of citizenship, the criticism for the majority of the students was linked to the inability of Pakistanis, especially the Pakistani state, to practice Islam in its 'true' sense. Answers to the question of what is the 'true' sense of Islam in relation to Pakistan also varied; teachers belonging to the Islamic Studies department of a government sector university in Lahore proposed 'true Islam' to be defined by a scholar whose interpretations Muslims agree to follow, while for others 'true' Islam was linked with honesty and lack of corruption. However, as discussed in this section, the responses nonetheless revolved around Islam as the defining feature of being a Pakistani citizen (see Nelson 2008; Dean 2005; Rahman 2004).

The Islamic Republic of Pakistan

What is the meaning of Pakistan? 'There is no God but Allah' is a predominant theme that emerged in this research, consistent with other studies (Afzal 2015; Dean 2005). This belief is not only promoted through the curriculum as the preceding section has highlighted, but also common in the unwritten curriculum of Pakistan, one that is repeatedly heard in public rallies organized by political figures, one that is chanted at the Wagha border during the popular 'Beating Retreat ceremony' when India and Pakistan lower their flags with the Pakistan side chanting 'What is the meaning of Pakistan? La illaha illAllah'[9]. The belief that Pakistan is an Islamic Republic is repeatedly engrained in the social psyche of Pakistanis, one that often fails to take into account the identity of non-Muslim Pakistanis, or those declared non-Muslim by the state. Simon (2013) in his exploration of citizenship highlights the danger of 'tying' 'citizenship to any kind of identity' as it is 'then tied to a particular conception of national identity, which, by its very nature precludes other conceptions of group entity' (p. 511), which in the case of Pakistan are non-Muslims, or those deemed non-Muslim by the state, hence occupying a different status of citizenship. '*Pak logoon kai rehnei ki jagha – Land of purity*' (Student, Female, Lahore); '*Our values, identity, flag, ideology and religion make us Pakistani*' (Teacher, Female, Hub2); '*Islamic Democratic state, who worships One Allah Almighty*' (Student, Female, Lahore). This belief in the Islamic purity of Pakistan is one that has been echoed by not just students in school, but by their teachers, and by adults studying in universities. The first quote for instance is by an academic who teaches at a university in Lahore, the second by a teacher who teaches in a government school in Hub, while the third is an undergraduate student of humanities in another university in Lahore. These adults are a product of an education and social system that reinforces this belief.

The problem with basing citizenship on Islam is that it removes any possibility of debate. However, there were exceptions to the narrative, albeit in a minority. At a private university in Karachi where a majority of the students were from private schools, where as undergraduate students they had been exposed to an alternative history of Pakistan, participants were questioning the reason behind Pakistan's creation, and the role of Islam in Pakistan:

> *As far as Pakistan was concerned Jinnah's demand was both tactical and practical given the circumstances. Until 1946 he was not expecting a separate nation. He thought when the British would leave the Muslims would have*

Indian flag to show his support for the cricketer for which he was arrested and 'charged under Pakistan's penal code' for 'acting against Pakistan's sovereignty', a charge that could lead to ten years of imprisonment and 'a fine' (Express Tribune 2016). Being anti-Indian as part of the citizenship discourse was also highlighted by Afzal's (2015) research on the Pakistan Studies curriculum and its role in shaping young students' perceptions about terrorism and intolerance in Pakistan. This anti-Indian sentiment is repeated in the discourse around Kashmir, which again is located in the pre-partition narrative that underlines the irreconcilable differences between Hindus and Muslims. This anti-Indian sentiment is also evident in the connection young people make to the 'sacrifices' of their forefathers for Pakistan, both at the time of partition and later on: '*Having [been] born here and holding the Pakistani NIC, but there is much more to it. I am a Pakistani more because my grandparents gave up everything in India and migrated to this land. It is their sacrifice that makes me Pakistani*' (Student, Male, Lahore); '*The fact that my grandparents were actively involved during partition and not being Pakistani is not an option*' (Student, Male, Lahore); '*Being born here, burying our relatives here and our attachment with our ancestors. The reason for which they laid their lives was to attain this piece of land. I think these things make us Pakistanis*' (Student, Male, Sahiwal); '*Our elders sacrificed so much for Pakistan; they got Pakistan as an Islamic state with a passion. We need to set limits for it, work hard for its success and should not stop oneself for sacrifices for it, all this explanation is a symbol that I am a Pakistani*' (Student, Male, Islamabad); '*Only those people were Pakistani who fought 1971 war and tied bombs on their chests and faced the cannons without any fear. But now this is not happening. We should show the youth this example of bravery and make them a true Muslim because this is what makes us Pakistani*' (Student, Male, Sahiwal).

The sacrifices of the older generation at the time of independence translate into a sense of unquestioned loyalty to the ideology of Pakistan. While partition did create over one million dead, especially in Punjab where Hindus, Sikhs and Muslims butchered each other once the Radcliffe line was drawn in the sand and communities fled across the new border, the interpretation of this generational sacrifice is not, strictly speaking, correct as those Muslims in the previously Muslim majority provinces of Sindh, Balochistan, the Frontier and East Bengal did not have to die for Pakistan's creation. The history of those who migrated from India, the Muhajirs, seems to underlie Pakistan's nationalism and seems to have become the history of the whole nation. Education has of course played a significant role in this development through the curricula of Pakistan Studies in particular.

Naqvi (2012) in his analysis of migration and sacrifice for the 'Muhajir community' observes how 'sacrificial narrative in the present … embody memories of loss and suffering that exceed the rationality of the high-political arena' amounting 'to a collective political claim for belonging and recognition' (p. 478). While Naqvi's focus was on Muhajir identity and the narrative of loss and sacrifice for the first-generation immigrants, his observation also rings true of the generations that follow, where the 'imagined' suffering of grandparents and great-grandparents became a uniting force in defining one's Pakistani identity. On the one level there is pride in the sacrifices of one's family for a Muslim homeland, while on another level there is the added frustration of living in a country where an average citizen is not given his/her due, despite the sacrifices of one's forefathers. Ironically, recognition of the sacrifices of non-Muslims is absent from any of these narratives, where the Pakistani citizen is once again the Muslim who migrated to Pakistan in search of a better future for his/her family.

Civic identity, citizenship and the counternarrative

The definition of citizenship, of being Pakistani, predominantly focused on a religious Islamic identity, was to be expected given the emphasis on Islamic nationalism in the education curriculum. However, despite belonging to an education system that seldom encouraged critical thinking and questioning, students from universities both government and private, as well as teachers, were nonetheless vocal about the limitations of being a Pakistani today. The most dominant theme was '*first of all being a Muslim and then not acting like one!!!*' (Male, Student, Lahore). While the Muslim–Pakistani nexus was far from questioned in relation to citizenship, the lack of knowledge about Islam, about being a Muslim was one that was repeated by students in both private and government universities, as the primary reason for the dismal state of affairs in Pakistan today. The response to the question of 'What is the meaning of Pakistan?' during focus groups was often qualified with the statement '*It is supposed to be There is no God but Allah*', '*it is supposed to be Land of the Pure*' but really Pakistanis are not there yet: '*Need right kind of Islamic education. People don't know about religion. Need to agree on basic tenants of Islam and teach them. If there is disagreement over something, that should be excluded. People should select a scholar and read the translation of the Quran*' (Focus Group, Government University)[12]; '*I think religious education needs to be reconsidered. We need to know what religion says. People say a lot but what is the true version*' (Focus Group, Private University[13]).

The notion that the 'right kind of Islamic education' is the solution to all of Pakistan's problems was echoed by students in universities and teachers alike. This is similar to the response of teachers in Nazir's research on democracy and education in Pakistan for whom 'a good teaching of Islam' was sufficient to guarantee 'human rights education' in schools (2010, p. 336). However, the belief that the 'right' Islamic education is the answer overlooks the problem of interpretation and sectarianism that Nelson (2009, 2008) highlights in his research on religious education in Pakistan. As Nelson (2009) observes, 'religious and sectarian differences' were often 'the proverbial "elephant in the living room"' which no teacher or parent wants to acknowledge (p. 601). In this study, the problem of sectarianism was discussed with students and academics at universities. Their responses ranged from the belief that the problem of the 'right kind of Islamic education' can be resolved by selecting 'a scholar' of one's choosing and following him, while for others sectarianism was a result of misunderstanding religion. As a female student in a focus group at a single-sex government university observed: '*Religion is not taught properly. Deen ka nahi pata. Firqoon ki baat karte hain*'[14] (Focus Group,[15] Government University). Others however pointed to the shortcomings of a strategy that aims to provide the '*right kind of Islamic education*'; '*Religion is also a problem when everyone thinks that their religion is right*' (Student, Female, Quetta). This is especially problematic when the state takes on the responsibility of defining what is the 'right Islamic education' and who qualifies as a Muslim. As one student in a focus group at a private university in Karachi highlighted: '*Look at our heroes. My parents in school knew about all the Ahmadi generals who fought in our wars, but during Zia's time all of them were removed from our books. We did not learn about them*' (Focus Group,[16] Private University). The solution of providing the right kind of Islamic education completely overlooks the non-Muslim Pakistani identity. As an academic from the Hazara community teaching at a university in Lahore observed: '*Look at our textbooks, nothing has changed. We don't know about minorities in our country. How many religions are there?*' He is right in pointing out that the textbooks do not teach about the different religions in Pakistan. Despite including a section on 'minorities' in the Pakistan Studies curriculum, the Grade 10 textbook published by the PCTB does not explain who the different minorities are. The only reference is to non-Muslim leaders or thinkers who are grouped together without distinguishing their religious identity. This is particularly problematic in the case of Abdus Salam who is included at the end of a paragraph on personalities in the field of law with one sentence – 'Doctor Abdus Salam rendered important services in physics' – and no mention of the fact that he is the first Nobel laureate of Pakistan (p. 139). This absence of recognition in the textbook that is meant to educate children about the achievements of different Pakistanis attests to the limitations of imagining the 'right kind of Islamic education' which is bound to exclude communities and identities that do not fall within the majority's 'version of Islam'. Abdus Salam belongs to the Ahmaddiya community.

While the need for the education system to teach the 'right kind of Islam' was one proposition in developing a better understanding of Pakistanis as Muslims, the education system was also seen as instrumental in promoting civic mindedness through citizenship education. As one student observed, '*Education could be made a lot more useful in (a) informing us about what the state does, (b) talking about rights and responsibilities*' (Student, Female, Karachi). There was a recognition by some that the existing education system '*upto high school barely does anything to instil citizenship within us, we might be provoked towards patriotism but not to citizenship*' (Student, Male, Islamabad). However, for many, fixing the education system that inculcates the importance of duties and responsibilities of citizens towards the state and vice versa, was the way forward. '*Education the only means of awareness*' (Student, Female, Quetta). The role of education also needs to be situated within the broader spectrum of inequality, poverty and corruption. This was clearly highlighted by a teacher in Sindh who observed: '*Education can go some way in clarifying what citizenship means but if the basic needs of food, water and security are not available to the people a concept is of no consequence in their lives.*'

The young people's voices show that education has not been successful in transferring the concept of citizenship from its primordial ethno-nationalist basis to an understanding of rights, responsibilities and political participation. This chapter demonstrates that the state has not managed to build a concept of citizenship among its citizens despite a strong sense of identity of what it means to be a Pakistani. In fact, the education system has over the decades since independence continuously narrowed what it means to be Pakistani, excluding increasing numbers of minority communities. Only those participants who belonged to minority identities raised the issue of non-Muslim Pakistanis and the absence of their narrative in the citizenship discourse of Pakistan. Moving forward the security state in Pakistan has further brought educational institutions into the security fold, with a national narrative that promotes resilience and tolerance being introduced in textbooks for Urdu, Islamiyat and English. However, given the deep ideological discourse on Islam and citizenship, this narrative on tolerance is also shaped through an Islamic lens.

In addressing inequalities between the various education system, the NCEPG 2018 have highlighted the importance of 'integrated education reforms' that would encompass the public, private and madrassa sector, creating 'vertical and horizontal linkages' across provinces and school systems (NACTA 2018, p. 5). The social contract between the citizen and the security state as discussed in Chapter 2 is further strengthened through such an uncritical education system. Far from challenging the fundamental ideological underpinnings of an exclusive Pakistani citizenship discourse in the curriculum as promoted by the education system, the security state in Pakistan is further normalizing its military-centric, Islamic narrative by bringing educational institutions into its counterextremism agenda.

Notes

1 Commonly known as the Sharif report.

2 This is still the case today: https://tribune.com.pk/story/333273/educational-bias-memorise-the-quran-for-twenty-extra-marks/

3 This is discussed in more detail below.

4 More recently the UNDP Human Development Report 2017 that surveyed youth across Pakistan said about its respondents: 'Most were schooled in a curriculum that forges an identity based exclusively on Islam, is discriminatory towards non-Muslim communities and cements an "us vs. them" mentality. Moreover, authority figures like parents, teachers and community leaders often discourage secular inquiry, critical thinking, and discussion of alternative visions of religion, society and state. It is worrying that almost half of all the NYPS respondents said they do not approve of having friendly relations with non-Muslims or Muslims of other sects, the right of these "other" communities to build places of worship, and especially, to preach their faith' (p. 110).

5 'You are free; you are free to go to your temples. You are free to go to your mosques or to any other places of worship in this State of Pakistan. You may belong to any religion, caste or creed – that has nothing to do with the business of the state.' – Mohammed Ali Jinnah, 8 November 1947.

6 P.b.u.h. – Peace be upon him.

7 'Clear differences between schools were observed here again with government schools focusing on the sacrifice of the previous generations, whilst madrassas couched being Pakistani in religious terms. Philanthropic schools had a wider definition encompassing culture, religion and parental sacrifice whilst private schools had more patriotic slogans. Anger, anti Indian sentiment and discontent

was most prevalent in the answers given by the students in [higher education]. In discussing their feelings of alienation and the elite's behaviour with regard to rights and duties, differences were observed based on school types again. Government schools and madrassas seemed to be most unhappy, expressing dismay at how the educated elite exploited the more disadvantaged. The students at private schools, mostly from the elites themselves gave explanatory style answers as to why the elites were taking advantage of their position vis-a-vis the poor. Interestingly there was less alienation or anger at the philanthropic schools, also reflected in their broad views of the elite' (Lall 2012, p. x).

8 The two madrassas chosen at random for the fieldwork all catered mainly to lower-middle-class and middle-class families. This was confirmed through the questionnaires where the students disclosed parental profession.

9 Translation: *'There is no God but Allah.'*

10 This focus group included participants from Hyderabad, Sukkur and Karachi.

11 Hafeez's lawyer Rashid Rahman was gunned down for defending him. In Pakistan, the accusation of blasphemy is akin to a death sentence, where the accused are known to have been lynched or murdered by mobs, or killed in prison. Often lawyers, judges, journalists and media personnel are fearful of defending the accused because of the danger of being killed in the process, especially in the aftermath of the assassination of Punjab Governor Salman Taseer who defended a Christian woman, Asia Bibi, accused of blasphemy, and was killed by his own guard. Hafeez continues to be imprisoned in a 'high-security ward', awaiting trial.

12 This focus group included participants from Lahore.

13 This focus group included participants from Hyderabad, Sukkur and Karachi.

14 Translation: *'Don't know about religion. They keep talking about sects.'*

15 This focus group included participants from Lahore, Sheikhupura, Muridke, Dera Ghazi Khan and Sargodha.

16 This focus group included participants from Hyderabad, Sukkur and Karachi.

4

Youth and Terrorism

Introduction

Taliban are terrorists. Politically motivated; scare and harm; want to impose an ideology.

It brings up the argument of security versus freedom. How much of our freedom are we willing to give up for that security.

In one of my local mosques Mumtaz Qadri (Salman Taseer's killer) is called Amin. It is a Barelvi mosque. In another Deobandi mosque they were praying for Bin Laden. This was happening in Karachi. These people are not even genuine aalim, but they are heading these mosques.

(Focus Group, Private University[1])

Pakistan has been transformed by terrorism. Passing through urban centres of Pakistan today, a common sight that one encounters is the presence of checkpoints; barbed wire fences around public institutions, especially government offices that have raised their boundary walls; educational institutions that have increased their security – in essence urban centres that have visually become securitized as a consequence of the constant threat of terror confronting these cities. Of course, such security measures are more evident in the rich neighbourhoods of cities such as Lahore, Karachi, Islamabad or Peshawar, since the level of both security and insecurity varies across neighbourhoods and different parts of Pakistan, and not every part of a city is considered equally at risk, or the people there equally worthy of protection. While certain parts of the country such as FATA, Provincially Administered Tribal Areas (PATA), Waziristan and certain areas in KP have at different points been at the frontline in the war against terrorism, this threat is nonetheless pervasive, evident in attacks on minority communities in urban cities, Sufi shrines, hotels, schools and universities as well as security establishments such as police offices or army barracks. According to the South Asia Terrorism Portal, Pakistan lost 62,421 lives to violence between 2002 and 2017. The number of violent civilian deaths spiked first in 2007 with 1,522 fatalities, increasing to well over 2,000 per annum in the 2 subsequent years, spiking again to over 3,000 deaths per annum in 2012 and 2013. Since 2014 the numbers have abated slowly but killings persist, and civilians and terrorist and security personnel continue to die at unusually high rates.[2] In effect this generation of Pakistani youths have experienced more violence than any generation before them.[3] The securitization of the day-to-day lives of Pakistanis is evident not only in the changing infrastructure of cities across Pakistan but also in the ideological narrative that is being promoted by a security state. While the military is fighting the physical threat of militancy and terrorism (yet pandering to certain strategic militant groups that would serve the state's interest), the security state is also allegedly attempting to focus on a softer approach to prevent terrorism from taking root in Pakistan. According to the Pakistani state and its security apparatus, the country faces 'traditional' and 'non-traditional' forms of threats that include 'extremism, sectarianism, terrorism and militancy' (Ministry of Interior 2014, p. 5). Pakistan's Ministry of Interior has responded to these threats with a National Internal Security Policy (NISP) 2014–2018[4] that adopts a multi-agency approach in combating these 'non-traditional' threats, and has included a 'soft component' through a 'Comprehensive Support Plan (CRP)' that will attempt to win the 'trust and confidence of general public to combat extremism and terrorism' (Ministry of Interior 2014, p. 6). In order to win this 'trust and confidence' NISP 2014–2018 has proposed the need for a national narrative to be constructed and promoted through the NACTA of Pakistan:

> An effective communication campaign will be of utmost importance and NACTA will be making all efforts to take NISP to all stakeholders and construct positive public opinion through integrated efforts. However, this is only possible if all key pillars of the state are prepared to develop a unified narrative and support each other for building a better future for the People of Pakistan. (p. 45)

In taking on board these different stakeholders, from civil society, academia, media, military and religious figures, the Ministry of Interior has formulated the NCEPG, with a focus on a strategy called 'CONNECT' that aims to reinforce citizens' confidence in the state, which is considered to be one of the reasons why Pakistanis are being radicalized (NACTA 2018). This chapter first examines terrorism in the various settings in Pakistan, looking at terror linked to sectarian groups, their effects across cities and the provinces before examining the nature of the NCEPG strategy and the 'non-traditional' threats that exist in the aftermath of 9/11 and Pakistan's involvement in America's 'war on terror'. It will explore the state's response to these threats, and how its policies have increasingly turned it into a security state, where ironically such policies work only so far as the citizen does not question the security apparatus. There are already pockets of resistance that are critical of the security state, but the student responses in this study show that the extent of this critique is limited. Those who do critique risk retaliation by the security services, where such retaliation may intimidate others. The students in this study in their assessment of the security apparatus have predominantly been in favour of the military and the state in its fight against terrorism, explaining the actions of the security state as a necessary response to the security situation that confronts Pakistan today.

Terrorism in Pakistan

Question: What makes you Pakistani?

Patience and the important toleration, important to tolerate everything, corruption, load shedding, terrorism.

(Student, Female, Lahore)

For many young Pakistanis in this study, the reality of the 'war on terror', the normalization of a security discourse in their everyday lives, from checkpoints to learning to distinguish between a fire alarm and a terrorist alarm (though mostly in private universities) is the only normality they know. For many, like this female student, being Pakistani is linked to this normality. Pakistan has been transformed by terrorism. The state and the people have been marked by the excesses of violent deaths that started to increase slowly during the 1980s and then gained momentum after 2002 as the after-effects of 9/11 swept across the region. However, even the face of terror has changed over the decades.

Early on Pakistan was racked by sectarian violence due largely to Zia's policies that made Sunni Islam the 'right' Islam to follow. The impact of sectarianism was felt across the country, as observed by this Hazara participant living in Lahore: '*We have always been with Pakistan but now at this moment because of target killings, sectarianism no place is safe. Only 40% of the Hazara community is left*' (Teacher, Male, Quetta); '*Sindh also has too diverse a culture which is a problem because there are too many minorities and no tolerance. We believe that Sunni Musalmaan should be on top, with the result those poor people are stuck with such beliefs*' (Focus Group, Private University[5]). While minority sects across the country fell victim to sectarianism, Karachi became a particular battleground, given its '*too diverse a culture*'. During the 1980s, under Zia's Islamization being a Muslim was no longer enough, one had to be a Sunni Muslim. Between 15 and 20 per cent of Pakistanis were at risk of attacks from the majority. This was nothing new as the anti Ahmadi movement had already led to sectarian violence. This time however a much larger community was in effect made 'fair game' for those who espoused purist Sunni views. One cannot lay all the blame at Zia's feet. Geopolitics played its role in increasing sectarian violence as well. The Iranian Revolution of 1979 influenced Shia Islam in Pakistan and returning Gulf workers found that one way of countering a rise in Shia madrassas was to build Sunni madrassas. This movement of madrassa building was actively supported by Saudi Arabia, keen to export its Wahhabi form of Islam. Over the next few decades the various sects, including the Deobandi, Barelvi and Ahle Hadith factions of Sunnism, built competing seminaries. Another element of geopolitics that supported increased anti-minority violence and supported the rise of an extremist interpretation of Sunni Islam was the creation of the mujahideen to fight off the Soviet invasion of Afghanistan. The radicalization was initially outward facing (and supported by the United States, including the University of Nebraska Omaha that printed related books to radicalize the youth); however, a parallel radicalization of Pakistan's education system occurred internally as discussed in Chapter 3 on education.

While sectarian violence was the major cause of violent death, and sectarian divisions were the major cause for terror in the 1980s and 1990s, 9/11 and the subsequent war in Afghanistan fuelled a new form of terror with the rise of the Taliban in Afghanistan and later the creation of the Pakistani Taliban whose main aim was to fight the Pakistani state. The face of terror changed post 2002 as different radical groups, many of which had bases across the border in Afghanistan or in the tribal areas of northern Pakistan, started a campaign against first military and then increasingly civilian targets.

For young Pakistanis in this study, the reasons for such violence ranged from Pakistan's involvement in the Soviet war to international conspiracies to destabilize Pakistan.[6] '*Well the origin of it can go back to the Soviet-US problem when the mujahideen were fighting against the Soviets. However today they are on a vengeance of some misguided sort against the state as a whole. On top of that you add religion to terrorism*' (Focus Group, Private University[7]). While the majority of participants believed terrorism to be one of the main problems facing Pakistan, the role of hostile countries, whether India and its intelligence service RAW,[8] even Israel and its intelligence service Mossad, along with the United States are held responsible for terror in Pakistan. '*But Taliban is a label to terrorize and manipulate you. ISIS, TTP titles created by media. The super power US is behind these titles. To create a sense of terrorising*' (Focus Group, Government University[9]). Respondents in this research constantly challenged the identity of the Taliban. '*But the people who join the Taliban came to Pakistan but not real Pakistanis. They are primarily from Afghanistan who settled in Pakistan. They do the dirty work but the people behind them are foreigners. You can see from the videos that are circulated all over the net. The Taliban is more white, definitely from the North or Afghanistan*' (Focus Group, Private University[10]). Young people were of course right that foreigners are involved, as Uzbek, Turkmen and Saudi fighters from the Afghan wars have joined the fight in Pakistan. However, the idea that fellow Muslims could unleash terror in the 'Islamic Republic' of Pakistan seemed unbelievable for many of the participants in this study. '*No Muslim would do this to other Muslims*' is a refrain heard often during the research over the years across all types of respondents. Nevertheless, as the extract from a focus group discussion below shows, there were other points of view: for some, groups such as the Taliban are 'tools' working for whoever pays them the most money, while for others they were following a misinterpretation of Islam, a misinterpretation propagated by Saudi Arabia, another country that was seen by some (mostly a minority) to be behind their existence in Pakistan and Afghanistan. '*I know this is a stretch and might sound silly but at one point there were rumours that the beggars on the streets were collecting money for the Taliban*' (People start laughing); '*I heard that the Indian advisor to Modi mention how it is about money, whoever offers more money to the Taliban*'; Q.: *But what about the Salafi ideology?* '*I think the ideology is to fool people. They work for whoever pays them*' (Focus Group, Private University[11]).

These theories of foreign forces are reinforced through media, by popular political analysts and political show hosts, whose references participants shared in their discussion on terrorism in Pakistan.[12]

The extent of the violence unleashed by different terrorist groups was captured by Ishrat Hussain (2018) in his analysis of terrorism in Pakistan that highlights how 'a variety of perpetrators – including the TTP, other Al-Qaeda-inspired groups, sectarian militants, and nationalist insurgents in

Balochistan – have succeeded in carrying out 7,311 terrorist attacks in Pakistan from January 2011 to mid-August 2016' that have 'claimed 9,689 lives and left 18,812 others injured' (2018, p. 352).[13] However, the security state's strategy of dealing with these terrorist threats have centred on strategic alliances which have historically backfired. During General Pervez Musharraf's term, attempts to counter extremist elements within Pakistan were led by his policy of 'enlightened moderation'. However, the policies of Musharraf towards right-wing political parties in Pakistan, his presumed strategic alliance with militants who were leading Pakistan's Kashmiri liberation strategy, and the complicated relationship with the Taliban, designated as the 'good' and 'bad' Taliban, resulted in creating further chaos and complicating the security situation in Pakistan. It was during Musharraf's rule that the Afghan Taliban and Al Qaeda–linked Arab and Uzbek fighters were able to enter KP, then known as the NWFP, and FATA. Sectarian and anti-Indian sectarian jihadi groups from Punjab were also able to establish bases in KP, sowing the seeds for what was to come. His alliance with the Muttahida Majlis-e-Amal (MMA) facilitated Islamic extremism in other ways. In his attempts to challenge the political status quo of the PML(N) and the PPP, Musharraf through rigging ensured that the six-party Islamic alliance of the MMA won the 2002 provincial elections in KP, sidelining the PPP and the PML(N), Musharraf's main political rivals. The MMA lent their 62 (out of 342) seats in the National Assembly to support Musharraf's Seventeenth Amendment to the constitution that resulted in concentrating power in the hands of the president, in return for his support of the Hisba Bill that sought to introduce Taliban-style government in KP (passed in 2005 but struck down by the supreme court). The mutual support did not end there. As of 2004 the MMA's largest constituent party – the Jamiat Ulema-e Islam (F) (JUI-F) – mediated talks between the military and FATA-based militant groups, resulting in amnesties and political space for these anti-India and anti-Afghanistan groups. The 2005 earthquake allowed Kashmir-based militant groups such as the Lashkar-e-Tayyaba (LeT) and Jaish-e-Mohammed to relocate training camps to the PATA. Both the amnesty and the earthquake allowed for the spread of Taliban-style governance (such as the court systems) in FATA and PATA settled areas and militancy to spread across the tribal areas between 2004 and 2009. The TTP, although a loose umbrella organization, was able to exert influence across FATA and in the NWFP's Malakand district, where it supported the Sunni extremist Tehrik-e-Nifaz-e-Shariat-e-Mohammadi (TNSM).

The support for such extremists resulted in more sectarian violence within the country. The majority of the students in this study believed that the military and its war were not to blame for sectarianism. Yet there were others who questioned the security state: '*Look at the Sipha e Sahaba. They openly say that Shias are not Muslims and can be killed. This happens openly in Pakistan*' (Focus Group, Private University[14]). These militant outfits have continued to wreak havoc in cities such as Karachi, especially in the 1980s and 1990s when Shia doctors, academics and other prominent members were strategically targeted by these outfits. For some students Pakistan is clearly a proxy for Iran and Saudi Arabia, though such observations are in a minority. However, there is a predominantly Sunni bias as prevalent in other institutions as well, from schools and the curriculum (as discussed in Chapter 3) to, some would argue, even media: '*Also look at the language used by the media. Recently a Shia mosque was attacked in Kuwait. In media they reported it as a "Shia mosque". Over here they call it "Imam bargha" as if Shias can't have a mosque, it has to be called something different. Even the language they use divides us*' (Focus Group, Private University[15]).

The participants were not completely wrong in blaming state policy for exacerbating sectarianism within the country. It was state appeasement of such extremist groups that strengthened their base support. Even the presence of the Taliban was the result of this 'good' versus 'bad' Taliban strategy under the Musharraf era. The valley of Swat was the first to experience direct Taliban rule. At first welcomed by some of the locals, Taliban governance quickly descended into brutality and chaos. The advance of the militants and their success in taking over the valley would have been impossible without the help of the MMA, which was in charge of KP at that time. Mullah Fazlullah used the FM radio stations to propagate his message of jihad against infidels at home and in the West, using this as a conduit to impose Sharia law in Swat. Women were banned from going outside and girls stopped from going to school, music shops were closed, tapes and videos destroyed and men were forbidden to shave. A new parallel court system resolved disputes resulting in public floggings and public executions. It was only in 2009 when the militants advanced to neighbouring Buner district (a five-hour drive from Islamabad) that the authorities decided to take action. The operation between May and July that year displaced almost three million people while many militants simply fled to neighbouring districts or to Afghanistan's Nuristan province bordering PATA to regroup. Others fled to Karachi, a move that would be repeated by many militants in the subsequent anti-terror campaigns led by the army. Although most of the three million internally displaced persons (IDPs) returned at the end of the summer, Swat's infrastructure had been badly affected, including 70 per cent of schools for girls having been destroyed.

In July 2009 the army declared Swat militant free and their operation a success. The violence seemed to reduce and ordinary Pakistanis hoped the problem had been resolved. However, a turning point came in October 2009 when shortly after Eid, a group of militants attacked the Army GHQ in Rawalpindi claiming 175 lives, with the COAS inside. The siege with hostages and shoot-out lasted eighteen hours, until the next morning. This was followed by almost daily bombings for the rest of the year, mainly in the major cities of Rawalpindi, Islamabad, Peshawar and occasionally in Lahore and Multan. In addition, a new form of fedayeen attacks where militants engaged directly with their targets by storming buildings and using suicide bombings started to become popular.[16] Lahore and other major cities had roadblocks every few kilometres. These roadblocks were the subject of further attacks. In response to the GHQ attack and the increasing violence in urban areas across Pakistan, the army launched a ground offensive entitled Rah-e-Nijat on 17 October in South Waziristan. However, not all militants were targeted and the military tried to gain the support of rival factions during this operation. North Waziristan, dominated by the Haqqani Network led by Afghan Taliban leader Sirajuddin Haqqani, which was focusing its attacks on Afghanistan, was also not targeted by the operation.

The Taliban became particularly problematic after the terror attacks on the APS Peshawar in December 2014. The attack happened after failed peace negotiations in February 2014 that instead emboldened jihadist groups further as the military continued its distinction between 'bad' and 'good' Taliban, such as the TTP's Gul Bahadur group and long-standing Afghan proxies, including Mullah Omar's Rahbari Shura, Gulbuddin Hekmatyar's Hizb-e-Islami and the Haqqani Network. Talks were abandoned after the June 2014 attack on Karachi airport which in turn led to the military operation of Zarb-e-Azb in June 2014, where the military finally went into North Waziristan to fight the TTP, the Islamic Movement of Uzbekistan, the East Turkestan Islamic Movement, Lashkar-e-Jhangvi and the Haqqani Network, who all had their bases there. Despite this operation the government was further weakened over the summer of August 2014 when both Imran Khan's PTI party and the cleric/politician Tahirul Qadri's Pakistan Awami Tehreek (PAT) led large demonstrations demanding Prime Minister Nawaz Sharif's resignation and parliament's dissolution. Sharif became dependent on the military to stay in power, abandoning his plans to improve relations with both Afghanistan and India.

Far from recognizing the APS attacks as a failure of the state and the military in protecting innocent civilians, another narrative evolved – the victims were described as martyrs who had sacrificed their lives for their country. Accounts of heroism of teachers and fellow students inundated media coverage of the tragedy, with the role of the army further strengthened in the fight against cowards who attack children. Government schools had put up posters of the 'martyrs', while children performed school plays re-enacting the tragedy, and recognizing the sacrifices of the students and teachers. Another intervention that was connected to the APS tragedy was introducing narratives of resilience and tolerance in schools through supplementary reading material and textbooks. Resilience was believed to be needed in order to re-establish the support of the Pakistani people in its military and security personnel, but to link intolerance with the APS attacks was clearly misleading. In discussing the APS tragedy with participants in this study, there was no clear narrative that emerged. Some very clearly held the TTP responsible as shown in the following quotes:

> *Q.: What about the Peshawar attack. A.: Obviously it was the Taliban. They took responsibility.*
>
> *Q.: Why did they do it? A.: As revenge against the army. They clearly gave their reasons.*
>
> (Focus Group, Private University[17])

But there were others who were hesitant in admitting that the TTP were behind these attacks. '*TTP not responsible. We don't know – if only we knew*' (Focus Group, Government University[18]).

In one government university in Lahore students blamed RAW and the United States rather than the TTP, claiming that there were forces behind the TTP who may have directed the attack: '*Let's call the attackers terrorists; Isn't that enough, calling them terrorist, why do we need to identify them?*' (Focus Group, Government University[19]). Others believed that the responsibility lay with the federal and provincial governments who had failed to protect the students and their teachers. However, there were other opinions such as '*I think the Peshawar attacks completely changed the thinking of the nation. It was a huge event that has completely changed politics in Pakistan. Raheel Sharif has emerged as a hero*' (Focus Group, Private University[20]). The student was right, there seemed to be a commitment from the government, and the army, that the long-time policy of distinguishing good versus bad Taliban had been abandoned. However, this resolve was tested in 2017 when the TTP spokesperson Ihsanullah Ihsan turned himself in. Ihsan is yet to be tried, with rumours that the army had given him amnesty. Families of the APS tragedy – which was labelled one of the worst attacks since Pakistan joined the war on terror – had to file a petition with the court demanding that Ihsanullah Ihsan be tried in a court of law or in a military court.

The war in Waziristan, FATA and PATA has also highlighted a problem of ethnic profiling. With the ongoing war innocent tribesmen from this region continue to be profiled by security agencies, often subject to target killings and 'disappearances'. A prominent victim of such target killing was Naqeebullah Mehsud, a twenty-seven-year-old shopkeeper and aspiring model who was accused of being a militant and killed through what the police often term 'encounter killings'. His murder by a well-known 'encounter specialist', Senior Superintendent Rao Anwar, unleashed outrage as news of his murder reached his Facebook fans who had been following Naqeebullah's modelling career (Ahmad 2018). This murder has resulted in an online campaign and spurred the PTM demanding justice and an end to ethnic profiling (Zahra-Malik 2018). They are also calling on the army to clear their tribal areas from landmines that have killed Pashtuns returning to their homes (Zahra-Malik 2018; Pashtun Long March 2018).

Terrorism in Pakistan also differs depending on where it takes place. Those living in Southern Punjab, Karachi, Balochistan or KP will experience violence perpetrated by different groups for a variety of reasons. While violence remains violence, no matter what justifications are given, young people did look at terrorism in different ways depending on where they had experienced it or where they came from.

South Punjab is one area where terrorism is linked to sectarian outfits. Hussain (2018) highlights how 'sectarian organizations and jihadi groups in Pakistan' had 'formed a nexus with the TTP and supported each other' (2018, p. 345). The state has patronized such militant groups for the distinct purpose of using these groups in Kashmir to fight against the Indian forces, or for its strategic interests in Afghanistan. Groups such as Jaish-e-Mohammed (responsible for the 2 January 2016 attack on India's Pathankot airbase, and more recently claimed responsibility for the attack in Pulwama on 14 February 2019) and the sectarian Lashkhar-e-Jhangvi (LeJ) have a strong presence. The military targets LeJ; however, the anti-India Jaish continues largely undisturbed.

LeJ's roots lie in Pakistan's first major radical anti-Shia Deobandi group SSP. SSP had emerged under Zia and was supported by Saudi Arabia to counter the

Iranian Revolution. Repressed by the PML(N) government between 1997 and 1999, LeJ sought refuge in Taliban-controlled Afghanistan, cultivating its ties with Al Qaeda. It re-emerged in Pakistan in May 2002 by bombing Karachi's Sheraton Hotel, killing fourteen (including eleven French engineers). The LeJ operatives have since conducted prominent anti-state attacks, including the bombing of the Marriott Hotel in September 2008 in Islamabad, the attack on the Sri Lankan Cricket team in March 2009 and the October siege of the GHQ in Rawalpindi.

LeJ was instrumental in the formation of the TTP and increasingly shapes the TTP agenda. This means that sectarian violence is part of the new mix of terror, affecting the Shia populations of KP and FATA. Not only are Shias targeted, non-Deobandi Sunni Muslims such as Barelvis, and Sufis are also targets.

The other Punjab-based group, Jaish-e-Mohammed, along with central Punjab-based Lashkar-e-Tayyaba/Jamaat-ud-Dawa (LeT/JuD), is among Pakistan's most important anti-India oriented jihadist groups and as such quite different from LeJ. However, according to Khaled Ahmed both are linked and united by their sectarian agenda: 'The SSP is the umbrella political group while Jaish-e-Mohammed and Lashkar-e-Jhangvi represented the organisation's [Kashmir] jihadi and domestic militant wings respectively' (International Crisis Group 2016, p. 6).

As mentioned at the start of the chapter and detailed in the dialogue on sectarianism at a private university in Karachi[21] below, the young respondents do see sectarianism as a problem:

> *I think the problem goes as far back as the 1970s.*
>
> *We are proxies of Iran and Saudi Arabia now.*
>
> *There is a way out. We need to stop taking their aid. That way they cannot control us.*
>
> *By the way the Shia-Sunni problem has also reached London. Did you read about how someone wrote Kaafir on a Shia mosque in London?*

Sectarian groups have found their way into mainstream politics. In the 2017 National Assembly by-elections for seat NA-120, a new political party was formed – Milli Muslim League, with a candidate by the name of Muhammad Yaqoob Sheikh (see Figure 4.1), who in 2012 was declared a terrorist for raising funds and operationally supporting the LeT (Hashim 2017a). The emergence of the MML and its links to LeT/JuD is believed to be part of the military's attempt at mainstreaming such militant groups, which became a point of contention between the army and the former prime minister Nawaz Sharif, who was

Figure 4.1 Poster for candidate Muhammad Yaqoob Sheikh representing Milli Muslim League in the NA-120 elections, 2017.

removed by the judiciary on charges of corruption. Instead of dismantling such anti-Indian militants, which had been proposed by Sharif before his removal, the military sought to normalize their presence through the political process. The fact that the MML stood for the NA-120 seat that has traditionally belonged to the PML(N), and managed to gain 6,000 votes in a by-election, winning more votes than the PPP, showed the possibility of such parties being successfully mainstreamed in Pakistani politics. It further reinforces the military's support for the 'good' militants, even though such militants have gone astray in the past. Another problematic group that has emerged in Punjab is the Tehreek-e-Labbaik Ya Rasool Allah (TLYR or TLP) as discussed in the introduction to this book.

Cities have been a particular target for terrorist attacks, including the capital Islamabad, especially in 2007 with the siege of the Lal Masjid (Red Mosque).

The direct impact of terrorism was felt again in March 2009 when Sri Lanka's cricket team was attacked by twelve gunmen in Lahore in the middle of a busy intersection. This became the last international cricket match Pakistan was able to host until 2017. The incident was followed by the attack on the Manawan Police Academy when gunmen armed with automatic weapons, grenades and rockets took over the main building during a morning parade. In October the same police academy was attacked again as part of a larger attack on three government buildings including the Elite Force Training Academy and the Federal Investigation regional headquarters in Lahore.

It was not only the security services that suffered. Life for ordinary civilians changed beyond recognition due to the roadblocks and the constant blast and threats of suicide attacks. The twin suicide attacks on Islamabad's International Islamic University in October 2009 killed six and injured twenty-nine (twenty-five were women) while over three thousand students were in the building. The first blast occurred next to the cafeteria and close to the girls' hostel, the second one only minutes later near the Sharia and law department. This attack changed things across the board for all education institutions. All schools and colleges closed to work on security improvements for several weeks. Private schools across the country employed security personnel while many government schools were issued with security cameras to monitor gates. Elite private institutions took extra security measures, hiring snipers for the protection of their students. Later that year, in December, two very large bomb blasts rocked the city in the Moon Market of Lahore's Allama Iqbal Town. The attack took place at 9 p.m., catching many who had changed their shopping habits to late evenings so as to avoid possible bomb attacks. It is estimated that 54 people were killed and well over 150 injured. This marked the end of a bloody year for Lahore that had seen regular terror attacks since the end of Ramadan that year in September.

In Karachi, Pakistan's commercial capital that generates around 70 per cent of national GDP, prior to 2004 violence had been the result of political turf wars between the MQM, Sindhi groups and the Pashtun Awami National Party (ANP). Many of the issues emanated from growing inequalities, the state's incapacity to meet the needs of the citizens in a growing megacity, and the growing influence of political gangs. Most of Karachi's katchi abadis (slums) are ethnically segregated with particular groups controlling different areas and industries; there is a roaring black-market economy worth over 830 million rupees generated by land mafia, police corruption, illegal gambling and the water mafia. '*You know Parveen Rehman (the Orangi Project person)*[22] *was killed by these water mafias because she was mapping the water system. There are around 151 unofficial water hydrants and she was killed because of that*' (Focus Group, Private University[23]).

Karachi was also regularly the target of sectarian violence led by anti-Shia groups such as the LeJ. As the violence engulfed Pakistan in 2009, Karachi was left relatively unaffected. Violence levels had been at a historic low since 2004. However, not for long. During the 2009 Rahe Nijad operation, many militants fled South Waziristan following those who had fled Swat and settled in Karachi's many katchi abadis to regroup. In May 2010 after a drive-by shooting marking a turf war between criminal gangs, a curfew was declared and Karachi was back at war. The various militant groups that had fled FATA were now terrorizing the city and at war with the groups that had controlled Karachi previously. Terror in Karachi also took the form of increased kidnappings for ransom to fund the various conflicts raging in the city and in the wider country. Ordinary civilians of all walks of life were being taken for ransom, so that with the money the groups could buy arms. Gangs representing the old ethnic political parties as well as the newly arrived jihadi outfits started to operate like warlords in the areas they controlled.

The deadliest year for Karachi was 2013 with 2,700 casualties, mostly victims of targeted attacks. According to the International Crisis Group 40 per cent of businesses fled the city to avoid growing extortion rackets. Young people were disgusted with the situation and especially with the involvement of politicians and their parties: '*Things are not really as they seem. Sau shaitaan martei hain tu aik siyasat daan banta hai*'[24] (Student, Male, Quetta); '*Target killings are all about money, not religion or ideology. People are paid a sum of money to kill and create chaos*', '*Politicians do it for money Create chaos and then ask foreign countries for money to fight*' (Student, Female, Quetta). The respondents saw the police and army as part of the same apparatus as the leading politicians: '*Same family. It is like in a family there is a head and other members, same case here. The head is the hukamraan that could be the politician. They keep saying "namaaloom afraad" (unknown individuals)*[25] *are responsible. How can they not know? Of course they are also involved in all these killings*' (Student, Male, Quetta).

The state's response to the rising levels of lawlessness in September 2013 was to empower the paramilitary Rangers to operate against the criminal gangs and jihadi networks across the city. The clashes had resulted in extrajudicial killings, torture and enforced disappearances reinforcing ethnic tensions. In 2015, the Ismaili community was targeted by Jundullah, a group that broke away from the Tehreek-i-Taliban Pakistan, killing forty-three people and injuring thirteen others (Ali 2015). As a result of the Rangers' operation, civilian deaths dropped to 40 per cent in 2014, to 65 per cent in 2015 and 74 per cent in 2016 (Hussain 2018).

Another terrorist campaign deserves a special mention in this chapter – the one waged against polio eradication campaigns and their workers. Since 2011 when the CIA designed a fake hepatitis campaign to find Osama Bin Laden, the Taliban have maintained that international immunization campaigns are fronts for espionage. With regard to polio in particular they claim that the vaccine will sterilize the children. As a result hundreds of polio workers have been killed across the country, but in particular in Karachi and Quetta, where both the vaccination centres and the door-to-door immunization workers are targeted (BBC News 2018b).

Beyond the mess in KP and the groups based in Punjab resulting in bombings, attacks and kidnappings in cities and across the country and a full-fledged war with the police and the army, an old ethnic-based conflict has re-erupted in Balochistan. Some of the violence is also sectarian, but the actual problem runs much deeper. In this case the disparity in security was captured by a student belonging to the Hazara community: '*What did you notice most about being in Lahore? There is no fear (khauf) in Lahore. In Quetta when we would have to go to the market I would wonder if I would get home alive, but Lahore is so safe. Here people go even for fun and can stay out till 10 p.m. without fearing for their life. In Quetta you only go out if you need to*' (Student, Female, Quetta). NCEPG 2018 in examining the problems in Balochistan highlight how '[s]parse location of populations, entrenched sense of deprivation, ethnic divisions, share in NFC[26] award, provision of basic amenities, education facilities, health facilities, dispute resolution mechanisms, abolition of office of District Magistrate as central grievance redress point at district level, lack of a coherent narrative for national integration are issues of disenchantment and extremism' (NACTA 2018, p. 13). Balochistan has been an ethnically diverse province of Pakistan. It had its problems with the centre since independence, resulting in three initial insurgencies and the fourth, also known as the 1974 war. While internal tribal conflict has been a constant feature, Baloch nationalism has also emerged, challenging the federal state. The problems, however, seemed to increase under the rule of General Musharraf, when the fifth insurgency started over the rape of a female doctor by a member of the military in Sui in 2005. Musharraf's feud with seventy-nine-year-old Baloch leader Nawab Akhbar Khan Bugti, who had been both former governor and chief minister of Balochistan, led to a revival of the Balochistan crisis. In August 2006 Musharraf ordered the Pakistan army to go after Bugti and his men, resulting in Bugti's death in a cave that collapsed, as well as the death of thirty-seven of his fighters and twenty-one Pakistani army soldiers. This made the Nawab[27] a hero, galvanizing Baloch national sentiments across the province. After the Nawab's death, Musharraf's government's way of dealing with Baloch dissidents was to let them 'disappear'. This Orwellian 'disappearance' was attributed to security forces, with tortured bodies appearing after days or weeks. Such acts clearly challenged the writ of the state with the former chief justice of Pakistan Iftikhar Muhammad Chaudhry taking the security establishment, especially General Musharraf, to task. The cases of these disappeared led to Chief Justice Chaudhry's dismissal and the rise of the lawyers' movement in 2007, resulting eventually in Musharraf's fall from power. The reignited issue in Balochistan refused to rest and today much of the province is off limits to ordinary civilians and the press as the military is fighting Baloch nationalists who they claim want independence from Pakistan. The Baloch insurgency of 2006–16 is different in nature, being led by more radical 'new players' (Rais 2017, p. 163). Balochistan has also strategically become more important in the China–Pakistan Economic Corridor (CPEC) through the development of the Gwadar port, with an investment of over $50 billion proposed by the Chinese president in 2015 for CPEC that will be instrumental in making trade more cost-effective (Hussain 2018). The military continues to be active in Balochistan, with operations that have included extrajudicial killings and enforced disappearances. The provincial government's efforts to negotiate a peace with Baloch insurgents have failed, since it cannot guarantee an end to the military violence. The military accuses the insurgents of collaborating with RAW – India's Intelligence Agency – making them prime targets (International Crisis Group 2015).[28] This narrative is also familiar to young Pakistanis.

For the young Pakistanis outside of Balochistan many are critical about the lack of information available about the province: '*I think the problem is that there is no information about what's happening in Balochistan. Also with regard to resource allocation. I check the government website about budget allocation to different provinces; there was nothing about Balochistan*' (Focus Group, Private University[29]). '*No one really knows what's going on inside which is the biggest problem. We are kept in the dark*' (Focus Group, Private University[30]). '*We don't know enough about Balochistan. There is a vacuum there left by political parties and then agencies are involved which is what they do. It is the same as the ISI*[31] *involved in Khalistan and Kashmir against India, and RAW involved in Balochistan*'

(Focus Group, Private University[32]). However, students did speculate about the problems facing the province, with the majority highlighting the issue of foreign interference: '*MQM, BLA (Baloch Liberation), Taliban all because of "bayroon-i-mulk" i.e. foreign forces, i.e. Mossad and RAW behind them*' (Focus Group, Government University[33]); '*Balochistan is rich in natural minerals. International players come and exploit as they have done in Afghanistan, linking the currency with the dollar, "currency politics"*' (Student, Male, Quetta); '*But other agencies are also involved, exploiting these issues. Yes, there is the missing persons issues but other agencies are funding him. We need to find out the real meaning behind what is happening. You cannot allow a separatist movement*' (Focus Group, Private University[34]) *Q.: Who is this other agency/agencies?* '*RAW – funding Mama Qadeer and BLA. RAW has been involved since independence*' (Focus Group, Private University[35]). Abdul Qadeer Baloch, known as Mama Qadeer, launched a nonviolent protest against the security state demanding the return of 'missing persons' after his son was picked up and killed by security forces. He launched a long march with a group of Baloch men and women travelling on foot from Quetta to Islamabad (News 2014). He was denied a platform to speak to the public on several occasions since his critique of the security state was perceived to challenge the Pakistani narrative. Balochistan is Pakistan's secret war. Trying to discuss the issue in public or through the electronic media can lead to arrests and even death. A new form of terror has emerged here; this time, however, it is the administration terrorizing the Baloch and ordinary citizens who might want to question what the army and police are doing in the province. Sabeen Mahmoud, a social activist, was shot dead in April 2015 after hosting a discussion on the war in Balochistan in the Karachi T2F social forum that she had founded. While her murderer in his confession claimed to have killed her for her liberal views, as discussed in Chapter 3, the timing of the murder after a controversial figure such as Mama Qadeer had been hosted at T2F was nonetheless considered suspicious by members of the civil society. Balochistan is a no-go area for human rights activists, media and even academic institutions as was evident when one of the premier universities of Lahore that planned to hold an event about Balochistan was asked to cancel the programme by the intelligence services. Subsequent discussions with the military have revealed that they expect universities to support what they call the 'national narrative' and do not want universities to support students and academics questioning the security state's role in Balochistan. Despite this suppression of information in Balochistan the participants in this study were questioning the experiences of the Baloch with some dismissing Mama Qadeer's movement: '*I went to the missing*

Baloch talk held outside (my university). ... After listening to Mama Qadeer I have become sceptical of what he is saying. He outrightly said that he wants a separate Balochistan. I cannot support that' (Focus Group, Private University[36]).

While the Baloch struggle is the most important part of the Baloch question, issues around local governance pertaining to delivery of basic amenities and services was also questioned by the participants, particularly in connection with Sui gas. Sui, a region located in Balochistan, is the main supplier of natural gas to the entire country (Surendra 2009). However, the province itself struggles with getting gas from its own neighbourhood: '*Balochistan is exploited. We take gas from Sui, send it to all the provinces and what is left is given back to people in Sui. We take their resources, so of course they have every right to feel exploited*' (Focus Group, Private University[37]). '*Yes I had a friend from Sui. She said they did not have enough gas, whereas Sui supplies everyone in the country*' (Focus Group, Private University[38]). While some participants in this study believed that the other provinces had 'ganged up' against Balochistan others questioned the provincial government, and the local structures that exist within the province: '*Balochistan problem over resources, blame Punjabis, government to blame*' (Focus Group, Government University[39]). Others blamed the corruption of the leaders in Balochistan that has resulted in the dismal conditions of the province. There were only a few instances in this research where participants were questioning the state-sponsored narrative of 'foreign interference' in the province. '*I don't agree with RAW being involved. The best way to win a conflict is to influence the narrative, so we blame everything on RAW. I think it is hypocritical to a certain extent if the state alleges that there is no ground reality for the Balochi demand*' (Focus Group, Private University[40]).

Beyond the anti-nationalist military operation Balochistan has suffered some of the worst sectarian violence in the country, which has particularly targeted the Hazara community.

> *Hazara community is imprisoned in its own neighbourhood. It took me 6 years to go from my neighbourhood to my own grandfather's neighbourhood who lives only a few kilometres away because it was so dangerous. We cannot speak the truth. We are jobless, innocent stuck in our neighbourhoods. There are twenty-eight different agencies operating, nobody knows. There is no place that is safe since we can't even hide because of our features.*
>
> (Student, Male, Quetta)

There have been many attacks, but two in 2013 in Quetta stand out: the 10 January suicide car bomb attack that killed more than a hundred, mostly Shias, and the 16 February terror attack that killed more than eighty, again mostly Shias, in Quetta's Hazara Town (International Crisis Group 2014b, p. i). In response to these attacks the Hazara community protested, refusing to bury their dead until the state provided protection to the community and punished the terrorists (BBC News 2013). The LeJ is mostly responsible for these attacks. '*The Lashkar-e-Jhangvi took responsibility for the attacks but where is the government. Why doesn't it do something? It is a government failure*' (Student, Female, Quetta). Because Balochistan borders on Iran, the province and its capital became a major SSP base, with LeJ leader Haq Nawaz Jhangvi moving to Quetta in the mid-1980s. The LeJ is now the most powerful sectarian organization in the city and province (International Crisis Group 2014, p. 18). According to the International Crisis Group, the TTP has attempted to 'woo Baloch dissidents, including by condemning the state's failure to recognise Baloch rights', but 'have found no takers within Baloch nationalist circles' (International Crisis Group 2014b, p. 20). However, TTP factions have targeted civilians in Quetta as well. Added to this cauldron of terrorist outfits is the appearance of Daesh in Pakistan around 2016. In 2016 seventy people were killed and ninety-two injured, in an attack that targeted lawyers who came together at the emergency department of a hospital when they accompanied the murdered body of their colleague (Al Jazeera 2016). A faction of the Pakistani Taliban, and Daesh, took responsibility for these attacks. One spokesperson for the Pakistan army claimed 'that the attack was aimed at undermining security in Balochistan in the light of China-Pakistan economic cooperation in the region' (Siddiqui and Dehghan 2016).

It is difficult to establish if it is despite or because of all of this that most of the young people who took part in the research support the Pakistani army and see the army as the only reliable institution: '*Army is everything here. The link between state and army is so vague. Foreign policy is run by the army*'; '*Army is the only stable institution we have.*' One student did however qualify that there is an ethnic element that plays a part: '*The army, government state is made up of Punjabis.*'

For a majority of the participants the army is the one institution that they can trust. Only a few participants, in both private and government universities, acknowledged that there were instances where the army had overstepped by interfering in the democratic process, but this was often followed by the majority claiming that the army was left with no choice, given the corrupt state of Pakistani politics. In the case of Balochistan as pointed out earlier, the participants were unclear about the ground realities in the province, the result of an information blackout related to Balochistan. Any criticism of the army was an exception not the norm across all students; that was clearly evident in the majority's support for military courts in providing swift justice.

Any discussion on terrorism in Pakistan is incomplete without examining the plight of its most vulnerable communities, the diverse 'non-Muslim' population. The nature of terror and extremism that the non-Muslim minority is subjected to in Pakistan can range from direct targeted attacks by militant outfits to an intolerant system of governance and laws that render them vulnerable to individual attacks. The Christian community in particular has been targeted. In 2013, two explosions in Peshawar at the All Saint's Church resulted in the deaths of nearly eighty people, with over a hundred injured (Sherazi 2013). In 2015, churches in Lahore were attacked by twin Taliban suicide attacks killing fifteen people and injuring over seventy (Gabol et al. 2015). The Christian community in Lahore was again targeted by the Taliban faction Jamaat ul-Ahrar on Easter in 2016 killing more than seventy people (Sherwood 2016). In Quetta in December 2017, nine people were killed and fifty injured after the Bethel Memorial Church was targeted, with Daesh taking responsibility for the attacks (Masood 2017). Christians are not only persecuted by Islamic terrorists, but also by the authorities through the use of the blasphemy law, which in the end plays into the hands of extremists. In November 2014 a Christian couple was burnt to death by a mob after being accused of blasphemy (Hashim 2015). In February 2018 a Christian man, Patras Masih, accused of blasphemy was apprehended by security forces and his cousin who was also interrogated by the police threw himself out of a window (Hashim 2018). The religious minorities continue to bear the brunt of an intolerant state and become easy targets for terrorist groups. The respondents were largely silent about the fate of minorities in Pakistan, showing again how marginalized these communities are.

The added complication to the problem of terrorism in Pakistan is the emergence of university-educated terrorists (see Appendix 2). According to Moeed Yusuf, young people are radicalized through 'socio-economic poverty, education systems based on curricula that breed close-mindedness, discouraging questioning and independent mindedness, and a religion-dominated ideological narrative' (UNDP 2017, p. 112), all factors present in Pakistan. Generally the narrative of a 'failed state due to the perceived weakness of the writ of the state – both geographical and ideological – will draw young people to extremism. However, it's not only the uneducated who are attracted to religious militancy' (UNDP 2017). Hussain (2018) argues that there are three reasons for the 'emergence of educated and urban militants': (1) 'unregulated cyberspace' that terrorist groups such as Daesh have 'exploited'; (2) Daesh's 'alternative jihadist platform, coupled with the excitement of creating a global "Sunni Caliphate" and the spiritual experience of fighting for the glory of Islam'; (3) generational differences that have created a 'rift' between the older and younger generation (2018, pp. 329–30). Panjwani and Khimani (2018) espouse that five factors have coalesced to make the educated youth attracted to extremism: a) religion as a defining framework of the education system in Pakistan, b) the lack of humanities-based critical education, c) the lack of ideological alternatives to contemporary economic and social problems, d) the construction of Islam as a solution to modern problems by the Islamist ideology and e) global interactions of extremist discourse through social media (2018, p. 82).

General Qamar Javed Bajwa's speech at the youth conference and the interior minister's observation (see this book's introduction) point to a recognition of the ideological problems linked to extremism and terrorism, especially among the educated youth. The war against terrorism continues in Pakistan. However, the war has moved beyond the physical domain, with a counterextremism strategy that aims to 'connect' citizens to the state through a state-sponsored 'national narrative'.

The national narrative

The NCEPG emerged out of the National Internal Security Policy (NISP) 2014 (Ministry of Interior 2014) and were published in January 2018.[41] They aim 'to strike at the ideological cobweb of extremism and terrorist propaganda based on falsehood and distortions manipulated to serve their aim for spreading unrest and dissonance in society'. The approach is one that 'connects' the citizen with the state 'predicated on citizen inclusion and engagement' (NACTA 2018, p. 9). In an interview in 2016[42] Ihsan Ghani, the director general for NACTA, stated that there were different stages to terrorism, which included intolerance and extremism. In order to challenge extremism NCEPG focused on six areas of intervention[43]: (1) rule of law and service delivery; (2) citizen engagement; (3) media engagement; (4) integrated education reform; (5) reformation, rehabilitation, reintegration, and renunciation; and (6) promotion of culture.

The director general also highlighted the importance of average citizens in this fight against terrorism, extremism and intolerance; NACTA had set up a helpline (1717) that can be called to report any suspicious behaviour but also any hate speech that one might encounter, whether it be in a Friday sermon at a mosque or in reading material distributed on the streets (Outlook Pakistan 2017).

A common factor behind these guidelines is the importance of strengthening the 'writ of the state'. While there is a recognition that poor service delivery (defined here as education, health and water) has eroded the citizens' confidence in the state, the issue of law, order and control is nevertheless seen as the most important tenet in any reforms that will lead to a reduction in extremism. According to this document, the relevance of the state for the common person is in their day-to-day lives at the level of the 'revenue district' – 'the meeting point between state and citizens' considered to be the 'most important unit in State hierarchy' (NACTA 2018, p. 10). It is this weakness that is exploited by terrorist groups, where citizens become vulnerable to extremist ideology as the state fails to provide the most basic provisions to its citizens. The NCEPG document provides a holistic approach in strengthening this weakness, recognizing a trust deficit between the citizens and the state, which can primarily be addressed at the district level.

In building a 'national narrative' the NCEPG further focuses on dismantling the 'militant's narrative'. For this purpose, the strategy includes a 'victim humanization approach' that involves media outlets which will show victims and their families as the real heroes, projecting 'their human side and realness of their suffering and pain'. 'Justification of violence may be countered with reinforced, continuous and repetitive portrayal of the reality of victim's pain, their existence, loss to their families, humanness and innocence of the presumed enemy, futility of violence in achieving the desired political and ideological goals, isolation and marginalization, difficulty to legitimize the human costs etc' (NACTA 2018, p. 23). The strategy will also include a 'messenger' or 'change agent' who could be a 'former' terrorist or extremist who can 'expose the ugly side of violence since they have commonality with the terrorist and extremist' (NACTA 2018). The education system will be used to create a counternarrative that promotes a rich cultural history and identity of Pakistan. A key part seems a further reform of the education system including teacher training and curricular content, as well as madrassa reform and exchanges between schools and madrassas. However, the responsibility for this is left at the provincial level, making change at best a slow process, provided provincial authorities get on board with the new strategy.

While the NCEPG 2018 attempts to address the weak social contract between the citizen and the Pakistani state, the extent to which these guidelines will be implemented remains to be seen. In education, whether this realization will lead to an education strategy that would encourage critical skills is questionable. Higher education institutions are increasingly becoming spaces of surveillance, rather than of critical thinking. The case of the Hazara University in Mansehra where 'liberal minded lecturers' are believed to be under surveillance by the administration (Basharat 2017); the case of the University of Engineering and Technology (UET) Taxila campus where students are fighting for their rights to be treated as adult students; the case of professors being picked up by security agencies, or arrested for holding political views (Express Tribune 2017c); and the case of bloggers disappearing and being tortured for criticizing the security state (BBC News 2017a), all testify to a strengthening 'security' state, rather than a strong social contract. Furthermore, the security state's record of continuing to mainstream extremist groups into Pakistani politics contradicts this sentiment. In keeping with tradition these are the groups that are not seen as a threat to the Pakistani state and are able to serve as proxies against India.[44] According to the International Crisis Group, there is still no clarity on who is banned:

> According to the January 2015 National Action Plan (NAP) implementation progress report, 72 organisations 'have been declared as proscribed by the MOI [Ministry of Interior], and a comprehensive analysis/assessment review is underway to identify how many of the proscribed organisations are active [and] working under changed names'. Interior Minister Chaudhry Nisar instructed the ministry to revise the national list of banned organisations in line with the UN list. This was apparently done, and the revised list, which included 60 banned under the ATA and twelve by the UN, was placed on the NATCA website just before U.S. Secretary of State John Kerry's January 2015 visit to Islamabad. The list was then taken off the website, because it included the Haqqani Network, the LeT/JD and the FIF charity front. On 20 January, a senior interior ministry official told the Standing Committee on the Interior that the LeT/JD and the Haqqani Network had not been banned. (International Crisis Group 2015, p. 11)

Until the Pakistani state together with its military disentangles itself from an ideology where geopolitical interests trump the security of its own citizens, the problem of terrorism in Pakistan will continue. In the words of a participant in this study: '*I think we have a delusional bubble about ourselves. We think everything is fine, everything is improving and if it isn't, it goes to India or God*' (Focus Group, Private University[45]).

Notes

1 This focus group included participants from Hyderabad, Sukkur and Karachi.

2 These horrifying numbers do not show the much larger numbers of injured and the very large numbers of kidnappings that have blighted the lives of millions.

3 According to the UNDP Human Development Report 2017 the number of terrorism-related deaths has declined in recent years in Pakistan, but it remains the world's sixth deadliest country. 'In 2016, it ranked fourth in the Global Terrorism Index of countries most impacted by terror, scoring 8.6 on a scale of 10. In 2013, nearly 1 out of every 4 young Pakistanis had been either victims of violence or had family or friends who were victims. Of those who had experienced a traumatic violent event, 41 percent reported suffering symptoms of post-traumatic stress disorder (PTSD). In FATA and Khyber Pakhtunkhwa, almost 62 and 35 percent of youth respectively were affected by violence. More alarmingly, of the youth affected by conflict in Balochistan, 80 percent were direct victims. Youth from Sindh have been so affected by violence that they believe it to be a serious threat to the country's very existence' (p. 113).

4 Launched in February 2014.

5 This focus group included participants from Lahore.

6 Also see Akhtar and Ahmad (2015).

7 This focus group included participants from Hyderabad, Sukkur and Karachi.

8 The arrest of Indian spy agent Kulbhushan Yadav in Balochistan reinforced these suspicions (Dawn 2016).

9 This focus group included participants from Lahore, Sheikhupura, Muridke, Dera Ghazi Khan and Sargodha.

10 This focus group included participants from Lahore.

11 This focus group included participants from Hyderabad, Sukkur and Karachi.

12 This focus group included participants from Lahore, Sheikhupura, Muridke, Dera Ghazi Khan and Sargodha.

13 Hussain cites the following numbers for this period: 9,689 dead and 18,812 injured. These numbers reflect the numbers from the South Asia Terrorism Portal, although it is unclear if Hussain is including the terrorists who have been killed and/or the security personnel who lost their lives.

14 This focus group included participants from Hyderabad, Sukkur and Karachi.

15 This focus group included participants from Hyderabad, Sukkur and Karachi.

16 Fedayeen attacks are suicide squad attacks. In 2007 there were 54 Fiyadeen attacks (up from 7 in 2006) with 765 dead and 1,677 injured. The peak came in 2009 with 76 attacks, 949 dead and 2,356 injured. As of 2010 these numbers have abated, with 15 in 2017 causing 325 dead and 992 injured (South Asia Terrorism Portal).

17 This focus group included participants from Hyderabad, Sukkur and Karachi.

18 This focus group included participants from Lahore, Sheikhupura, Muridke, Dera Ghazi Khan and Sargodha.

19 This focus group included participants from Lahore, Sheikhupura, Muridke, Dera Ghazi Khan and Sargodha.

20 This focus group included participants from Hyderabad, Sukkur and Karachi.

21 This focus group included participants from Hyderabad, Sukkur and Karachi.
22 The Orangi Pilot Project collectively designates three Pakistani NGOs working together in the squatter areas of Orangi Town, Karachi, Pakistan.
23 This focus group included participants from Hyderabad, Sukkur and Karachi.
24 Translation: *'100 devils die to make one politician.'*
25 Translation: *'unknown individuals.'*
26 National Finance Commission award – distribution of financial resources between federal and provincial governments.
27 Who had a brutal reputation for not tolerating dissent himself and torturing his opponents.
28 Kulbhushan Yadav arrest in Balochistan reinforced these suspicions (Dawn 2016).
29 This focus group included participants from Hyderabad, Sukkur and Karachi.
30 This focus group included participants from Lahore.
31 Inter Services Intelligence – Pakistan's Intelligence Agency.
32 This focus group included participants from Hyderabad, Sukkur and Karachi.
33 This focus group included participants from an Islamic Studies department from across Lahore.
34 This focus group included participants from Hyderabad, Sukkur and Karachi.
35 This focus group included participants from Hyderabad, Sukkur and Karachi.
36 This focus group included participants from Hyderabad, Sukkur and Karachi.
37 This focus group included participants from Hyderabad, Sukkur and Karachi.
38 This focus group included participants from Lahore.
39 This focus group included participants from Lahore, Sheikhupura, Muridke, Dera Ghazi Khan and Sargodha.
40 This focus group included participants from Hyderabad, Sukkur and Karachi.
41 Yusuf says in the 2017 UNDP report that 'what is clear is that Pakistan urgently needs a national counter-narrative independent of religion and promoted through state-society linkages' (p. 112). This narrative now has been provided – however, given the role of the security forces it is, as this chapter shows, unlikely to help much in countering terrorism.
42 Director General NACTA, 4 October 2016. www.youtube.com/watch?v=4LEYxSkhDaE
43 NACTA (2018, p. 5).
44 For example: 'Although banned in Pakistan and included in the UN sanctions list, Hafez Saeed's Lashkar-e-Tayyaba (LeT, now renamed Jamaat-ud-Dawa, JD) and Maulana Masood Azhar's Jaish-e-Mohammed are among the "good banned groups", since India is their primary target. The LeT/JD not only continues to operate freely, but has also expanded its activities to Karachi and elsewhere through its so-called charity front, the Falah-e-Insaniyat Foundation (FIF). … While continued support for Afghan jihadi proxies is evident, with the Haqqani Network also excluded from

Pakistan's list of terrorist groups, several home-grown Sunni extremist outfits also appear to be considered among the "good banned groups". These include the Sipah-e-Sahaba Pakistan (SSP, banned in 2002, now renamed Ahle Sunnat Wal Jamaat, ASWJ) Sunni extremist LeJ, several of whose activists have been arrested, tried and, in the case of those convicted in the late 1990s to mid-2000s, even hanged. Yet, no action has been taken against its leader, Malik Ishaq, or Asmatullah Muawiya, head of the so-called Punjabi Taliban, who announced in September 2014 that his group would end attacks on Pakistani security forces and focus on Afghanistan. He was reportedly allowed to return to his home in Punjab' (International Crisis Group 2015, pp. 8–10).

45 This focus group included participants from Hyderabad, Sukkur and Karachi.

5

Youth and Social Media

It's like in the essay 'the revolution will not be tweeted'. You just click on a button and think you have done your part.'

(Student, Male, Karachi)

Facebook makes you aware of the political parties situation going on and it's just not the reason why I use Facebook. I have to be active on Facebook so that I can contact my siblings who aren't in Pakistan right now.

(Student, Female, Sialkot)

Activism is the next step after awareness. The knowledge you actually have in which you believe.

(Focus Group, Private University[1])

In Pakistan, around 15 to 17.8 per cent of the population is estimated to be internet users, the majority of whom are young Pakistanis (Internet Live Stats 2016; Pew Research Center 2016). The nature of internet access may also be determined by class (see Bolognani 2011). This access is predicted to increase, as mobile companies have started offering internet connectivity packages to their customers, with the aim of reaching Pakistanis across the country (Freedom House 2016). The use of social media sites such as Facebook is popular among the youth (Yusaf 2015). According to Facebook's Audience Insights there are 25 to 30 million active users of Facebook in Pakistan; 22 per cent are women and 78 per cent are men (Facebook Audience Insights 2017).[2] Fifty-seven per cent of these women and 48 per cent of these men are between the ages of eighteen and twenty-four, while 30 per cent and 35 per cent, respectively, are between the ages of twenty-five and thirty-four.[3] The majority of these users are in Lahore (29 per cent) and Karachi (23 per cent). In examining Facebook data, the nexus between mobile companies and Facebook usage is further evident in the number of 'likes'[4] that the page 'Facebook for Every Phone' has received, as it is the most popular site, with 6.1 million people having 'liked' the page.

Social media can be instrumental in helping young people stay connected, as is evident in the quote from the student in Sialkot; awareness of politics or current affairs, to the extent that this information translates into a political conscience that would result in political action, often varies across individuals, as evident in the student quotes. However, the response of Pakistan's security state, its need to control social media and online platforms, which are perceived to be spaces that can promote anti-state and terrorist propaganda, implies that the space has the potential to disrupt the 'national narrative'; therefore these platforms are considered dangerous by the security state.

There have been cases such as Noreen Leghari's in which young people have been radicalized online through social media. Leghari, a nineteen-year-old student who left home, married a militant and joined Daesh; she blamed social media for her radicalization, in particular Facebook and Instagram through which she was recruited, and exposed to militant and extremist content (Daily Times 2017; Dawn 2017a). In order to prevent such online spaces, the Prevention of Electronic Crimes Act (PECA) introduced in 2016 increased control and surveillance of the internet. However, given the discussion in Chapter 4, the nature of this terrorist or anti-state threat is determined more by strategic interests, where certain extremist groups are allowed to flourish, while civil society and human rights groups are considered anti-state. The surveillance further targets content that is deemed blasphemous by the authorities. In June 2017, Taimoor Raza became the first Pakistani to be sentenced to death by an anti-terrorism court for 'allegedly committing blasphemy on Facebook' (Rasmussen and Gillani 2017). Belonging to the minority Shia community, Raza was involved in 'a debate about Islam on Facebook' with a man who turned out to be an employee of the Counterterrorism Department (CTD). Raza's arrest was part of a wider crackdown on social media activism by the Ministry of Interior. In March 2017 the interior ministry asked the social media site Facebook 'to help investigate "blasphemous content" posted on the social network by Pakistanis' (BBC News 2017a). The Ministry has further moved to criminalize any activity on social media that is critical of the Pakistani army (Dawn 2017b).

This chapter examines the presence and policing of social media in Pakistan. It highlights how state policy towards preserving a 'national narrative' about the country that glorifies the army, criminalizes dissent and promotes an exclusive religious identity, is also reinforced on social media. Such criminalization of activity online is also problematic in a context where law enforcement authorities are ill-equipped and lack training in dealing with 'online' crimes committed by individuals. It further leads to a securitization of online spaces, evident in cases of bloggers and activists being abducted by '*namaloom afraad*' or the '*khalai makhlouq*'[5] for their online activity. The chapter also examines student narratives from the 2015–16 student survey in Lahore and Karachi in relation to social media, especially Facebook, to understand how students (among the urban youth) use social media, and the extent to which this medium of communication has the potential to promote political activism offline.

Social media engagement

> *Yes, Facebook posts and statuses keep us aware about political situation to some extent.*
>
> (Student, Female, Lahore)

The Janus-faced nature of social media is evident in the role of social networking websites such as Facebook in the Cambridge Analytica scandal[6], and its ability to promote real-world activism and reporting during the Arab Spring (Brown et al. 2012; Eltantawy and Wiest 2011); the anti-austerity protests in Europe (Cristancho 2015); and the live streaming of police brutality in the Black Lives Matter movement in the United States. India is another example where social media was instrumental in promoting mobilization for the 2011 anti-corruption movement and the mass mobilization against sexual violence and rape during the Delhi gang rape case in 2012. Yet, in the same year it also proved lethal in spreading fake news that resulted in exacerbating the ethnic conflict in Assam and the Muzzafarnagar riots in 2013[7] (Bute 2014). In Pakistan, social media sites such as Twitter have been instrumental in promoting the PTM as broadcasting media were banned from airing any reports about the movement. It has also provided a space for journalists to circulate news articles or op-eds that were blocked from being printed by news conglomerates. Kleinhans et al.'s (2015) research highlights the power of 'ICT [information and communication technology], social media and mobile technologies' to 'alter the larger context of public participation' by opening 'up new possibilities for policy-makers' as well as empowering and fostering 'the self-organization of citizens' (2015, p. 240). It is not meant to replace 'real-world' activities and participation but rather provide another avenue through which these activities can be improved. This is evident in the use of social media by political actors (see Howard et al. 2016). Blogs, 'the Social Media equivalent of personal web pages' (Kaplan and Haenlein 2010, p. 63), and Twitter, 'an information transmission channel'

(Kim et al. 2015, p. 330), also provide an online space for individuals to directly convey their messages to other users. Kim et al. (2015) highlighted how 'microblogs' are used by the United States as 'tools to communicate with citizens, to learn about ideas, and to establish a network of people, in addition to serving as a new outlet for important announcements' (2015, p. 330). They further explored the use of Twitter by the Korean government and concluded 'that services for transparency/openness through social media can positively affect people's trust in the government directly and that services for engagement/participation and communication/relationship enhance the trust and perceived reliability of the government agency that provides the service, which indirectly enhances trust in the central government' (2015, p. 348). The use of Twitter by the president of the United States, Donald Trump, for communicating not only with the citizens of his country but also with world leaders demonstrates both the potential and the danger of such social networking websites, which are meant to allow uncensored freedom of expression (though these websites have the ability to censor their own users depending on the nature of the message).

In the case of Pakistan, Hussain (2014) has studied the use of social media by the chief secretary's office of Gilgit Baltistan to show the possibility of strengthening the state–citizen relationship through social media sites like Facebook. The chief secretary set up a Facebook page for the purpose of providing 'an additional channel of public communication, to enhance government outreach, to increase transparency and to counter corruption in order to improve governance in Gilgit-Baltistan' (Hussain 2014, p. 2). With the number of 'followers' increasing to '22,754 people', the chief secretary provided the citizens an opportunity to directly correspond with him and his office. The success of this initiative is evident in the way the chief secretary was able to address direct complaints of his constituents, 'improve citizens' participation in project planning', and 'tackle corruption' as citizens could share their complaints about local officers directly with the chief secretary (Hussain 2014).

Yusaf (2015) highlights the importance of 'new media technologies' during the lawyers' movement when 'anti-Musharraf activists used SMS networks to organize flash mobs; university students used a combination of blogs, e-mail lists, and SMS messages to organize protests; and protestors used cameras on their mobile phones to document and archive their action on Flickr and YouTube' (2015, p. 159). Members of the Pakistani diaspora were connected to the movement 'through Facebook'. The use of social media by political parties like the PTI is also highlighted by Yusaf. As she observes, Imran Khan's 'official Facebook page had attracted 487,000 "likes" and had 100,000 more followers than the PTI's official website' by October 2012 (2015, p. 156). In fact, as part of their campaign strategy, PTI 'mobilized a twenty-five-member social media team comprised of volunteers from around the world to keep the party's online platform buzzing', a move that pushed other political parties to also use online platforms more effectively (2015). Ironically, Yusaf also notes how Pervez Musharraf after being ousted from power boasted about 'his social media following – 825,000 Facebook "likes" in March 2013' as an indicator of his popularity, 'far more than Khan's' (2015, p. 160). Despite the fact that PTI won seats in KP, a province where mobile and internet penetration had yet to gain momentum, the party's presence on social media nonetheless was important in gaining local and international traction, where 'Khan was better able to position himself as a political outsider and revolutionary' (2015, p. 157).

However, any discussion on the use of social media in Pakistan needs to first examine the nature of these 'users'. Khan and Nisbet's (2016) research related to 'online censorship' that included 3,720 Pakistani internet users, revealed that 'heavy internet users in Pakistan', that is those 'who use the internet every day', are predominantly 'very young (72% under 30 years of age), largely male (59%), and highly educated (72% with at least some university schooling)' (also see Durrani et al. 2015). Seventy-seven per cent of all internet users accessed social media websites such as Facebook and Twitter. For the participants in the 2015–16 survey the majority used social media sites, where Facebook was more popular than Twitter.[8]

However, social media can also be used as a mechanism of surveillance. This surveillance can range from strategies developed to gauge consumer behaviour and preference based on 'a complex set of data collection, tracking, and targeting systems that monitor and monetize individual users' behaviors as well as their interactions with friends and acquaintances' (Montgomery 2015, p. 773; also evident in the Facebook's Cambridge Analytica scandal), or to gauge the potential of online political dissent that can translate into real-world activism, thereby providing an opportunity to crack down on such activity before it is implemented offline (Rahimi 2011). According to a Freedom House (2017) report Pakistan's 'Freedom on the Net' status is 'not free'; the country's level of internet openness is ranked at 71 out of 100, and that place has fallen from 2016 when it was 69 out of 100.[9] Yusaf highlights how 'in the years following the liberalization of broadcast media, the SPR, the public relations wing of the Pakistan army, was expanded to comprise separate wings to monitor and engage with print media, FM radio, private television channels, and social media outlets such as Facebook and Twitter' (Yusaf 2015, p. 162). By 2016 online dissent and critique had been criminalized under the PECA 2016. While human rights and digital rights activists voiced their concern about the unlimited nature of the power given to security agencies under this law, it aimed to garner support by claiming to address 'the need to check extremist content, prosecute hate speech, and curb online harassment of women' (Aziz 2018). The law continues to be broad and loosely defined. Article 37(1) referring to 'unlawful on-line content' states:

> The Authority shall have the power to remove or block or issue directions for removal or blocking of access to an information through any information system if it considers it necessary in the interest of the glory of Islam or the integrity, security or defence of Pakistan or any part thereof, public order, decency or morality, or in relation to contempt of court or commission of or incitement to an offence under this Act. (National Assembly Secretariat 2016, p. 762)

The words used in Article 37(1), and throughout PECA 2016 – phrases such as 'in the interest of the glory of Islam' or the 'integrity, security or defence of Pakistan' to ensure 'public order, decency or morality' – provide a wide space for interpretation by the security state. This piece of legislation is in line with the NCEPG 2018 that recognize how 'transferring of cultural identity to next generations involves a process of socialization' in which a 'society must reflect the values it intends to pass on, factoring in all modes of socialization including family, education system and the electronic and social media' (2018, p. 38). The security state in the interest of 'national security' has normalized its presence in every institution, formal or informal, of the country. Democracy, citizen rights and freedoms are secondary where any form of dissent to the national narrative, online or offline, is projected as an existential threat to the survival of the country.

PECA 2016 shows a pattern of control and surveillance that exists across Pakistani society, especially in relation to what the state considers 'legitimate' knowledge or activity. The vagueness of the language, especially in Article 37(1), opens up the possibility of abuse of power against online critique and debate under this piece of legislation. In Pakistan today, any form of dissent that may challenge state authority, whether in the education curriculum, as shown in Chapter 3, or through student activism on university campuses, as discussed in Chapter 2, is immediately crushed. Online forums are no different. PECA 2016 claims to meet the challenge of the age of the internet by providing legislation to 'prevent unauthorized acts with respect to information systems and provide for related offences as well as mechanisms for their investigation, prosecution, trial and international cooperation' (p. 745). This act has been criticized for giving unlimited powers to 'authorized personnel' who may confiscate data and 'information systems' under the guise of ensuring law and order, and security of the Pakistani public, while also threatening 'free speech' (Freedom House 2016; Digital Rights Foundation 2015; Human Rights Watch 2017). A report by the Jinnah Institute that examined PECA against similar laws in India, the United Arab Emirates and the United States concluded that this legislation 'has the highest number of crimes included under law, specifies harsher penalties and awards unrestricted authority to investigate and prosecute' compared to the other three countries in their study (Kamal 2017, p. 9). Citizens are further vulnerable as 'ISPs [internet service providers] and mobile companies are not obliged to maintain or comply with data protection policies that protect consumers', thereby allowing the government easy access to citizen data online (Freedom House 2017, p. 15).

However, such draconian legislation is not new to Pakistan. 'The 1996 Pakistan Telecommunications Act already' supported 'censorship for the protection of national security' primarily for 'religious reasons'. In fact, 'Section 99 of the penal code' allowed 'the government to restrict information that might be prejudicial to the national interest, to justify filtering antimilitary, blasphemous or antistate content' (Freedom House 2016). According to a report by the Citizen Lab at the University of Toronto, Pakistan had been using 'Netsweeper technology' to block not just 'blasphemous and anti-Islamic content' but also 'sites promoting Balochi, Sindhi, and Pashtun human rights and political autonomy in Pakistan' (Citizen Lab 2013, p. 2; also see Yusaf 2015). Furthermore, in order to control the 'national narrative', as highlighted by Yusaf (2015), 'websites of religious minorities' have also been banned in the past. Examples include websites or blogs launched by the Shia and Ahmadiyya communities 'to document instances of sectarian violence and campaign for their rights', two of which were 'temporarily blocked' by the government in July 2012 (Yusaf 2015, p. 170).

The threat of terrorism, and the use of mobile phones as detonators, has also resulted in greater control of mobile services. Such control increased inequalities in access across Pakistan; for example, in Balochistan 'in late 2016 and early 2017, mobile internet was suspended in the province for undefined security reasons', and in the FATA 'mobile internet service was shut down for more than a year' beginning in June 2016 (Freedom House 2016, pp. 1, 3). The Freedom House (2016) report highlights greater surveillance of citizens in Pakistan through the registration of 'fingerprint' and 'other identifying information when applying for broadband internet packages and mobile services', which can be monitored for security reasons. In essence, the security state through the National Database Registration Authority (NADRA) has digitized citizens' identification data where all mobile accounts are connected to this data with the security state able to monitor citizens' online and offline activity without any effective checks and balances.

In relation to anti-military statements online, the Federal Investigation Agency (FIA) has been working with its Counterterrorism Department (CTD) to track down social media users who have been critical of the army. As of May 2017, it 'has identified dozens of suspects involved in what it calls an "organised" campaign against the country's armed forces on social media' (Wasim and Tahir 2017). However, as identified by an FIA agent, the cybercrime division lacks 'modern equipment to deal with such offences'. Furthermore, opposition parties had also accused Nawaz Sharif's government of abusing the law to target its party supporters, especially given that '23 Pakistan Tehreek-e-Insaaf (PTI) supporters were detained and threatened with action under' PECA 2016 (Al Jazeera 2017). The arrests further included one individual arrested 'for sharing a satirical picture of Prime Minister Nawaz Sharif', and journalists complaining of being harassed and threatened under this law. According to a 2017 report by Harvard's Berkman Klein Center for Internet & Society, Pakistan is among seven countries in the world that 'pervasively filter political content', the others being China, India, Indonesia, Saudi Arabia, Uzbekistan and Yemen (Clark et al. 2017). The website of the MQM was banned in August 2016 by the Pakistani government after its leader was accused of delivering 'an "anti-Pakistani" speech' (Freedom House 2017, p. 9). According to Freedom House (2017), 'political dissent and secessionist movements in areas including Baluchistan and Sindh province have been subject to systematic censorship for years' (2017). In 2018, after the PTM gained momentum across Pakistan, the security state started its crackdown on online publication of newspaper articles by journalists, as well as forcing a news channel, Geo News, to go offline for its coverage of PTM (Al Jazeera 2018). Geo News had issues with the security state in the past, being forced off the air for its criticism of Pakistan's army. The moral policing of the population is also evident in pornographic sites being banned. Freedom House (2017) highlights how in the beginning of 2016 alone PTA blocked '429,343 supposedly pornographic websites' without publicizing either 'the list' or the vetting process. Often such measures also impact websites that provide sex education, further policing individual behaviour through such actions (Freedom House 2017, p. 10).

In light of such measures Khan and Nisbet (2016) attempted to gauge young Pakistanis' response to state surveillance and censorship of the internet. They differentiated between heavy users of the internet, 'moderate users' – who use the internet 'several times a week' and light users – who use the internet 'several times a month or less'. Their research demonstrated differences in user opinion about government surveillance across these categories: 'In general, light users are substantially more willing to support government censorship and blockage of online content as compared to moderate and heavy internet users, especially considering sensitive political and religious topics' (2016, p. 7). However, in examining the perceived reason for government censorship, 'the plurality of Pakistani internet users (45%) believe that the government's primary motivation for internet regulation is to protect themselves from criticism while about one-third selected it was to curtail freedom of expression (35%)' (2016, p. 8). The level of trust in the government's regulation of the internet also varied across the different groups, indicating a diversity of opinion and trust in the government. While the internet provides a medium for greater connectivity, Durrani et al.'s (2015) research illustrates how for Pakistani youth 'greater connectedness may not automatically mean greater connection and better social cohesion but it appeared to give young people greater visibility and voice' (2015, p. 199). For Durrani et al. (2015) young people's experiences with social media and its relation to society, in particular the idea of 'social cohesion', are shrouded in 'fear' and 'excitement':

> There is fear that social media may be used to promote extremism among the youth; the state may fear that the social media may be used to subvert government position; the civil society may fear that Pakistan's Inter-state Intelligence may use social media to obtain personal information of the youth to spy on them; some elements in the society fear that social media may promote blasphemous material against Islam and youth may fear harassment and bullying online. (Durrani et al. 2015, pp. 197–8)

Given the implementation of PECA 2016, and the arrests of individuals like Taimoor Raza, this 'fear' is not irrational. Such arrests and detentions become especially life-threatening when individuals are accused of committing blasphemy.

Silencing dissent

In January 2017 five prominent bloggers and activists disappeared, once again abducted by '*namaloom afraad*', only later was it discovered that they had been taken away by the Intelligence Agency (Al Jazeera 2017). These activists included 'prominent poet Salman Haider, bloggers Waqas Goraya, Aasim Saeed, and Ahmad Raza Naseer, and social rights activist Samar Abbas' (HRW 2017). These activists had been 'vocal critics of militant Islamist groups and Pakistan's military establishment'. After their disappearance 'the government immediately blocked access to their websites and blogs' (HRW 2017). In an interview with the BBC, one of the bloggers, Aasim Saeed, talked about his involvement with a 'Facebook page' that was 'critical of Pakistan's military establishment, called Mochi, "because since the inception of Pakistan they've always been ruling us directly or indirectly"' (BBC News 2017d). According to Saeed, he was questioned about Mochi, especially 'why he was critical of the army' and his connection to the Indian Intelligence Agency, the RAW. Saeed claims that he was tortured during his incarceration. Waqas Goraya in another interview with the BBC also claimed he was picked up by '"a government institution" with links to the military' because 'he ran a satirical Facebook page critical of the influence of the Pakistani military in the country's political system' and was tortured (BBC News 2017c). Salman Haider's article in BBC Urdu also highlights the torture and questioning about his blog, in particular his 'sympathy' for the Baloch plight. While the bloggers were eventually returned after protests by civil rights activists, their disappearance was further complicated, where their lives were put at risk, when a 'counter-campaign' against them that was 'backed by a number of TV anchors' accused them of blasphemy (BBC News 2017c). Ironically, the campaign against the bloggers included online pages that could have fallen under hate speech, but 'despite reports to both the PTA and the FIA, no action was taken against the people operating the accounts and pages running such campaigns, nor were measures taken to block the sites themselves, thereby putting the activists' reputations and lives at risk' (Aziz 2018). The case of the bloggers in particular highlights the extent to which online activism is being silenced in Pakistan by the security establishment. Most of the bloggers who spoke out eventually fled the country seeking asylum elsewhere. The refusal of the state to crack down on hate speech against the bloggers further highlights the indiscriminate application of PECA 2016, which has become yet another tool of surveillance in an increasingly securitized Pakistan.

In the case of the blasphemy laws, the government of the PML(N) ironically through its crackdown on social media and the internet the PML(N) government further 'weaponised' the blasphemy laws (Inayat 2017). Instead of addressing the draconian nature of blasphemy laws in Pakistan, Nawaz Sharif in March

2017 ordered 'a ban on all blasphemous material online', while the interior minister termed all 'blasphemers as enemies of humanity' (HRW 2017). The state already had power to block what it termed 'blasphemous' material online as evident in the ban of YouTube in 2012 after the 'anti-Islam film "Innocence of Muslims", was uploaded to the site sparking violent protests' (Wilkes 2016). But the weaponization of the blasphemy laws has resulted in further abuse, sanctioning what is akin to a witch hunt to find blasphemers online, or enabling further abuse of the blasphemy laws to settle other disputes.

The dangerous intersection between blasphemy laws and social media surveillance was evident in the April 2017 murder of Mashal Khan that highlights the danger associated with such accusations and social media. The accusation that sparked the violent lynching by his fellow students was linked to his activities on Facebook (Akbar 2017). On further investigation it was discovered that the student had been targeted because of his activism against corruption in his university, his murder instigated by university officials (Rasmussen and Baloch 2017). In another case in the same month 'police intervened to prevent a mob from killing a Hindu man accused of sharing blasphemous content on social media in Hub, Balochistan province' (HRW 2017). Blasphemy laws implicate both Muslim and non-Muslim citizens where the accusation may stem from personal vendettas or disputes. This misuse of the blasphemy laws has been further exacerbated through technology. Another example is the case of a Christian man known as 'Nadeem or Nasim James' who went into hiding after his 'Muslim friend' accused him of blasphemy when he shared a poem that was perceived to be insulting of Islam through the instant messaging service WhatsApp, despite the fact the accused in question was said to be illiterate and had no knowledge of using the app, according to his brother (Constable 2016). With the case of Taimoor Raza as the first Pakistani to be sentenced to death for committing blasphemy online, the existing problem of abuse of blasphemy laws against innocent individuals will only be exacerbated. Furthermore, the issue of freedom of speech will continue to be compromised, where any criticism of even the blasphemy laws themselves has resulted in accusations of blasphemy and death (The Economist 2017; Amnesty International 2016). The normalization of such surveillance of online content is further evident in Figure 5.1, which shows a text message sent by the PTA to all customers of mobile networks (this message was received by the co-author). Advising citizens to report blasphemous 'content', in a Pakistani context where such laws have been abused in the past, where, as admitted by an FIA official (Wasim and Tahir 2017) the state does not have the appropriate

Figure 5.1 PTA SMS sent via mobile networks.

tools to examine online offences, such policies will only curtail free speech, while increasing the possible abuse of the blasphemy laws.

In its 2017 annual report PTA clearly outlines the 'nuisance of blasphemous content' (2017, p. 39), and how it 'informed the general public' about ways of reporting such content (as indicated in Figure 5.1). 'In response, PTA received, processed and blocked thousands of web links, Facebook pages etc. and the cases were also referred to the LEAs[10] for further investigation' (2017, p. 40). In using technology as a means of fighting against blasphemy, hate speech and extremism, the government under the NACTA has also launched a mobile app, available to download on Google and Apple Play stores, that 'enables citizens to report extremist content and activities anonymously and securely whenever they notice it in their areas and also on the internet. The data and information received will be shared with the Police, FIA and other law-enforcement and regulatory authorities in Pakistan' (Express Tribune 2018). In essence, citizens have become increasingly part of the state's counter-extremism agenda, instrumental not only in assisting the security state's fight against extremism, but also in upholding the national narrative (also discussed in Chapter 3).

However, PECA 2016 is useful in the manner by which it has codified laws to punish online abuse, especially sexual harassment and bullying. According to Kamal (2017), in KP 'a man was arrested for blackmailing women by uploading fake videos on social media websites' while 'a University professor was arrested for harassing a female teacher' (2017, p. 1). Yet Aziz (2018) highlights how after the initial 'hype, progress was slow' as 'citizens routinely complained of not hearing back for long periods after submitting their complaints – in cases that, to them, required urgent attention'. In situations that made it to courts, the procedures for trying such cases were still being streamlined. The case of Naila Rind especially highlights the disconnect between such laws and their implementation. Naila Rind was a graduate student at Sindh University who committed suicide after being blackmailed with 'pictures and videos' by a man whom she met on Facebook. In her case, the police were clueless about the nature of PECA 2016 in relation to sexual harassment. As the founders of the Digital Rights Foundation highlighted, the state was 'in a rush to pass perfunctory laws such as the PECA without thinking over the implementation or plan to educate law enforcement agencies and the judiciary on the law' (Dad and Khan 2017). While it is important to have laws that address the problem of online sexual harassment, the security state has spent more time mainstreaming its surveillance strategy under PECA 2016, rather than streamlining the process of complaints and prosecution in cases of online sexual harassment and abuse.

In essence, the scope of the cybercrime law is largely undefined, giving almost unlimited powers to state officials in their surveillance of the internet. As Kamal highlights, any 'act of displaying or transmitting information that harms the reputation of a person' can 'be construed to penalize satire, political expression or any other form of journalism' (Kamal 2017, p. 8). The action against a satirical news website 'the Khabaristan Times' highlights this problem, since the website was blocked 'on the grounds that it published "anti-state" content' (Aziz 2018).

This normalization and increased surveillance are further evident in the requests made by the Pakistani government to Facebook administration in its efforts to crack down on blasphemy and anti-state activity (Dawn 2015). For the purpose of transparency Facebook releases a Government Request Report (GRR) every six months that 'lists the number of requests for content removal, restriction, user data, and any other requests made by governments worldwide' (Kamran 2017). Between January to June 2017, as a result of such data sharing, Facebook restricted 177 pieces of content 'based on legal requests from the Pakistan Telecom Authority and Federal Investigative Agency' since the content violated 'local laws prohibiting blasphemy and condemnation of the country's independence' (Facebook 2018; see Table 5.1 and Table 5.2).

Such accusations of statements or activity against the 'independence' of the country, where the nature of these statements is open to interpretation, can lead to further curtailment of dissent and free speech. With the implementation of PECA 2016, and attempts by the interior ministry to work with Facebook to gain access to detailed information about individuals posting 'blasphemous' content

Table 5.1 Facebook's Pakistan Government Request Report Data: Pakistan Requests for Data response 'to valid requests relating to criminal cases … checked for legal sufficiency' and accordingly accepted, rejected or asked for more information by Facebook

Report Period	Total Requests	Users/ Accounts Requested	Requests Where Some Data Produced (%)
July 2016–December 2016	1,002	1,431	67.56
January 2016–June 2016	719	1,029	65.09
July 2015–December 2015	471	706	66.45
January 2015–June 2015	192	275	58.33
July 2014–December 2014	100	152	42.00
January 2014–June 2014	116	160	35.34
July 2013–December 2013	126	163	47.62
January 2013–June 2013	35	47	77.00

Note: https://transparency.facebook.com/government-data-requests/country/PK

Table 5.2 Pakistan Content Restrictions: These restrictions are 'based on legal requests from the Pakistan Telecom Authority and Federal Investigation Agency'

Report Period	Reason for Content Restriction	Number of Pieces of Content Restricted
July 2016–December 2016	'alleged to violate local laws prohibiting blasphemy and condemnation of the country's independence'	6
January 2016–June 2016	'allegedly violating local laws prohibiting blasphemy, desecration of the national flag, and condemnation of the country's independence'	25
July 2015–December 2015	'alleged to violate local laws prohibiting blasphemy'	6
January 2015–June 2015	No data on restrictions	
July 2014–December 2014	'under local laws prohibiting blasphemy'	54
January 2014–June 2014	'under local laws prohibiting blasphemy and criticism of the state'	1,773
July 2013–December 2013	'under local laws prohibiting blasphemy and criticism of the state'	162
January 2013–June 2013	No data on restrictions	

Notes: https://transparency.facebook.com/content-restrictions/country/PK; https://govtrequests.facebook.com/country/Pakistan/2013-H1/

online, policing of social media will further restrict free speech and activism in Pakistan. These questions of freedom and rights are important as the powers of the security state are strengthened. However, for the participants in this study in 2015–16, the question of state censorship and the possibility that social media could be a space for promoting political activism were seldom mentioned. If anything, social media could promote political awareness but the extent to which that awareness translates into action is questionable.

Using social media in Pakistan

As with the participant quotes in the beginning of this chapter, the use of social media for participants in this study was similar to that identified by Khan and Nisbet (2016). In their study they point to the use of the internet for the purposes of 'email (91%), communicating on social networking sites (77%), reading international newspapers (68%), posting videos or video clips online (68%), downloading or listening to music or watching videos online (65%), and using internet telephony (63%)' (2016, p. 10). Social media as discussed in the present study was a space predominantly for connecting with friends and family. In relation to political activism, the narratives in this study highlight both the *potential* of social media as a source to promote political literacy, and its *limitation* in encouraging students to act on this literacy offline, in the 'real' world. Howard et al.'s (2016) 'slacktivism hypothesis' takes a new form among social media users in Pakistan. 'Slacktivism' draws on 'the supposition that if internet or social media use increases, civic engagement declines' (Howard et al. 2016, p. 56). Howard et al. challenge this hypothesis in their study of Mexico, but the participants in this research reaffirm it.

While students gave mixed responses to the question of activism on social media, often their responses were dependent on how they defined political activism as discussed in Chapter 2. Some participants at a private university in Karachi argued how social media was one form of activism '*It is about being vocal about your political ideology through social media, by attending rallies, vigils, vocally condemning something*' (Focus Group, Private University[11]). However, the problem was in participants differentiating between awareness and activism. For some '*putting up a comment over something political makes one politically active in my opinion*' (Student, Female, Karachi). With the sentencing of Taimoor Raza over a Facebook argument, or the arrest of bloggers, or attempts by the Pakistani state to gain the personal data of Facebook users – in other words, in an age where dissent of any kind may be labelled anti-state or treasonous – such actions on social media cannot simply be dismissed. As another student in Lahore highlighted, social media activism allows '*ordinary people an agency or a voice*' (Student, Female, Lahore). If that voice is perceived to be suppressed, then social media sites such as Facebook definitely provide an avenue for that voice to be heard. However, the extent to which young people even engage in social media debate or discussion varies across individuals, as does their level of political awareness. This political awareness is defined in the following ways: '*Yes [I am politically aware] because of political posts which have been uploaded by someone*' (Student, Male, Lahore); '*Yeah, after all it makes all of us aware of the circumstances all around*' (Student, Female, Sialkot); '*Yes because you can share information with everyone and people do use it on a daily basis*' (Student, Female, Lahore).

The potential that social media has in raising such political awareness cannot be discounted, especially in a context like Pakistan where a lack of political literacy, let alone activism, among the majority of the youth continues to be a problem. However, contrary to such narratives there were others who on further probing provided insights about the limitations of being active online: '*Yes, it makes people aware of others' political views and thus enhances your information*' (Student, Female, Sheikhupura). Others also highlighted these limitations in offline activism in their narratives: '*Because only liking any post doesn't make you politically aware*' (Student, Female, Lahore); '*Facebook does make you politically active. You can change profile pics, take a stand … . I think people can take out their aggression on Facebook and TV but don't come out*' (Focus Group, Private University[12]); '*No, because after letting out steam, they lose all interest and develop a this-is-not-my-problem attitude*' (Student, Female, Karachi); '*No it encourages complacency by making people believe they are politically active by simply posting articles rather than initiating in any tangible change*' (Student, Male, Karachi); '*Because after tweeting, people believe they have done their part in showing their disapproval but they don't take any actions or deduce practical solutions. It's a ranting place*' (Student, Female, Karachi). These responses reflect the 'slacktivism' hypothesis, where there is a danger that such online expression will not translate into offline action (Howard et al. 2016, p. 56).

In response to the participants who believe that online activism is nothing more than a place to rant, where people remain complacent or develop a '*this-is-not-my-problem attitude*', the response of the security state to online activism may seem quite exaggerated. However, it is the potential that the online space has to challenge the national narrative and critique the actions of the security state that threatens the security establishment. The role of social media in the Arab Spring, in the way it helped spread the message and assisted young activists in mobilizing support, turns it into a thorn in the side of the security establishment. Its role in promoting PTM in Pakistan is another instance where social media has the potential of mobilizing citizens. This is particularly true in instances where political parties have been using social media to promote their message: the use of Twitter by individuals like Maryam Nawaz, the daughter of Nawaz Sharif and his predicted heir, in her criticism of Panamagate and her father's dismissal (and her sudden silence); the use of social media by political parties such as the PTI to spread its agenda and mobilize young people for its rallies (Yusaf 2016; Kolsy 2013; Farooq 2014). Even in India, Kanungo (2015) observes how the Bharatiya Janata Party (BJP) used social media in the 2014 Lok Sabha elections, arguing that while it was important it was not necessarily a 'game changer'. Similarly, Ullah (2013) argues for its potential in Bangladesh where youth engagement on social media may not directly influence 'political decision-making' but could play a role in the 'policy-making process'. While it is unclear the extent to which social media impacts political participation of young people, Kahne and Bowyer's research on social media and participatory politics in the United States found that a connection between 'offline political activity to online participatory politics was statistically significant' in their research, compared to 'online participatory politics to offline political activity', which, though 'positive', was 'not statistically significant' (2018, p. 490). It is clear that young people who are already politically active become better organized through online activity; the question still remains to what extent are politically inactive people encouraged to become active offline. However, in Pakistan the disconnect between online activism and offline participation in political rallies or movements is evident in the fact that often only a fraction of the individuals who agree to take part in such rallies online actually show up to the event, once again indicative of Howard et al.'s 'slacktivism' hypothesis (2016).

For the majority of the participants then, the main role of social media sites such as Facebook was simply networking with friends and family, socializing through posting photographs or following celebrities, or simply as '*time pass*', that is, a medium of procrastination (Student, Male, Kanganpur). Only a handful (8 in total) from the 2015–16 sample did not use Facebook because they felt it was a waste of time. More problematic was the idea that Facebook was a useful source of news about the country and the world: '*Yes, we get most of the news from there. A platform where people exchange views*' (Student, Female, Lahore): '*Yes, you can say that because nowadays whatever happens around the world it's all on Facebook in a second*' (Student, Female, Quetta).

There were, however, survey participants who were critical of the nature of the news that was shared on Facebook, highlighting how one needs to be wary of 'fake news'. In an international context, with Facebook's Cambridge Analytica scandal and the 2016 American elections in which the role of social media in spreading 'fake news' was highlighted, the danger of young people relying on such sites for information about their country and the world is highly problematic. The ease of access in an age when convenience has become a necessity, when information is available at the click of a button, that has made the problem particularly intractable. Students across the sample highlighted the importance of accessibility: '*With newspapers, going and reading a newspaper feels like a job. You have to take out time for that. Other mediums are constantly available with you (such as your phone/Facebook)*' (Focus Group, Private University[13]). This stance was also reflected by a student in Lahore: '*Because nowadays people find no time to read newspapers and watch news. They can easily see the current problems on social media*' (Focus Group, Private University[14]). While social media was considered a source of news, some argued that it went beyond newspapers, owing to its interactive user interface: '*Yes, because unlike news it's not one sided but all sorts of ideas, opinions and evidences are entertained which allows one to process and have their own point of view*' (Student, Female, Lahore); '*Well yes because people get to listen/analyse other people's perspectives and this is what makes them more politically active*' (Student, Male, Karachi).

However, the idea that such interaction and exchange of points of view is possible has repeatedly been questioned, with Facebook being defined as an 'echo chamber' (Allcott and Gentzkow 2017; Sanders 2016; Pariser 2011), or a medium following the logic of 'trench warfare' (Karlsen et al. 2017). For Karlsen et al. (2017) 'the architecture of the internet creates a particularly good environment for reinforcement through contradiction' (2017, p. 260). This is what they describe as 'trench warfare dynamics: people will interact and engage in debate with others who hold opposing political views, but this will only serve to strengthen their initial beliefs' (2017, pp. 260–1). Sanders (2016) argues that 'Facebook's News Feed, which is how most users see content through the app and site, is more likely to prominently display content based on a user's previous interests, and it also conforms to his or her political ideology.' The extent to which young people in our study engaged in online debate was also limited.

There was one prominent example of a young woman in a private university in Lahore who discussed being active on Facebook:

> Q.: *Are you politically active on social media, Facebook?*
>
> *Not anymore. We got banned from the NATO page (two girls). So on the NATO page they were saying how successful they were in Afghanistan. First my brother just posted a comment, saying we do not like your presence here, and the admin kept deleting his comment. We actually wrote and included textual evidence related to the problems of their operation, we did our research and gave them proper evidence but they also kept deleting us, and then they blocked us from their page. This was also during the time when NATO forces were passing through the Pakistani border, during Gilani's period.*
>
> Q.: *Why did you stop being politically active?*
>
> *No point. We might just end up like Sabeen.*
>
> (Focus Group, Private University[15])

The problem of Facebook as a potential 'echo chamber' is clearly evident in this example where the administrator of the NATO page kept deleting the comments posted by these young people, instead of engaging in a debate with them. This further raises the question of who decides what is offensive or threatening in a space such as Facebook. While the laws of a country are taken into consideration in banning Facebook pages or individuals as evident in the preceding discussion, administrators of specific pages also have the space to block or delete comments. Individuals have the ability to block or delete 'friends', especially in instances where they might be offended by their friends' comments. The level of supposed engagement between individuals with diverse viewpoints is therefore suspect. What is also more alarming in this participant narrative is the fear that this young woman and her brother describe of ending 'up like Sabeen'; the participant is referring to Sabeen Mahmood's murder as discussed earlier in the book (see Ali and Zaman 2016).

The extent to which social media provides a forum where one is preaching to the choir (the 'echo chamber') or engaging in a debate ('trench warfare') depends on the individual. Whether such engagement will result in action offline again may vary among individuals. But the extreme efforts taken by the state to crack down on any form of online activity, and the real-world consequences of posting opinions online that have led to lynching and death sentences, reveal that even online activism in Pakistan is both under threat and poses a threat to the State. The national narrative of Pakistan cannot be challenged, even by a minority, even by those whose only point of action is a 'status update' on Facebook or changing a profile picture while remaining indoors. But it is the potential to mobilize and express dissent where the audience is global that has caused the internet and social media sites such as Facebook to become dangerous.

The potential of social media in Pakistan

Obar and Wildman (2015) have argued that 'as social media services further integrate into our societal systems and personal lives, scholars, advocates and policymakers must continue to wrestle with the extent to which legal and regulatory innovations can ensure the protections and freedoms that will at certain points harness and at other points reign in the transformative possibilities implicit in social media" (p. 749). In Pakistan, the potential of social media – to ignite debate and discussion, to challenge the state narrative on Pakistaniat, to translate into real-world action – is far from being harnessed. While organizations such as the Digital Rights Foundation, along with human rights activists, journalists and civil society members, have resisted and challenged the state by bringing international attention to the issue of freedom of speech and rights online, such actions have been successful only to a limited extent. PECA 2016 was implemented with limited changes, and continues to curtail any form of activism online, with the situation only worsening as the existing government clamps down on dissent that is perceived to be against the state, the army or Islam, that is, the national narrative. Yusaf (2015) describes 'cyberspace' in Pakistan as 'increasingly' reflecting 'the polarization and intolerance that plagues Pakistani society' (2015, p. 172). She gives the example of the reaction to the assassination of the Governor of Punjab Salman Taseer by his bodyguard Mumtaz Qadri 'on account of his support for amending Pakistan's controversial blasphemy laws'. The reaction on Facebook included people who condemned Qadri and those who celebrated his actions by creating and supporting (through 'likes') Facebook pages celebrating him. When those pages were reported by Facebook users as hate speech and banned, those same Qadri supporters replaced their profile pictures with his photograph to show their support (Yusaf 2015, pp. 172–3). The online space therefore reflects the offline reality, an uneven contest for a narrative about Pakistan that the military state and right-wing (often militant) groups dominate, where human rights activists, even politically active citizens who take part in movements such as the PTM, are labelled rogue elements of an 'engineered protest'.[16]

The most dangerous aspect of this surveillance of social media activity is the reinforcement of the blasphemy laws, where citizens are being encouraged to report on fellow citizens who have committed blasphemy online. In Pakistan killing in the name of blasphemy is already a problem that the state has been unable to control, as evident in the Human Rights Commission of Pakistan (HRCP) 2016 and the Amnesty International 2016 reports. Instead of curtailing or amending the blasphemy laws that legitimize the criminalization of speech deemed blasphemous to the extent that individuals take the law into their own hands as in the killing of Salman Taseer, Shama and Shahzad Masih, Mashal Khan and countless others, the state has 'weaponized' this law. Such actions could be perceived as PML(N)'s attempt to pander to a deepening conservatism within Pakistani society for votes in the elections of 2018, but whatever the rationale behind such policing, the PML(N) has widened the scope for these laws to be abused.

Furthermore, the extent to which young people are truly active online varies among individuals, with the majority of young people using social media sites such as Facebook to connect with friends and family both in Pakistan and abroad; the level of political activism is often limited to an online comment or reading the news. Such activism will not gain momentum, especially given the responses of participants who feel threatened by the actions of the state, which have only worsened after the implementation of PECA 2016. However, with PTM gaining traction and social media promoting the movement while broadcasting channels are prevented from doing so, demonstrates the potential of social media as a medium to garner support for indigenous, civil rights movements.

Ironically, social media can also be a platform for greater engagement between the state and its citizens. But the persistence of 'fear' that Durrani et al. (2015) alluded to continues to influence state–citizen interaction online. It is a space where citizens can express dissent, or voice opposition against the state and the security apparatus, but also where the state through its direct interaction can ensure greater transparency and effectiveness in governance. The internet and social media have the potential to become an important tool in strengthening the state–citizen relationship. Yet, given the global nature of the World Wide Web, the citizen can also become a potential threat to the state, transcending boundaries and physical spaces, in communication with a global audience. In Pakistan the internet, and in particular social media, has become yet another space to be controlled, through which the state denies its citizens freedom of speech and protest (Digital Rights Foundation 2015; HRW 2017), upholding a national narrative that citizens are forced to blindly follow.

Notes

1 This focus group included participants from Hyderabad, Sukkur and Karachi.
2 Also see Internet World Stats (2018) (www.internetworldstats.com/stats3.htm).
3 These are self-reported details.
4 An option on a Facebook Page that allows users to follow information being posted on the Page. It is often associated with the popularity of a particular Facebook Page.
5 'unknown individuals' – this term is often used by state officials related to such abductions but civil society and human rights activists claim that these 'unknown individuals' are not that 'unknown' since they are part of the intelligence community.
6 Cambridge Analytica, a 'data analytics firm that worked with Donald Trump's election team and the winning Brexit campaign harvested millions of Facebook profiles of US voters, in one of the tech giant's biggest ever data breaches, and used them to build a powerful software program to predict and influence choices at the ballot box' (Cadwalladr and Graham-Harrison 2018).
7 In Assam ethnic conflict broke out in which '70 people died and around 4,85,000, people' were 'displaced'; in a communal dispute leading to the Muzzafarnagar riots in 2013 '43 people were killed, 93 injured and 50,000 were relocated'. (For more information see Bute 2014.)
8 It is important to note that according to Pew Research Center's survey of 1,201 Pakistanis in 2013, only 3 per cent used their cell phones to access social media sites (Pew Research Centre 2014, p. 6). This number will have increased with the push towards 3G and 4G networks provided by mobile companies in Pakistan.
9 0 is most free while 100 is least free.
10 Law enforcement agencies (LEA).
11 This focus group included participants from Hyderabad, Sukkur and Karachi.
12 This focus group included participants from Hyderabad, Sukkur and Karachi.
13 This focus group included participants from Hyderabad, Sukkur and Karachi.
14 This focus group included participants from Lahore.
15 This focus group included participants from Lahore.
16 A comment made by the Chief of Army Staff General Qamar Javed Bajwa in which he did not directly mention PTM but was perceived to have alluded to that particular movement (Syed 2018).

Epilogue

PTI and the Disillusioned 'Naya' Pakistan: One Year On

A year into PTI's government, Pakistan has gone back to the International Monetary Fund (IMF) for the thirteenth time in thirty-one years. As the government struggles with a collapsing economy, further budget cuts have been introduced to education and health. The elected members of the National Assembly, Mohsin Dawar and Ali Wazir, who were associated with a predominantly peaceful PTM movement, have been arrested and accused of instigating an attack by PTM protestors on an army checkpoint in Waziristan. Media outlets and journalists are facing unprecedented censorship, as news channels have intermittently been forced to go off air for showing interviews of opposition leaders or discussions related to the PTM. One year on, the pretence of human rights that was a key part of Prime Minister Imran Khan's inaugural speech seems to have been abandoned, with the security state stronger than ever before as the interests of both the civilian government and the military clearly align.

Imran Khan had promised Pakistan would not resort to the IMF but with a foreign debt burden of more than US$105 billion, and a current account deficit that 'reached a peak level of $19 billion in 2017–18' (Pasha et al. 2019), the country has had to accept the new structural adjustment plan of the IMF which will result in more welfare cuts, unemployment and inflation (See Shalal 2019; BBC News 2019). The promise of quality education and opportunity to the youth of the country will be far from fulfilled as the budget expenditure reveals severe cuts in education, with Rs. 77,262 million provided in budget estimates from 2019–20, against Rs. 97,420 million in budget estimates for 2018–19, and Rs. 97,155 million in revised estimates for 2018–19 (see Government of Pakistan 2019). The Higher Education Commission has been bracing for budget cuts nearing 50 per cent in its development expenditure. These cuts will particularly impact scholarship students from the most vulnerable parts of the country. Along with a weakening economy and rising inflation, unemployment figures are also predicted to increase; the prices of basic necessities, including food items, are increasing as well.

PTI's attempt to fix the taxation system has yielded less than favourable results. Far from punishing tax evaders, taxes levied on the salaried class and on everyday items, including medicine, has shot up. Under this government, Pakistanis will be faced with severe economic difficulties, at least for the foreseeable future. While the PTI argues that such difficulties are an outcome of the corruption and inefficiency of the previous governments, an outcome that is unavoidable given the weak political, economic and social infrastructure of the country, the PTI government is going further into debt, without providing any sufficient safeguards to the 'second youngest population in the world'.[1]

The security state under the PTI government has also intensified its reach, with journalists and media coming under greater surveillance and censorship. In June 2019 the Pakistan Electronic Media Regulatory Authority (PEMRA) issued a notice to all satellite television channels advising them against airing 'satirical content' that mocks political leadership and personalities or law enforcement agencies. Reporters Without Borders (RSF) reported how three Pakistani news channels were 'suspended from cable networks at the behest of the authorities in reprisal for broadcasting an opposition leader's news conference' (RSF 2019). The opposition leader in this case was Maryam Nawaz, the daughter of the imprisoned former prime minister Nawaz Sharif. BBC Monitoring reported how under the new government media censorship has moved beyond harassing individual journalists, to pressurizing 'organisations that are seen to be critical of the establishment' (Mushtaq 2019). This was also echoed by the Pakistan Federal Union of Journalists (PFUJ) that held nationwide protests in July 2019 against censorship and budget cuts that resulted in journalists being laid off. The protest highlighted not just the issue of increasing censorship but also that 'the country's newly-elected government is slashing its advertising budget, squeezing a key source of revenue for private newspapers and TV stations' (Dawn News 2019). Journalists and human rights activists are also targeted on social media, in one case for putting up 'defamatory and obnoxious posts' on Twitter that were 'against the "judiciary, government institutions and intelligence agencies"' (See CPJ 2019).

Despite this current economic crisis and the increasing surveillance and monitoring of journalists, human rights activists, students and academics in 'naya' Pakistan, the new government has attempted to normalize relations with its neighbours and build stronger partnerships with former allies. Two cases particularly stand out in this regard: the peace gesture by Prime Minister Imran Khan's government to India when it returned their pilot Wing Commander Abhinandan Varthaman, and the prime minister's visit to the United States to meet President Trump in order to restore relations between the two allies. Varthaman's fighter jet was shot down in February 2019 when Indian jets bombed what they claimed to be a rebel camp inside Pakistani territory, a claim Pakistan denied. As a peace gesture, the Pakistani government returned the Indian pilot, with Imran Khan reiterating his call for talks and improving relations with India. In July 2019, Imran Khan led a seemingly successful meeting with President Trump who 'spoke of possibly restoring $1.3 billion in American aid that he had cut last year, depending upon the results of the meeting, and offered to mediate in the longstanding dispute between Pakistan and India over the Kashmir region' (Rampton and Chiacu 2019). Both Pakistan's chief of army staff (COAS) and Pakistan's intelligence chief accompanied Khan, presenting a united front to the United States. This attempt at rekindling old alliances has resulted in the prime minister clearly stating that his government will no longer allow 'armed militias to operate', on Pakistani soil. While one may see some truth in this statement, with the arrest of Hafiz Saeed, and the crackdown on the TLP, Pakistan's history has clearly illustrated how the security state often backtracks on such actions.

Given the state of affairs one year on, where is the youth of Pakistan in the policy of the PTI government? With budget cuts to higher education and record-level inflation, the need for quality education and for jobs that young Pakistanis demanded are far from being met. In a July 2019 poll on public opinion about the PTI government by Gallup Pakistan, which included 1,400 households across the country, the approval rating of Imran Khan had dropped 'from 58% in April 2019 to 45%' after the announcement of the Budget for 2019. However, the same poll highlights how the PTI still enjoys strong support, with respondents claiming that they would still vote for PTI in the next elections. With increasing austerity under the IMF structural adjustment programme, the PTI's popularity will be tested in the coming years. The crackdown on PTM, a peaceful movement, is a lost opportunity for this government. Addressing the grievances of PTM supporters could have been instrumental in uniting citizens across ethnic lines, in parts of the country that have previously been ignored if not violated. This lost opportunity is indicative of a security state that can only tolerate one national narrative that is under its control. The crackdown on human rights activists, journalists and free speech in general will continue under a current government that cannot tolerate dissent, which was evidenced in the continued silencing of elected MNAs.

Yet, as the narratives in this book have illustrated, such crackdowns will not necessarily impact the wider support given to the security state. The predominant view of the most of 1,900+ respondents of this book is that the security state can do no wrong. The assumption remains that it is acting in the interest of the law-abiding citizen, even when it infringes on the rights of its citizens. However, what will impact the support of this government and its future is its economic performance and its ability to ensure employment and education for the Pakistani youth who are still hoping for a real 'naya' Pakistan.

Note

1 PM Imran Khan reiterated the importance of this 'second youngest population' in his inaugural speech – See prologue.

Appendix 1: Pakistani Terror Groups[1]

JI: Jamaat-e-Islami, the vanguard of modernist political Islam and the most organized and politically active religious party.

JUI: Jamiat Ulema-e-Islam, the main Sunni-Deobandi political party and successor in Pakistan to the Jamiatul Ulema-e-Hind in pre-partition India. The party is divided into three factions, denoted by the initials of their leaders: JUI-Samiul Haq (JUI-S), JUI-Fazlur Rahman (JUI-F), and JUI-Ajmal Qadri (JUI-Q). The three factions control most Pakistani madrassas. The JUI madrassas were also the main supply line of Afghan jihadis in the 1980s.

Jaish-e-Mohammed: Deobandi jihadi group whose main aim is to unite Kashmir with Pakistan. They have acted as the military's proxy in Kashmir.

Lashkar-e-Islami: A Deobandi extremist group based in FATA's Khyber agency.

Lashkar-e-Tayyaba (LeT), renamed Jamaat-ud-Dawa (JD): Punjab-based jihadi outfit responsible for the 2008 Mumbai attacks.

Sipah-e-Sahaba Pakistan (SSP): A Deobandi militant organization, which pioneered organized sectarian militancy in the country.

Tehrik-e-Nifaz-e-Shariat-e-Mohammadi (TNSM): A Swat-based Sunni radical group, responsible for sending thousands of fighters to help the Taliban after US-led attacks on Afghanistan in October 2001.

Tehrik-i-Taliban Pakistan (TTP): Formed in December 2007 by senior leaders of some forty militant groups, a loose alliance of Pakistani Taliban groups and movements crusading for the implementation of Sharia law mainly in the tribal areas of NWFP, setting up private courts and prisons in areas under their influence. Originally led by South Waziristan-based Baitullah Mehsud until his death on 5 August 2009 in a US drone attack, and then led by his former deputy Hakimullah Mehsud, the TTP is loosely allied to Lashkar-e-Tayyaba and the Jaish-e-Mohammed (which are both seen by the military as 'good' militants).

There are also a few foreign jihadi outfits, including the Islamic Movement of Uzbekistan (IMU) and the East Turkestan Islamic Movement, both of which are present in the tribal areas on Pakistani soil and have operated on both sides of the Pakistan–Afghanistan border.

Notes

1 Taken from various International Crisis Group reports.

Appendix 2: Cases of Students Turning to Terrorism

1. **Omar Sheikh**, a British citizen, completed his education from a university in London. He was convicted in Pakistan for the murder of journalist Daniel Pearl. www.theguardian.com/world/2002/jul/15/pakistan.simonjeffery
2. **Saad Aziz** completed his education from IBA Karachi in 2011. He was convicted for killing The Second Floor (T2F) director Sabeen Mahmud, as well as being involved in Safoora Goth bus attack (forty-six dead). An anti-terrorism court (ATC) acquitted him of the Safoora massacre. www.dawn.com/news/1257959 and https://tribune.com.pk/story/1698805/1-atc-acquits-saad-aziz-police-encounter-case/ and https://dailytimes.com.pk/234308/safoora-massacre-convict-saad-aziz-acquitted-in-police-encounter-case/
3. **Hafiz Nasir** was a graduate student of the Karachi University. Nasir and his brother confessed to have killed eighteen people in the city over sectarian differences. The revelations were made by the suspect allegedly involved in attacks on Muttahida Qaumi Movement (MQM) offices and Safoora attack. http://dunyanews.tv/en/Pakistan/378197-Tanzeem-ulIslami-amir-Nasir-confesses-to-have-kil and http://jworldtimes.com/jwt2015/magazine-archives/jwtmag2018/jan2018/militancy-and-pakistans-highly-educated-youth/
4. **Azfar Ishrat / Mohammad Azfar Ishrat, alias Maajid,** is an engineer having graduated from the Sir Syed University of Engineering and Technology. Involved in terrorist activities since 2011, Ishrat is a trained terrorist who has expertise in making bombs and electronic circuits used as timers in such bombs. https://discuss.pkpolitics.com/topic/31951/from-iba-graduate-to-terror-suspect/2?page=1
5. **Hammad Adil** was arrested along with his brother Adnan Adil from Barakahu in September 2013 in connection with the Chaudhry Zulfiqar murder case. Hammad Adil had confessed to his involvement in the assassination of federal minister for minorities Shahbaz Bhatti in the

capital city in March 2011. www.dawn.com/news/1191338 and www.dawn.com/news/1043484

6. **Tanveer Gondal / Tanvir Gondal, alias Qari Nasir**, is in charge of Al Qaeda's Punjab chapter. www.dawn.com/news/1101286
7. **Haafiz Nasir / Hassan bin Nazeer, alias Yasir**, who completed an MA in Islamic Studies at Karachi University, has been involved in terrorist activities since 2013. A trained terrorist, Nasir has expertise in brainwashing and motivating people for jihadi activities. https://discuss.pkpolitics.com/topic/31951/from-iba-graduate-to-terror-suspect/2?page=1
8. **Sarosh Siddiqui:** The tale of Abdul Karim Sarosh Siddiqui and Sheharyar, alias Abdullah Hashmi, who are suspected of being top commanders of a mysterious Pakistani version of the Ansarul Sharia militant group, begins at a university. Sarosh is considered to have been the mastermind of an attack on the MQM MPA and leader of the opposition in the Sindh Assembly, Khawaja Izharul Hassan. At one time the two friends and neighbours who both studied at the department of applied physics at the University of Karachi were simply associates of Masood Azhar's Jaesh-e-Muhammad. https://tribune.com.pk/story/1501380/tale-two-terrorists/
9. **Noreen Jabbar Laghari** was a student of Jamshoro's Liaquat University of Medical Sciences and disappeared on 10 February 2017 while going from her home to the university. It is insinuated that she had joined Islamic State of Iraq and Syria (ISIS) and had spent two weeks in Daesh training camp in Syria. She reportedly returned to Pakistan on 10 March 2017. www.newspakistan.tv/hyderabad-girl-noreen-jabbar-laghari-join-daesh/

References

A

Adeney, K. (2004) 'Between federalism and separatism: India and Pakistan'. In U. Schneckener and S. Wolff (eds), *Managing and Settling Ethnic Conflicts: Perspectives on Successes and Failures in Europe, Africa and Asia*. London: Hurst & Company.

Adeney, K. (2009) 'The limitations of non-consociational federalism – the example of Pakistan'. *Ethnopolitics*, 8(1): 87–106.

Afzal, M. (2015) *Education and Attitudes in Pakistan: Understanding Perceptions of Terrorism*. United States Institute of Peace Special Report 367.

Afzal, M. (2018a) *Order from Chaos. Did Pakistan's Imran Khan Win a "Dirty" Election or a Real Mandate?* Available: www.brookings.edu/blog/order-from-chaos/2018/ 07/27/did-pakistans-imran-khan-win-a-dirty-election-or-a-real-mandate/ (accessed 5 November 2018).

Afzal, M. (2018b) *Order from Chaos. A Volatile Election Season in Pakistan*. Available: www.brookings.edu/blog/order-from-chaos/2018/07/20/a-volatile-election-seas on-in-pakistan/ (accessed 5 November 2018).

Ahmed, I. (2002) 'The 1947 partition of India: A paradigm for pathological politics in India and Pakistan'. *Asian Ethnicity*, 3(1): 9–28.

Ahmad, M. (2018) 'The slain "militant" was a model, and a Karachi police commander is out'. *New York Times*. Available: www.nytimes.com/2018/01/23/world/asia/ka rachi-police-rao-anwar-naqeebullah-mehsud.html (accessed 30 April 2018).

Ahmed, Z. S. and M. J. Stephan (2010) 'Fighting for the rule of law: Civil resistance and the lawyers' movement in Pakistan'. *Democratization*, 17(3): 492–13.

Akbar, A. (2017) 'Mardan university student lynched by mob over alleged blasphemy: Police'. *Dawn*. Available: www.dawn.com/news/1326729 (accessed 1 July 2017).

Akhtar, A. S. (2018) *The Politics of Common Sense: State, Society and Culture in Pakistan*. Cambridge: Cambridge University Press.

Akhtar, A. S. and A. N. Ahmad (2015) 'Conspiracy and statecraft in postcolonial states: Theories and realities of the hidden hand in Pakistan's war on terror'. *Third World Quarterly*, 36(1): 94–110.

Al Jazeera (2013) 'How important is Pakistan's youth vote?' *The Stream*. Available: http: //stream.aljazeera.com/story/201305080011-0022739 (accessed 10 June 2017).

Al Jazeera (2016) 'Quetta attack: ISIL and Taliban claim suicide bombing'. Available: www.aljazeera.com/news/2016/08/pakistan-blast-quetta-hospital-lawyer-killed-1608 08050839643.html (accessed 10 April 2017).

Al Jazeera (2017) 'Pakistani crackdown on online anti-army campaigners'. Available: www.aljazeera.com/news/2017/05/pakistani-crackdown-online-anti-army-campaigners-170522103450072.html (accessed 23 June 2017).

Al Jazeera (2018) 'Geo goes dark: Media and the military in Pakistan'. *The Listening Post*. www.aljazeera.com/programmes/listeningpost/2018/04/geo-dark-media-military-pakistan-180413213149760.html

Ali, I. (2015) '43 killed in attack on bus carrying Ismailis in Karachi'. *Dawn*. Available: www.dawn.com/news/1181698 (accessed 30 April 2018).

Ali, U. (2016) 'Junaid Hafeez: Condemned forever?' *DAWN*. Available: www.dawn.com/news/1258426 (accessed 2 June 2016).

Ali, N. S. and F. Zaman (2016) 'Anatomy of a murder'. *Herald*. Available: http://herald.dawn.com/news/1153209 (accessed 23 June 2017).

Allcott, H. and M. Gentzkow (2017) 'Social media and fake news in the 2016 election'. *Journal of Economic Perspectives*, 31(2): 211–36.

Altbach, P. G. (1970) 'Student movements in historical perspective: The Asian case'. *Journal of Southeast Asian Studies*, 1(1): 74–84.

Amnesty International (2016) *"As Good as Dead": The Impact of the Blasphemy Laws in Pakistan*. London: Amnesty International Ltd.

Anderson, B. (1983) *Imagined Communities: Reflections on the Origin and Spread of Nationalism*. London: Verso.

Aziz F. (2018) 'Pakistan's cybercrime law: Boon or bane?' *Heinrich Böll Foundation*. Available: www.boell.de/en/2018/02/07/pakistans-cybercrime-law-boon-or-bane (accessed 12 April 2018).

Aziz, K. K. (2010) *The Murder of History. A Critique of History Textbooks used in Pakistan*. Lahore: Sang-e-Meel Publications.

B

Bajwa, S. (2015) 'Agents and articulators of change: Student politics and the state in West Pakistan 1940s–1971'. *Masala, Jahrgang*, 10(1): 12–18.

Balibar, E. (2010) 'Antinomies of citizenship'. *Journal of Romance Studies*, 10(2): 1–20.

Ball, S. (2003) *Class Strategies and the Education Market: The Middle Classes and Social Advantage*. London: Routledge.

Bano, M. (2009) 'Marker of identity: Religious political parties and welfare work – The case of Jama'at-i-Islami in Pakistan and Bangladesh'. *Religions and Development Working Paper 34*. University of Birmingham.

Barker, M. (2018) 'Former Pakistani PM Nawaz Sharif sentenced to 10 years in jail'. *The Guardian*. Available: www.theguardian.com/world/2018/jul/06/former-pakistani-leader-nawaz-sharif-sentenced-to-10-years-in-jail (accessed 5 November 2018).

Basharat, R. (2017) 'Liberal faculty fears being under "surveillance" at Hazara University'. *Nation*. Available: https://nation.com.pk/28-Oct-2017/liberal-faculty-fears-being-under-surveillance-at-hazara-university (accessed 15 April 2018).

BBC News (2013) 'Quetta: Shia Hazaras refuse to bury Pakistan bomb dead'. Available: www.bbc.com/news/world-asia-21495975 (accessed 30 April 2016).

BBC News (2017a) 'Pakistan blogger Aasim Saeed says he was tortured'. Available: www.bbc.com/news/world-asia-41662595 (accessed 25 December 2017).

BBC News (2017b) 'Pakistan asks Facebook to help fight blasphemy'. Available: www.bbc.com/news/world-asia-39300270 (accessed 23 May 2017).

BBC News (2017c) 'Pakistan activist Waqass Goraya: The state tortured me'. Available: www.bbc.com/news/world-asia-39219307 (accessed 23 May 2017).

BBC News (2017d) 'Pakistan blogger Aasim Saeed says he was tortured'. Available: www.bbc.com/news/world-asia-41662595 (accessed 25 December 2017).

BBC News (2018a) 'The "angels" at play in Pakistan election'. Available: www.bbc.com/news/world-asia-44899054 (accessed5 February 2019).

BBC News (2018b) 'Pakistan polio: Mother and daughter killed giving vaccinations'. Available: www.bbc.com/news/world-asia-42738360 (accessed 30 April 2018).

BBC News (2019), 'Pakistan to get $6bn IMF lifeline to ease economic crisis', *BBC*, 13 May. Available online: https://www.bbc.co.uk/news/business-48250399 (accessed 20 July 2019).

Benhabib, S. (2005) 'Borders, boundaries and citizenship'. *Political Science and Politics*, 38(4): 673–7.

Birmani T. S. (2018) 'Seraiki province a solution to many problems: Zardari'. *Dawn*. Available: www.dawn.com/news/1386361 (accessed 15 April 2018).

Bolognani, M. (2010) 'Virtual protest with tangible effects? Some observations on the media strategies of the 2007 Pakistani anti-Emergency movement'. *Contemporary South Asia*, 18(4): 401–12.

Bolognani, M. (2011). 'Rang de Basanti in Pakistan: Elite student activism in 2007 Pakistan State of Emergency'. In M. Bolognani and S. M. Lyon (eds), *Pakistan and its Diaspora: Multidisciplinary Approaches*. New York: Palgrave.

Bolognani, M. and S. Lyons (eds) (2011) *Pakistan and Its Diaspora: Multidisciplinary Approaches*. New York: Palgrave Macmillan.

Boone, J. (2015) 'Peshawar school attack: One year on "the country is changed completely"'. *Guardian*. www.theguardian.com/world/2015/dec/16/peshawar-school-attack-one-year-on-the-country-is-changed-completely (accessed 26 December 2017).

Braungart, R. G. (1971) 'Family status, socialization, and student politics: A multivariate analysis'. *American Journal of Sociology*, 77(1): 108–30.

British Council (2013) *Pakistan: The next generation goes to the ballot Box*. Islamabad: British Council Pakistan.

British Council (2013) Pakistan: Next Generation Voices in Conflict & Violence Youth Survey 2012-2013 National Data. Available: www.britishcouncil.pk/programmes/so ciety/next-generation (accessed 30 October 2018).

British Council NGBB Report (2013) *The Next Generation Goes to the Ballot Box*. Available: www.britishcouncil.pk/sites/default/files/next_generation_goes_to_the_ballot_box.pdf (accessed 30 October 2018).

Brown, H., E. Guskin and A. Mitchell (2012) 'The role of social media in the Arab uprisings'. *Pew Research Center*. Available: www.journalism.org/2012/11/28/role-social-media-arab-uprisings/ (accessed 23 May 2017).

Buncombe, A. (2014) 'Pakistani academic accused of blasphemy shot dead in Karachi'. *Independent*. Available: www.independent.co.uk/news/world/asia/pakistani-academic-accused-of-blasphemy-shot-dead-in-karachi-9744154.html (accessed 2 February 2016).

Bute, S. (2014) 'The role of social media in mobilizing people for riots and revolutions four case studies in India'. In B. Pătrut and M. Pătrut (eds), *Social Media in Politics. Case Studies on the Political Power of Social Media (Public Administration and Information Technology Vol. 13)*. London: Springer.

C

Cadwalladr, C. and E. Graham-Harrison (2018) 'Revealed: 50 million Facebook profiles harvested for Cambridge Analytica in major data breach'. *Guardian*. Available: www.theguardian.com/news/2018/mar/17/cambridge-analytica-facebook-influence-us-election (accessed 12 April 2018).

Centre of Civic Education Pakistan (2009) *Political participation of youth in Pakistan*. Islamabad: CCE and NDI.

Cheema, A. and A. Liaqat (2017) 'Political attitudes in Lahore and the 2018 elections – policy brief'. *Institute of Development and Economic Alternatives (IDEAS)*. Available: https://ideaspak.org/images/Publications/Governance-Institutions/PoliticalAttitudesLahore2018Election-PolicyBrief-April2017.pdf (accessed 12 April 2019).

Citizen Lab (2013) *O Pakistan We Stand on Guard for Three: An Analysis of Canada-based Netsweeper's Role in Pakistan's Censorship Regime. Research Brief*. University of Toronto.

Clark, J., R. Faris, R. Morrison-Westphal, H. Noman, C. Tilton and J. Zittrain (2017) *The Shifting Landscape of Global Internet Censorship*. Berkman Klein Center for Internet & Society Research Publication.

Cohen, S. (2011) *The Future of Pakistan*. Washington DC: Brookings Institution Press.

Committee to Protect Journalists (CPJ) (2019), 'Pakistani journalist arrested for critical Twitter posts', *CPJ*, February 9. Available online: https://cpj.org/2019/02/pakistani-journalist-arrested-for-critical-twitter.php (accessed 20 July 2019).

Constable, P. (2016) 'Police in Pakistan hunt Christian accused of blasphemy for online poem'. *Washington Post*. Available: www.washingtonpost.com/news/worldviews/wp/2016/07/12/police-in-pakistan-hunt-christian-accused-of-blasphemy-for-online-poem/?noredirect=on&utm_term=.679d3334e986 (accessed 30 September 2017).

Crick, B. (1998) *Education for Citizenship and the Teaching of Democracy in Schools.* Final report of the Advisory Group on Citizenship. London: Qualifications and Curriculum Authority. Available: http://dera.ioe.ac.uk/4385/1/crickreport1998.pdf (accessed 15 June 2015).

Crick, B. (2000) *Essays in Citizenship*. London: Continuum.

Cristancho, C. (2015) 'Social media in the mobilisation of anti austerity protest'. In EU-LAC Foundation (ed.), *Social Protests and Democratic Responsiveness: Assessing Realities in Latin America and the Caribbean and the European Union*. Hamburg: EU-LAC Foundation.

D

Dad, M. and S. Khan (2017) 'Naila Rind killed herself because Pakistan's cybercrime laws failed her'. Available: www.dawn.com/news/1306976 (accessed 20 February 2018).

Daily Times (2017) 'Noreen blames social media for her radicalization'. Available: https://dailytimes.com.pk/12187/noreen-blames-social-media-for-her-radicalisation/ (accessed 18 February 2018).

Davies, I. (2008) 'Political literacy'. In J. Arthur, I. Davies, and C. Hahn (eds), *The Sage Handbook of Education for Citizenship and Democracy*. London: Sage, 377–87

Dawn (2015) 'The Pakistan govt is asking Facebook for user data – and the giant is complying'. Available: www.dawn.com/news/1220071 (accessed 21 January 2018).

Dawn (2016) *Transcript of RAW Agent Kulbhushan's Confessional Statement.* Available: www.dawn.com/news/1248786 (accessed 24 March 2018).

Dawn (2017a) '"Terrorist" killed, wife held in Lahore encounter'. Available: www.dawn.com/news/1327252/terrorist-killed-wife-held-in-lahore-encounter (accessed 18 February 2018).

Dawn (2017b) 'Interior minister says wants to track each social media user's activities online'. Available: www.dawn.com/news/1334930 (accessed 20 June 2017).

Dawn (2018) 'Paigham-i-Pakistan'. Available: www.dawn.com/news/1383642 (accessed 15 April 2018).

Dawn News (2019), 'Journalists stage protests to denounce censorship', *Dawn*, 16 July. Available online: https://www.dawn.com/news/1494418 (accessed 27 July 2019).

Dean, B. L. (2004) 'Pakistani conceptions of "Citizenship" and their implications for democratic citizenship education. In K. Muendel and D. Schugurensky, *Lifelong Citizenship Learning, Participatory Democracy and Social Change*. Toronto: TLC.

Dean, B. L. (2005) 'Citizenship education in Pakistani Schools: Problems and possibilities'. *International Journal of Citizenship and Teacher Education*, 1(2): 35–55.

Dean, B. L. (2007) *The State of Civic Education in Pakistan*, Research Report, IED. Karachi: Aga Khan University.

De Souza, R., S. Palshikar and Y. Yadav (2008). 'The democracy barometers, surveying South Asia'. *Journal of Democracy*, 19(1): 84–96.

Dewey, J. (1910) *How We Think*. USA: Heath and Co.

Digital Rights Foundation (2015) *Pakistan: New Cybercrime Bill Threatens the Rights to Privacy and Free Expression*. Available: https://digitalrightsfoundation.pk/new-cybercrime-bill-threatens-the-rights-to-privacy-and-free-expression-in-pakistan/ (accessed 5 November 2018).

Dorsey, J. M. (2018) 'Crunch time in Pakistan'. *South Asia Journal*. Available: http://southasiajournal.net/crunch-time-in-pakistan/ (accessed 5 November 2018).

Durrani, N., A. Halai, L. Kadiwal, S. K. Rajput, M. Novelli and Y. Sayed (2015) *Education and Social Cohesion in Pakistan: An Analysis of Policies, Teachers and Youth*. Pakistan Country Report.

E

Eltantawy, N. and J. B. Wiest (2011) 'Social media in the Egyptian revolution: Reconsidering resource mobilization theory'. *International Journal of Communication*, 5: 1207–24.

European Union Election Observation Mission (EU EOM) (2018) *Islamic Republic of Pakistan. European Union Election Observation Mission. Final Report General Elections, 25 July 2018*. Available: https://cdn1-eeas.fpfis.tech.ec.europa.eu/cdn/farfuture/7OsUPfcoQp4IOwOLiZfEi1dOhrRtwb_1lar-9AxZvQk/mtime:1540558548/sites/eeas/files/final_report_pakistan_2018_english.pdf (accessed 30 November 2018).

Express Tribune (2012) 'PTI to target youth for next elections: Imran'. Available: https://tribune.com.pk/story/348814/pti-to-target-youth-for-next-elections-imran/ (accessed 15 June 2015).

Express Tribune (2016) 'Kohli's Pakistani fan arrested for hoisting Indian flag on rooftop'. Available: http://tribune.com.pk/story/1035006/kohlis-pakistani-fan-arrested-for-hoisting-indian-flag-on-rooftop/ (accessed 2 February 2016).

Express Tribune (2017a) 'Army museum opens doors to public in Lahore'. Available: https://tribune.com.pk/story/1502658/army-museum-opens-doors-public-lahore/ (accessed 15 January 2018).

Express Tribune (2017b) 'Curbing terrorism: Youth being exploited by terrorist groups, says army chief'. Available: https://tribune.com.pk/story/1412867/nature-character-extremism-changed-dg-ispr/ (accessed 25 March 2018).

Express Tribune (2017c) 'Karachi University's associate professor "whisked away by LEAs"'. Available: https://tribune.com.pk/story/1522036/karachi-universitys-associate-professor-whisked-away-leas/ (accessed 30 April 2017).

Express Tribune (2018) 'Mobile app to report hate speech launched'. Available: https://tribune.com.pk/story/1658274/1-safe-city-project-mobile-app-report-hate-speech-launched/ (accessed 13 April 2018).

F

Facebook (2018) *Pakistan January 2017–June 2017*. Available: https://transparency.facebook.com/country/Pakistan/2017-H1/ (accessed 30 January 2018).

Facebook Audience Insights (2017) taken from https://www.facebook.com/business/insights/tools/audience-insights

Fair, C. C. (2008) 'The educated militants of Pakistan: Implications for Pakistan's domestic security'. *Contemporary South Asia*, 16(1): 93–106.

Farooq, U. (2014) 'Alternate mobilisation: PTI's secret weapon – their social media team'. *The Express Tribune*. Available: https://tribune.com.pk/story/660080/alternate-mobilisation-ptis-secret-weapon-their-social-media-team/ (accessed 2 July 2017).

Feyyaz, M. (2015) 'Why Pakistan does not have a counterterrorism narrative'. *Journal of Strategic Security*, 8(1–2): 63–78.

Finkel, S. E. and H. R. Ernst (2005) 'Civic education in post-apartheid South Africa: Alternative paths to the development of political knowledge and democratic values'. *Political Psychology*, 26(3): 333–64.

Fogel, J. and E. Nehmad (2009) 'Internet social network communities: Risk taking, trust, and privacy concerns'. *Computers in Human Behavior*, 25: 153–60.

Freedom House (2016) *Freedom on the Net 2016*. Available: https://freedomhouse.org/report/freedom-net/2016/pakistan (accessed 23 May 2017).

Freedom House (2017) *Freedom on the Net*. Available: https://freedomhouse.org/sites/default/files/FOTN%202017_Pakistan.pdf

Freire, P. (1972) *Pedagogy of the Oppressed*. M. B. Ramos, trans. New York: Penguin Books.

G

Gabol I., N. Haider, W. Riaz, A. Akbar and A. Haider (2015) '15 killed in Taliban attack on Lahore churches'. *Dawn*. Available: www.dawn.com/news/1169713/15-killed-in-taliban-attack-on-lahore-churches (accessed 20 March 2017).

Gallup Pakistan (2019), *Public Opinion Report on Federal Government and Politics July 219*. Islamabad: Gallup Pakistan.

Gayer, L (2007) 'Guns, slums, and "yellow devils": A genealogy of urban conflicts in Karachi, Pakistan'. *Modern Asian Studies*, 41(03): 515–44.

Giroux, H. A. (2003) 'Selling out higher education'. *Policy Futures in Education*, 1(1): 179–200.

Government of Pakistan (1947) *Proceedings of the Pakistan Educational Conference, held at Karachi, from 27th November to 1st December 1947*. Karachi: Ministry of the Interior (Education Division), Govt. of Pakistan [1952].

Government of Pakistan (2019), *Budget in Brief 2019-20*. Available online: http://www.finance.gov.pk/budget/Budget_in_Brief_2019_20.pdf (accessed July 27, 2019).

H

Haider, S. (2013) 'Youth to play decisive role in coming election, shows ECP data'. *Dawn*. Available: www.dawn.com/news/796759/youth-to-play-eciding-role-in-upcoming-eleftions-shows-ecp-data (accessed 15 June 2015).

Haider, S. (2018) 'Salman Haider: "Tafsheesh karne waali nei warning dee dekho baahir jakar maulvi na ban jana" (The interrogator gave me a warning: look don't turn into a maulvi once you are released)'. *BBC Urdu*. Available: www.bbc.com/urdu/pakistan-42577193 (accessed 20 February 2018).

Hanif, M. (2010) 'Why Pakistan's Ahmadi community is officially detested'. *BBC News*. Available: http://news.bbc.co.uk/2/hi/8744092.stm (accessed 4 May 2016).

Hasan, A. (2002) 'The roots of elite alienation'. *Economic and Political Weekly*, 37: 44–5. Available: www.epw.in/journal/2002/44-45/special-articles/roots-elite-alienation.html (accessed 15 June 2015).

Hashim, A. (2015) 'Blasphemy in Pakistan: Anatomy of a lynching'. *Al Jazeera*. Available: http://america.aljazeera.com/articles/2015/6/20/blasphemy-in-pakistan-anatomy-of-a-lynching.html (accessed 30 April 2018).

Hashim, A. (2017a) 'Pakistan ruling party wins key by-election in Lahore'. *Al Jazeera*. Available: www.aljazeera.com/news/2017/09/voting-concludes-key-pakistan-election-170917124556192.html (accessed 30 April 2018).

Hashim, A. (2017b) 'Parched for a price: Karachi's water crisis'. *Al Jazeera*. Available: https://interactive.aljazeera.com/aje/2017/parched-for-price/index.html (accessed 29 March 2018).

Hashim, A. (2018) 'Suspect in Lahore blasphemy case fighting for his life'. *Al Jazeera*. Available: www.aljazeera.com/news/2018/03/suspect-lahore-blasphemy-case-fighting-life-180303085358736.html (accessed 30 April 2018).

Hayes, L. D. (1987) *The Crisis of Education in Pakistan*. Lahore: Vanguard Books.

Holston, J. (2008) *Insurgent Citizenship. Disjunctions of Democracy and Modernity in Brazil*. Bradford: Princeton University Press.

Hoodbhoy, P. (2007) Pakistan: The threat from within. Research Briefing No. 13, *Pakistan Security Research Unit (PSRU)*, University of Bradford, United Kingdom.

Hooks, B. (1994) *Teaching to Transgress Education as the Practice of Freedom*. London: Routledge.

Hoskins, B., J. G. Janmaat and E. Villalba (2012) 'Learning citizenship through social participation outside and inside school: An international, multilevel study of young people's learning of citizenship'. *British Educational Research Journal*, 38(3): 419–46.

Howard, P. N., S. Savage, C. F. Saviaga, C. Toxtli and A. Monroy-Hemandez (2016) 'Social media, civic engagement, and the slacktivism hypothesis: Lessons from Mexico's "El Bronco"'. *Journal of International Affairs*, 70(1): 55–73.

Human Rights Commission of Pakistan (HRCP) (2016) *State of Human Rights in Pakistan 2016*. Available: http://hrcp-web.org/hrcpweb/wp-content/uploads/2017/05/State-of-Human-Rights-in-2016.pdf (accessed 30 April 2018).

Human Rights Watch (HRW) (2017) *Pakistan: Escalating Crackdown on Internet Dissent*. Available: www.hrw.org/news/2017/05/16/pakistan-escalating-crackdown-internet-dissent (accessed 30 April 2018).

Hussain, A. (1976) 'Ethnicity, national identity and praetorianism: The case of Pakistan'. *Asian Survey*, 16(10): 918–30.

Hussain, I. (2018) *Governing the Ungovernable: Institutional Reforms for Democratic Governance*. Pakistan: Oxford University Press.

Hussain, Y. (2014) 'Social media as a tool for transparency and good governance in the government of Gilgit-Baltistan, Pakistan'. *Crossroads Asia Working Paper Series*, 22. https://bonndoc.ulb.uni-bonn.de/xmlui/handle/20.500.11811/155

I

Imam, Z. (2016) 'The day I declared my best friend kafir just so I could get a passport'. *DAWN*. Available: www.dawn.com/news/1261622 (accessed 10 June 2016).

Inayat, N. (2017) 'Pakistanis say their government has "weaponized" its blasphemy law'. *Public Radio International*. Available: www.pri.org/stories/2017-05-19/pakistanis-say-their-government-has-weaponized-its-blasphemy-law (accessed 1 June 2017).

International Crisis Group (ICG) (2004) 'Pakistan: Reforming the education sector'. *Asia Report No. 84*.

International Crisis Group (ICG) (2014a) 'Education reform in Pakistan'. *Asia Report No. 257*.

International Crisis Group (2014b) Policing urban violence in Pakistan. *Asia Report No. 255*: 1–49.

International Crisis Group (2015) 'Revisiting counter-terrorism strategies in Pakistan: Opportunities and pitfalls'. *Asia Report No.* 271: 1–38.

International Crisis Group (2016) 'Pakistan's Jihadist heartland: Southern Punjab'. *Asia Report No. 279*: 1–26.

Internet Live Stats (2016) *Pakistan Internet Users*. Available: www.internetlivestats.com/internet-users/pakistan/ (accessed 1 July 2017).

Iqbal, M. (2013) 'To vote or not to vote: Will the youth decide the country's future?' *Express Tribune*. Available: https://tribune.com.pk/story/546292/to-vote-or-not-to-vote-will-the-youth-decide-the-countrys-future/ (accessed 15 June 2016).

Iqtidar, H. (2011) *Secularizing Islamists. Jama'at-e-Islami and Jama'at-ud-Da'wa in Urban Pakistan*. Chicago: Chicago University Press.

Islam, N. (1981) 'Islam and national identity: The case of Pakistan and Bangladesh'. *International Journal of Middle East Studies*, 13(1): 55–72.

J

Jahangir, R. (2018) 'Religious parties clinch over 9pc share of votes in National Assembly'. *Dawn*. Available: www.dawn.com/news/1424235 (accessed 5 November 2018).

Jinnah Institute (JI) (2013) *Apolitical or depoliticised? Pakistan's Youth and Politics*. Islamabad: Friedrich Naumann Stiftung and Jinnah Institute.

Joppke, C. (2007) 'Transformation of citizenship: Status rights, identity'. *Citizenship Studies*, 11(1): 37–48.

Jorgic, D. (2018) "'Aliens" and "angels": Euphemisms mask Pakistani election fears'. *Reuters*. Available: https://in.reuters.com/article/pakistan-politics-language/aliens-and-angels-euphemisms-mask-pakistani-election-fears-idINKCN1J21US (accessed 5 February 2019).

Justice Project Pakistan (2017) 'Trial and terror. The overreach of Pakistan's anti-terrorism act'. Available: www.jpp.org.pk/wp-content/uploads/2017/11/2017_11_13_PRIV_ATA-Report-Final.pdf (accessed 25 March 2018).

K

Kahne, J. and B. Bowyer (2018) 'The political significance of social media activity and social networks'. *Political Communication*, 35(3): 470–93.

Kamal, D. (2017) 'Policing cybercrime: A comparative analysis of the prevention of electronic crimes bill'. *Jinnah Institute Policy Brief*. Available: https://jinnah-institute.org/opinions/policy-brief-a-comparative-analysis-of-the-prevention-of-electronic-crimes-bill/

Kamran, H. (2017) 'Facebook releases government transparency report and it's worrying'. *Digital Rights Foundation*. Available: http://digitalrightsfoundation.pk/facebook-releases-government-transparency-report-and-its-worrying/ (accessed 21 February 2018).

Kanungo, N. T. (2015) 'India's digital poll battle: Political parties and social media in the 16th Lok Sabha elections'. *Studies in Indian Politics*, 3(2): 212–28.

Kaplan, A. M. and M. Haenlein (2010) 'Users of the world, unite! The challenges and opportunities of social media'. *Business Horizons*, 53: 59–68.

Karlsen, R., K. Steen-Johnsen, D. Wollebæk and B. Enjolras (2017) 'Echo chamber and trench warfare dynamics in online debates'. *European Journal of Communication*, 32(3): 257–73.

Keating, A., D. Kerr, T. Benton, E. Mundy and J. Lopes (2010) *Citizenship Education in England 2001-2010: Young People's Practices and Prospects for the Future: The Eighth and Final Report from the Citizenship Education Longitudinal Study (CELS)*. Available: https://assets.publishing.service.gov.uk/government/uploads/system/uploads/attachment_data/file/181797/DFE-RR059.pdf (accessed 21 February 2018).

Khamsi, G. S. (2014) 'Cross-national policy borrowing: Understanding reception and translation'. *Asia Pacific Journal of Education*, 34(2): 153–67.

Khan A. H. (1997) 'Education in Pakistan: Fifty years of neglect'. *The Pakistan Development Review*, 36(4): 647–67.

Khan, A. and Erik C. Nisbet (2016) 'Benchmarking demand: Pakistan and the internet users' perspective'. Internet Policy Observatory. Retrieved from http://repository.upenn.edu/internetpolicyobservatory/21

Khyber Pukhtunkhwa Textbook Board (2015–16a) *Islamiyat 8*. Peshawar: University Book Printers and Publishers (Pvt) Ltd.

Khyber Pukhtunkhwa Textbook Board (2015–16b) *Muashriti Aloom Jamaat Panjum (Social Studies Grade 5)*. Peshawar: Leading Books Publisher.

Kim, S. K., M. J. Park and J. J. Rho (2015) 'Effect of the government's use of social media on the reliability of the government: Focus on Twitter'. *Public Management Review*, 17(3): 328–55.

Kirstein, R. and S. Voigt (2006) 'The violent and the weak: When dictators care about social contracts'. *The American Journal of Economics and Sociology*, 65(4): 863–90.

Kivisto, P. and T. Faist (2007) *Citizenship: Discourse, Theory and Transnational Prospects*. Oxford, UK: Blackwell Publishingbook.

Kleinhans, R., M. V. Ham and J. Evans-Cowley (2015) 'Using social media and mobile technologies to Foster engagement and self-organization in participatory urban planning and neighbourhood governance'. *Planning, Practice & Research*, 30(3): 237–47.

Kolsy, U. (2013) 'How a fringe Pakistani politician is using Obama's campaign strategies'. *The Atlantic*. Available: www.theatlantic.com/international/archive/2013/04/how-a-fringe-pakistani-politician-is-using-obamas-campaign-strategies/274553/ (accessed 1 June 2017).

Korson, J. H. (ed.) (1974) *Contemporary Problems of Pakistan*. The Netherlands: Brill.

Kugelman, M. (2012) *Prospects for Youth-led Movements for Political Change in Pakistan*. Policy Brief. Oslo: NOREF.

Kuisma, M. (2008) 'Rights or privileges? The challenge of globalization on the values of citizenship'. *Citizenship Studies*, 12(6): 613–27.

Kymlicka, W. and W. Norman (eds), (2000) *Citizenship in Diverse Societies*. Oxford: Oxford University Press.

L

Lall, M. (2009) 'Education dilemmas in Pakistan: The current curriculum reform'. In M. Lall and E. Vickers (eds), *Education as a Political Tool in Asia*. Oxford: Routledge.

Lall, M. (2010) 'What role for Islam today? The political Islamisation of Pakistani society'. In A. Khan (ed.), *Shaping a Nation: An Examination of Education in Pakistan*, part of the series Oxford in Pakistan Readings in Sociology and Social Anthropology edited by Steven Lyon. Lahore: Oxford University Press.

Lall, M. (2012) 'Citizenship in Pakistan: State, nation and contemporary faultlines'. *Contemporary Politics*, 18(1): 71–86.

Lall, M. (2014) 'Engaging the youth – citizenship and political participation in Pakistan'. *Commonwealth & Comparative Politics*, 52(4): 535–62.

Lall, M. et al. (2014) *Citizenship in Myanmar: Contemporary Debates and Challenges in Light of the Reform Process.* Yangon and Bangkok: Myanmar Egress and FNS.

Lall, M. and G. Nambissan (eds), (2011) *Education and Social Justice in the Era of Globalisation – India and the UK.* New Delhi: Routledge.

Lall, M. and E. Vickers (eds), (2009) *Education as a Political Tool in Asia.* UK: Routledge.

Lieven, A. (2011) *Pakistan: A Hard Country.* London: Penguin.

Lloyd, M. (1999) 'Violence recedes at U. of Karachi, but Pakistani politics persists'. *The Chronicle of Higher Education*, 45: 29. Available: www.chronicle.com/article/Violence-Recedes-at-U-of/28417 (accessed 1 March 2019).

Lyon, S. M. (2002). *Power and Patronage in Pakistan* (PhD thesis). Available: www.dur.ac.uk/s.m.lyon/Publications/Lyon.pdf (accessed 1 March 2019).

M

Masood, S. (2017) 'Pakistan church attacked by 2 suicide bombers'. *New York Times.* Available: www.nytimes.com/2017/12/17/world/asia/pakistan-quetta-church-attack.html (accessed 28 March 2018).

Ministry of Education (1961) *Report of the Commission on National Education January–August 1959.*Karachi: Government of Pakistan.

Ministry of Education (1966) *Report of the Commission on Student Problems and Welfare.* Karachi: Government of Pakistan.

Ministry of Education (1992) *Development of Education, 1990–1992 National Report of Pakistan.* Islamabad: Ministry of Education.

Ministry of Education (2006) *National Curriculum for Pakistan Studies Grades IX–X 2006.* Islamabad: Government of Pakistan.

Ministry of Education (2009) *National Education Policy 2009.* Government of Pakistan.

Ministry of Interior (2014) *National Internal Security Policy 2014–2018.* Government of Pakistan.

Ministry of Interior (2014) *National Internal Security Policy (NISP).* Available: https://nacta.gov.pk/nisp-2014/. Government of Pakistan.

Mirza, S. H. (1991) *The Punjab Muslim Students Federation 1937–1947.* Islamabad: National Institute of Historical and Cultural Research.

Mirza, S. H. (1989) *Muslim Students and Pakistan Movement: Selected Documents (1937–1947) Volume 3.* Lahore: Starlite Press.

Mitra, S. (2008) 'Level playing fields: The post-colonial state, democracy, courts and citizenship in India'. *German Law Journal*, 9(3): 343–66.

Mohammad-Arif, A. (2005) 'Textbooks, nationalism and history writing in India and Pakistan'. In V. Benei (ed.), *Manufacturing Citizenship: Education and Nationalism in Europe, South Asia and China*. UK, London: Routledge.

Montgomery, K. C. (2015) 'Youth and surveillance in the Facebook era: Policy interventions and social implications'. *Telecommunications Policy*, 39: 771–86.

Mullick, H. A. H. (2008) 'Towards a civic culture – student activism and political dissent in Pakistan'. *Georgetown Journal of International Affairs*, 9(2): 5–12.

Mushtaq, W. (2019), 'Analysis: Pakistani media face growing censorship', *BBC Monitoring*, 12 July. Available online: https://monitoring.bbc.co.uk/product/c200y1ly (accessed 20 July 2019).

N

Naqvi, T. (2012) 'Migration, sacrifice and the crisis of Muslim nationalism. *Journal of Refugee Studies*, 25(3): 474–90.

Nasr S. V. R. (1992). 'Students, Islam, and Politics: Islami Jamiat-i-Tuleba in Pakistan'. *Middle East Journal*, 46:1, 59–76.

National Assembly Secretariat (2016) *Prevention of Electronic Crimes Act 2016*. Available: www.na.gov.pk/uploads/documents/1472635250_246.pdf (accessed 1 June 2017).

National Commission for Justice and Peace (NCJP) (2013) *Education vs Fanatic Literacy. A Study on the Hate Content in the Textbooks in Punjab and Sindh Provinces.*

National Counter Terrorism Authority (NACTA) Pakistan (2018) *National Counter Extremism Policy Guidelines*. Government of Pakistan.

Nayyar, A. H. and Salim A. (eds), (2003) *The Subtle Subversion: The State of Curricula and Textbooks in Pakistan – Urdu, English, Social Studies and Civics*. Sustainable Development Policy Institute.

Nazir, M. (2010) 'Democracy and education in Pakistan'. *Educational Review*, 62(3): 329–42.

Nelson, M. J. (2008) 'Religious education in non-religious schools: A comparative study of Pakistan and Bangladesh'. *Commonwealth & Comparative Politics*, 46(3): 271–95.

Nelson, M. J. (2009) *Religion, Politics and the Modern University in Pakistan and Bangladesh* (NBR Project Report). Washington DC: The National Bureau of Asian Research.

Nelson, M. J. (2009) 'Dealing with difference: Religious education and the challenge of democracy in Pakistan'. *Modern Asian Studies*, 43(3): 591–618.

Nelson, M. J. (2011) 'Embracing the Ummah: Student politics beyond state power in Pakistan'. *Modern Asian Studies*, 45(3): 565–96.

News (2014) '72-year-old Mama Qadeer Baloch breaks record of Gandhi after 84 years'. Available: www.thenews.com.pk/archive/print/636350-72-year-old-mama-qadeer-baloch-breaks-record-of-gandhi-after-84-years (accessed 15 June 2016).

Niens, U. and M. Chastenay (2008) 'Educating for peace? Citizenship education in Quebec and Northern Ireland'. *Comparative Education Review*, 52(4): 519–40.

O

Obar, J. A. and S. Wildman (2015) 'Social media definition and the governance challenge: An introduction to the special issue'. *Telecommunications Policy*, 39: 745–50.

Olsen, M. and M. A. Peters (2005) 'Neoliberalism, higher education and the knowledge economy: From the free market to knowledge capitalism'. *Journal of Education Policy*, 20(3): 313–45.

Outlook Pakistan (OP) (2017) 'NACTA briefs CM KPK on national counter extremism policy'. Available: www.outlookpakistan.com/nacta-cm-kpk-national-counter-extremism-policy/13882/ (accessed 15 April 2018).

P

Pakistan Army (2017) *Role of Youth in Rejecting Extremism Seminar 18.05.2017.* Available: www.pakistanarmy.gov.pk/AWPReview/pDetails.aspx?pType=PressRelease&pId=994 (accessed 29 March 2018).

Pakistan Telecommunications Authority (PTA) (2017) *Annual Report 2017.*

Pakistan Today (2017a) 'A timeline of Faizabad sit-in'. Available: www.pakistantoday.com.pk/2017/11/28/a-timeline-of-faizabad-sit-in/ (accessed 29 March 2018).

Pakistan Today (2017b) 'FixIt founder leads protest over poor quality of education'. Available: www.pakistantoday.com.pk/2017/11/19/fixit-founder-leads-protest-over-poor-quality-of-education/ (accessed 29 March 2018).

Pakistan's Youth: Apolitical or Depoliticised? (2013). Available: https://tribune.com.pk/story/594169/pakistans-youth-apolitical-or-depoliticised/

Panjwani, F. and Z. Khimani (2018) 'Misplaces Utopia. education and extremism – the case of Pakistan'. In F. Panjwani, L. Revell , R. Gholami and M. Diboll (eds), *Education and Extremisms: Rethinking Liberal Pedagogies in the Contemporary World.* London: Routledge.

Paracha, N. F. (2000) 'Student politics in Pakistan: A celebration, lament, and history'. Available: http://nadeemfparacha.wordpress.com/student-politics-in-pakistan-a-celebration-lament-history/ (no longer accessible, but abridged version https://www.dawn.com/news/print/1116782) (accessed 20 May 2015).

Pariser, E. (2011) *The Filter Bubble: What the Internet Is Hiding from You.* London: Penguin.

Pasha, H. A., Kardar, S. and Imran, M. (2019), 'Economic impact of IMF program', *Business Recorder*, 20 May. Available online: https://fp.brecorder.com/2019/05/20190520477186/ (accessed 20 July 2019).

Pashtun Long March (2018) Twitter. Available: https://twitter.com/pashtunmarch?lang=en (accessed 28 March 2018).

Peace and Education Foundation (2016) *Teaching Intolerance in Pakistan: Religious Bias in Public School Textbooks*. United States Commission on International Religious Freedom, pp. 2–3.

Pew Research Centre (2014) *Emerging Nations Embrace Internet, Mobile Technology*. Available: www.pewglobal.org/2014/02/13/emerging-nations-embrace-internet-mobile-technology

Pew Research Center (2016) *Most Adults in Advanced Economies Use Internet, Developing Countries Less So*. Available: www.pewglobal.org/2016/02/22/internet-access-growing-worldwide-but-remains-higher-in-advanced-economies/technology-report-02-08/ (accessed 1 July 2017).

Powell, J. (2014) 'Risk, welfare, education and youth international letters of social and humanistic sciences'. *International Letters of Social and Humanistic Sciences*, 7: 22–30.

Print, M. (2007) 'Citizenship education and youth participation in democracy'. *British Journal of Educational Studies*, 55(3): 325–45.

Punjab Curriculum and Textbook Board (2014–15) *Muashriti Aloom Jamaat Panjum (Social Studies Grade 5)* Professor Aftab Ahmad Daar. Lahore: Gohar Publishers.

Punjab Curriculum and Textbook Board (2015–16a) *Islamiyat 8*.

Punjab Curriculum and Textbook Board (2015–16b) *Urdu Quaid o Insha 9–10*. Lahore: Gohar Publishers.

Punjab Curriculum and Textbook Board (2016–17) *Mutaalaeh Pakistan Jamaat Daham* (Pakistan Studies Grade 10), Professor Aftab Ahmad Daar. Lahore: Gohar Publishers.

Q

Qin, B., D. Strömberg and Y. Wu (2017) 'Why does China allow freer social media? Protests versus surveillance and propaganda'. *Journal of Economic Perspectives*, 31(1): 117–40.

R

Rahimi, B. (2011) 'The agonistic social media: Cyberspace in the formation of dissent and consolidation of state power in postelection Iran'. *The Communication Review*, 14(3): 158–78.

Rahman, T. (1998) 'Language-teaching policies in Pakistan'. Research Report Series #14. Sustainable Development Policy Institute.

Rahman, T. (2004) *Denizens of Alien Worlds: A Study of Education, Inequality and Polarization in Pakistan*. UK: Oxford University Press.

Rais, R. B. (2007) 'Identity politics and minorities in Pakistan', *South Asia: Journal of South Asian Studies*, 30(1): 111–25.

Rais, R. B. (2017) *Islam, Ethnicity, and Power Politics: Constructing Pakistan's National Identity*. Pakistan: Oxford University Press.

Rampton, R. and Chiacu, D. (2019), 'Trump, Pakistan's Khan discuss way out of Afghanistan war', *Reuters*, 22 July. Available online: https://uk.reuters.com/article/uk-usa-pakistan/trump-pakistans-khan-discuss-way-out-of-afghanistan-war-idUKKCN1UH20O (accessed 27 July 2019).

Rasmussen, S. E. and K. Baloch (2017) 'Student's lynching sparks rare uproar in Pakistan over blasphemy killings'. *The Guardian*. Available: www.theguardian.com/world/2017/apr/26/lynching-of-a-student-sparks-uproar-in-pakistan-against-blasph emy-laws (accessed 3 June 2017).

Rasmussen, S. E. and W. Gillani (2017) 'Pakistan: Man sentenced to death for blasphemy on Facebook'. *The Guardian*. Available: www.theguardian.com/world /2017/jun/11/pakistan-man-sentenced-to-death-for-blasphemy-on-facebook (accessed 1 July 2017).

Reporters without Borders (RSF) (2019), 'Three Pakistani TV news channels suddenly taken off the air', *RSF*, 9 July. Available online: https://rsf.org/en/news/three-pakistani-tv-news-channels-suddenly-taken-air (accessed July 25, 2019).

Richards, J. (1993) *Mohajir Subnationalism and the Mohajir Qaumi Movement in Sindh Province, Pakistan*. Unpublished doctoral thesis, University of Cambridge.

Ritter, N. and J. Bondanella (1988) *Rousseau's Political Writings*. New York: W. W. Norton & Company.

Ryan, M. (2011) 'Productions of space: Civic participation of young people at university'. *British Educational Research Journal*, 37(6): 1015–31.

S

Saigol, R. (2003) *Becoming a Modern Nation: Educational Discourse in the Early Year of Ayub Khan (1958-64)*. Islamabad: Council of Social Sciences, p. 2

Saigol, R. (2005) 'Enemies within and enemies without: The besieged self in Pakistani textbooks'. *Futures*, 37: 1005–35.

Salim, A. and Z. Khan (2004) *Messing Up the Past: Evolution of History Textbooks in Pakistan, 1947–2000*. Sustainable Development Policy Institute.

Sanders, S. (2016) 'Did social media ruin election 2016?' *NPR*. Available: www.npr.or g/2016/11/08/500686320/did-social-media-ruin-election-2016 (accessed 3 June 2017).

Sant, E. (2014) 'What does political participation mean to Spanish students?' *Journal of Social Science Education*, 13(4): 11–25.

Sarwar, B. (2009) '*Three Days that Shook the Country' – Students' Herald, January 19, 1953*. Available: https://drsarwar.wordpress.com/2009/11/16/three-days-that-shook-the-country-students-herald-jan-19-1953/ (accessed 16 February 2016).

Sattar, M. (2013) 'The youth vote: More hype than reality?' *Dawn*. Available: www.dawn.com/news/801996/the-youth-vote-more-hype-than-reality (accessed 16 February 2016).

Sayeed, S. (2018) 'In blow to minorities, Pakistani court orders citizens to declare religion'. *Reuters*. Available: www.reuters.com/article/us-pakistan-religion-law/in-blow-to-minorities-pakistani-court-orders-citizens-to-declare-religion-idUSKCN1GL28T (accessed 2 May 2018).

School Education Department (2014) *Curriculum Implementation Framework – Punjab 2014*. Punjab Curriculum and Textbook Board, Government of Punjab, p. 4.

Shah, A. (2019) 'Pakistan: Voting under military tutelage'. *Journal of Democracy*, 30(1): 128–42.

Shalal, A. (2019), 'IMF says Pakistan needs to mobilise tax revenue, cut debt', *Reuters*, 22 July. Available online: https://uk.reuters.com/article/uk-imf-pakistan/imf-says-pakistan-needs-to-mobilise-tax-revenue-cut-debt-idUKKCN1UH01P (accessed 25 July 2019).

Sherazi, Z. S. (2013) 'Twin church blasts claim 80 lives in Peshawar'. Available: www.dawn.com/news/1044668 (accessed 28 March 2017).

Sherwood, H. (2015) 'Lahore attack: Christian leaders express horror at massacre'. *Guardian*. Available: www.theguardian.com/world/2016/mar/28/pakistan-christian-leaders-express-horror-at-lahore-massacre (accessed 19 February 2016).

Siddiqa, A. (2007) *Military Inc.: Inside Pakistan's Military Economy*. England: Pluto Press.

Siddiqi, A. (2013) 'The emerging social contract: State–citizen interaction after the floods of 2010 and 2011 in Southern Sindh, Pakistan'. *IDS Bulletin*, 44(3): 94–102.

Siddiqi, A. (2014) 'Climatic disasters and radical politics in Southern Pakistan: The non-linear connection'. *Geopolitics*, 19(4): 885–910.

Siddiqi, F. H. (2010) 'Intra-ethnic fissures in ethnic movements: The rise of Mohajir identity politics in post-1971 Pakistan'. *Asian Ethnicity*, 11(1): 25–41.

Siddiqui, T. and S. K. Dehghan (2016) 'Pakistan: Dozens dead as bomb hits mourners at Quetta hospital'. *Guardian*. Available: www.theguardian.com/world/2016/aug/08/pakistan-dozens-feared-dead-as-bomb-targets-mourners-at-hospital (accessed 28 March 2017).

Simon, T. (2013) 'Citizenship as a weapon'. *Citizenship Studies*, 17(3–4): 505–24.

Sindh Textbook Board (2015) *Muashriti Aloom Paanchween Jamaat ke liye* (Social Studies for Grade 5). Jamshoro: Government of Sindh.

Sindh Textbook Board (2016) *Urdu Lazmi Noween aur Dasween jamaaton ke liyei* (Urdu Compulsory for grades 9 and 10). Islamabad: Department of Education.

South, A. and M. Lall (eds), (2017) *Citizenship in Myanmar: Ways of Being in and from Burma*. Thailand: ISEAS, Singapore and Chiang Mai University Press.

Surendra, S. D. (2009) 'Explaining social mobilization in Pakistan: A comparative case study of Baluchistan and Azad Kashmir'. *Comparative Studies of South Asia, Africa and the Middle East*, 29(2): 246–58.

Syed, B. S. (2018) '"Engineered protests" won't be allowed, says army chief'. *Dawn*. Available: www.dawn.com/news/1401345 (accessed 19 April 2018).

T

Talbani, A. (1996) 'Pedagogy, power, and discourse: Transformation of Islamic education'. *Comparative Education Review*, 40(1): 66–82.

Talbot, I. A. (1980) 'The 1946 Punjab elections'. *Modern Asian Studies*, 14(1): 65–91.

Talbot, I. A. (1998) *Pakistan, A Modern History*. Pakistan: Vanguard.

Tankel, S. (2016) 'Beyond the double game: Lessons from Pakistan's approach to Islamist militancy'. *Journal of Strategic Studies*, 41(4): 545–75. https://warontherocks.com/2016/07/pakistani-militants-and-the-state-friends-foes-and-frenemies/

Tariq, K. K. (2016) 'Junaid Hafeez and Pakistan's laws of darkness'. *The World Post*. Available: www.huffingtonpost.com/khwaja-khusro-tariq/junaid-hafeez-pakistan-laws_b_9621280.html (accessed 2 June 2016).

The Economist (2017) 'Why doesn't Pakistan reform its blasphemy laws?' Available: www.economist.com/blogs/economist-explains/2017/04/economist-explains-14 (accessed 3 June 2017).

Twitter (2017) Available: https://about.twitter.com/company (accessed 3 June 2017).

U

Ullah, M. S. (2013) 'ICTs changing youths' political attitudes and behaviors in Bangladesh'. *International Communication Gazette*, 75(3): 271–83.

UNESCO (1997) 'Study on primary school curriculum and textbooks in Pakistan'. Available: http://nhdr.undp.org.pk/

United Nations Development Programme (UNDP) (2016a) *Human Development Report 2016*. New York: UNDP.

United Nations Development Programme (UNDP) (2016b) *Development Advocate Pakistan. Inequality: Missing from the Public Agenda*. UNDP Pakistan.

United Nations Development Programme (UNDP) (2017) *Unleashing the Potential of a Young Pakistan, Pakistan National Human Development Report*. Pakistan: UNDP.

United Nations Development Programme (UNDP) (2018), *Human Development Indices and Indicators: 2018 Statistical Update*. New York: UNDP.

V

Verba, S., K. L. Schlozman and H. E. Brady (1995) *Voice and Equality*. Cambridge: Harvard University Press.

Vincent, C. and S. Ball (2007) 'Making up the middle-class child: Families, activities and class dispositions'. *Sociology*, 41(6): 1061–77.

W

Warsi, A. (2018) "'Fired for political views', Ammar Ali Jan to take PU to court'. *Daily Times*. Available: https://dailytimes.com.pk/228047/fired-for-political-views-ammar-ali-jan-to-take-pu-to-court/ (accessed 18 May 2018).

Wasim, A. and Z. Tahir (2017) 'FIA launches crackdown on "anti-army campaigners"'. *DAWN*. Available: www.dawn.com/news/1334626 (accessed 3 June 2017).

Weinbaum, M. G. (1996) 'Civic culture and democracy in Pakistan'. *Asian Survey*, 36(7): 639–54.

Welzel, C. and Inglehart, R. (2008) 'The role of ordinary people in democratization'. *Journal of Democracy*, 19(1): 126–40.

Whaites, A. (1998) 'Political cohesion in Pakistan: Jinnah and the ideological state'. *Contemporary South Asia*, 7(2): 181–92.

Whitely, P. (2014) 'Does citizenship education work? Evidence from a decade of citizenship education in secondary schools in England'. *Parliamentary Affairs*, 67: 513–35.

Wilkes, T. (2016) 'Pakistan lifts ban on YouTube after launch of local version'. *Reuters*. Available: www.reuters.com/article/us-pakistan-youtube-idUSKCN0UW1ER (accessed 3 June 2017).

Winthrop, R. and C. Graff (2010) *Beyond Madrasas: Assessing the Links between Education and Militancy in Pakistan*. Centre for Universal Education at Brookings. Available: http://www.jceps.com/wp-content/uploads/PDFs/05-2-01.pdf

Wrigley, T. (2007) ''Rethinking education in an era of globalisation', *Journal for Critical Education Policy Studies*, 5(2): 1–27.

World Economic Forum (2017) *The Global Competitiveness Report 2017–2018*. Available: http://www3.weforum.org/docs/GCR2017-2018/05FullReport/TheGlobalCompetitivenessReport2017–2018.pdf (accessed 20 April 2018).

Y

Yasmeen, S. (2013) 'Pakistan, militancy and identity: Parallel struggles'. *Australian Journal of International Affairs*, 67(2): 157–75.

Yusaf, H. (2015) 'New media in Naya Pakistan: Technologies of transformation or control?' In C. C. Fair and S. J. Watson (eds), *Pakistan's Enduring Challenges*. Pennsylvania: University of Pennsylvania Press, 156–77.

Yusuf, M. (2011) 'Youth and the future'. In S. Cohen (ed.), *The Future of Pakistan*. Washington DC: Brookings Institution Press, 257–83.

Z

Zahra-Malik, M. (2018) 'In Pakistan, long-suffering Pashtuns find their voice'. *New York Times*. Available: www.nytimes.com/2018/02/06/world/asia/pakistan-pashtun-long-march.html (accessed 29 April 2018).

Zaidi, A. (2013). 'The old and the new in naya Pakistan'. *Economic and Political Weekly*, 48: 24. Available: www.epw.in/journal/2013/24/web-exclusives/old-and-new-naya-pakistan.html (accessed 11 January 2016).

Zaidi, S. M. A. (2011) 'Polarisation of social studies textbooks in Pakistan'. *The Curriculum Journal*, 22(1): 43–59.

Index

Note: Page numbers in 'italics' refers to figure.